THE DISSIDENT

THE DISSIDENT

ALEXEY NAVALNY: PROFILE OF A POLITICAL PRISONER

DAVID M. HERSZENHORN

12
TWELVE
NEW YORK BOSTON

Twelve
Hachette Book Group
1290 Avenue of the Americas, New York, NY 10104
twelvebooks.com
twitter.com/twelvebooks

First Edition: October 2023

Twelve is an imprint of Grand Central Publishing. The Twelve name and logo are trademarks of Hachette Book Group, Inc.

Library of Congress Control Number: 2023940118

ISBNs: 978-1-5387-0945-0 (hardcover), 978-1-5387-0947-4 (ebook)

Printed in Canada

MRQ-C

10 9 8 7 6 5 4 3 2 1

To my wife, partner, and best friend, Christina Pan Marshall, whose own work internationally as a U.S. lawyer specializing in compliance and ethics proves that the fight against corruption is universal and, as Alexey Navalny maintains, a core pillar of democracy. It is thanks to Christina and our sons, Miles, Isaac, and Ellis—to whom this book is also dedicated—that I was able to live my dream as a foreign correspondent, and to witness firsthand some of the key events described in these pages.

And to my parents, Jaime and Janet, and my teachers in the New York City public schools—P.S. 32, I.S. 227, and Townsend Harris High School—who made writing a joy worthy of professional pursuit.

CONTENTS

THE DISSIDENT

INTRODUCTION

Alexey Navalny wouldn't die. He wouldn't stay away from Russia. And, even more vexing for the Kremlin, he just wouldn't shut up.

After Russian government assassins allegedly poisoned him with a deadly nerve agent in late August 2020, Navalny, the foremost political opponent of President Vladimir V. Putin, spent more than two weeks in a coma in a German hospital. When he woke up, he declared that he would return home to Moscow as soon as he recovered. He would not be cowed into exile.

Barely three weeks after regaining consciousness, while still suffering tremors and other aftereffects of the poisoning and the heavy medications that saved him, Navalny sat for a long interview with Yury Dud, a popular journalist and YouTuber, in which he accused Putin of presiding over the impoverishment and degradation of Russia, and even mocked the government for its incompetent assassination program.

At first, Dud and Navalny chuckled about the strange parallels with an interview they did three years earlier. In 2017, Dud noted, Navalny had just come out of detention after being arrested at a protest. In 2020, he had just emerged from a coma. In 2017, Navalny noted, someone had splashed antiseptic in his face, staining him bright green. In 2020, special service operatives had splashed Novichok, a chemical nerve agent, on his underwear.

Dud asked how Russia had changed since their conversation three years earlier. Navalny answered like a candidate campaigning for office, which is basically how he always speaks—as if his future hinges not on the whims of a despot but on voters deciding if they are better off now than before the last election.

"Russia has become impoverished," Navalny said, citing failed projects, including efforts to develop a Russian-built passenger jet that no one wanted to buy, and to build a new space center for rocket launches that had yet to materialize.

"None of Putin's projects were successful."

"Russia is degrading in every sense," Navalny said, adding: "And by the way, on the question of whether they poisoned or they didn't poison [me], the system cannot degrade everywhere and develop—excellently—in the area of murders. In the area of murders, apparently, it is also degrading. But that's just lucky."

After emerging from his coma, Navalny had to relearn how to walk, to write, and perform other basic tasks. But in November 2021, while still recuperating, Navalny testified by video link before the European Parliament. He urged European Union governments to get tougher on Putin's regime, in part by sanctioning Kremlin-connected oligarchs who, Navalny griped, were permitted to conduct business and own lavish assets in the West, including luxury homes, megayachts, and even professional sports teams.

Within a month after that, working with the investigative news outlets *Bellingcat* and the *Insider*, he identified by name most of the Russian government operatives who tried to poison him to death. Pretending to be an aide to the head of Russia's National Security Council, Navalny even tricked one agent into admitting his role in the assassination plot and subsequent cover-up. In a nearly hour-long phone conversation, the agent blamed Navalny's survival on bad luck, including paramedics who administered emergency treatment.

* * *

Navalny just won't stop. So, it was no surprise that upon returning to Russia in January 2021, his plane was diverted to a different airport—thwarting throngs of supporters who came out to greet him—and he was arrested before he could cross passport control.

There are many ways to take a life. Poison had failed. Prison was now the fallback.

Two weeks after his arrest, Navalny stood in a packed courtroom in Moscow, defiant as ever, to address the Russian government's latest absurd accusation against him: he failed to check in with parole officers while in a coma.

Navalny wore a dark blue hoodie and khaki green pants. His light brown hair was combed perfectly in place, his angular jaw and dimpled chin uncovered while nearly everyone else in court wore masks as protection against coronavirus.

Watching him, jaunty and flashing ironic smiles from inside the locked glass-enclosed dock that Russians call "the Aquarium," it was hard to believe that just five months earlier, he was nearly killed with an internationally banned chemical weapon. The tricked FSB officer was right. Navalny's life was saved thanks to a combination of stupidly lucky events: the bumbling of the security agents who tried to kill him; the quick emergency landing by the pilots of the plane he was on; and the professionalism of an ambulance crew and doctors in the Siberian city of Omsk, who were never told that they were supposed to just let him die.

As he spoke, Navalny's voice was firm, edged with his trademark tone—a mix of supreme confidence and abject disbelief—that has come from years of tangling with the inane illogic of the Russian judicial system. It is a system that makes sense only when recognized as beholden to political masters, delivering preordained outcomes disconnected from laws and facts.

Navalny perfected that tone of voice and his bemused, friendly, storytelling style, by narrating YouTube videos, viewed millions of times, in which he revealed spectacular corruption by Russian government officials. In one such video, he exposed his own would-be assassins—providing a surreal dispassionate account of how they plotted his death.

In court, as was made obvious by his captivity in a glass box, Navalny was the defendant, charged with parole violations that could—and would—lead to a sentence of nearly three years in a notorious Russian penal colony.

But as he delivered his statement that subfreezing February afternoon,

Navalny turned the absurdity of the Russian court system to his advantage. He transformed himself from accused into accuser, and his defendant's statement into a prosecutor's closing argument, in which he leveled charges against the one man he held responsible for his poisoning and imprisonment: Vladimir Vladimirovich Putin, Russia's modern-day czar.

The judge, a last-minute replacement named Natalya Repnikova, the prosecutor, Yekaterina Frolova, and a representative of the Federal Penitentiary Service, Alexander Yarmolin, were secondary objects of Navalny's dismissive, derisive scorn. The case that he presented was directed squarely at Putin, the ex-KGB chief who has served as Russia's supreme leader since Boris Yeltsin's resignation on New Year's Eve, 1999.

Dispensing quickly with the court's accusations, Navalny pointed out that he was charged with parole violations in a case that the European Court of Human Rights had already found baseless, and for which the Russian government had paid him compensation. On top of that, he noted that in 2014, he had been given a suspended sentence of three and a half years in the case. "A little bit of mathematics," Navalny said, flashing his trademark acerbic irony. "It's now 2021."

"Nevertheless," he continued, turning his attention to Putin, "someone really wants, really wanted, that I not take a single step across the territory of our country, returning as a free person. From the moment I crossed the border, I was a prisoner. And we know who. We know why this happened. The reason for all this is the hatred and fear of one person living in a bunker. Because I inflicted a mortal offense against him by the fact that I just survived after they tried to kill me on his orders."

Frolova, the prosecutor, tried to interrupt, but Navalny barreled over her.

"I don't need your remark," he snapped. "The fact that the representative of the prosecution is trying to interrupt me, to shut my mouth, also perfectly characterizes everything that is happening... So, I will continue. I inflicted a mortal offense by the fact that I survived. Thanks to good people—pilots and doctors. Then, I offended him even more, by the fact that, having survived, I did not hide, living somewhere under guard in some smaller bunker that I could afford."

Navalny was no longer addressing Judge Repnikova, whose decision to sentence him to prison was already made, and who was merely a prop in a long-running script. Navalny was playing to his own audience—millions of followers—in Russia and around the world.

"Then something terrible happened," he said. "Not only did I survive, not only did I not get scared and hide, I also participated in the investigation of my own poisoning. And we have shown and proved that it was Putin, using the Federal Security Service, who carried out this assassination attempt. And I was not the only one. And now everyone knows it, and they will learn a lot more. And this is what drives this thieving little man in his bunker crazy. It is precisely this fact—the fact that everything was revealed. Do you understand? . . .

"It turned out that in order to cope with a political opponent who has neither [access to] television nor a political party, merely requires trying to kill him with chemical weapons," Navalny continued. "And of course [Putin] is just going crazy about it. Because everyone realized that he was just a bureaucrat randomly appointed to the presidency. He never participated in debates or elections, and this is the only way he knows how to fight—to try to murder people. And no matter how much he pretends to be a great geopolitician, some great world leader, his main resentment towards me now is that he will go down in history precisely as a poisoner."

In the most memorable, oft-quoted line from his speech that day, Navalny reached across centuries to invoke two legendary Russian leaders. One was Yaroslav I, who reigned as grand prince of Kievan Rus from 1019 to 1054 and implemented the first system of codified laws in what would become the Russian Empire. The other was Czar Alexander II, who ruled from 1855 to 1881 and was renowned as a reformer of the judicial system who ended corporal punishment, and emancipated Russia's serfs.

"You know, there was Alexander the Liberator, or Yaroslav the Wise," Navalny declared in a tone of scathing, unvarnished contempt. "And we will have Vladimir, the Poisoner of Underpants."

* * *

Alexey Anatolyevich Navalny doesn't want to be known as a dissident.

He has been jailed repeatedly for his political views, survived several state-sponsored assassination attempts, and undertaken a hunger strike to protest conditions of his imprisonment. He has crusaded relentlessly against public corruption and led an opposition movement against Russia's autocratic, warmongering government, resulting in the imprisonment of many of his associates and supporters. That crusade has even led to the targeting of some of their family members—including Navalny's brother, Oleg. Nonetheless, Navalny recoils from the term "dissident."

Navalny is the archnemesis of Putin, the former KGB agent who has ruled the country as president, prime minister, and president again for more than twenty-three years, with an ever-tightening iron fist. To prolong his hold on power, Putin has manipulated election results and rewritten the country's constitution. And Putin regards Navalny with such visceral disdain that he refuses to say his name, referring to him instead with euphemisms like "the Berlin clinic patient" or "the character you mentioned."

Coming from Putin, these weird, clumsy references are a badge of honor—proof, as if any were needed, that Navalny has managed to get under the skin of Russia's all-powerful leader. But in post-Soviet Russia, the word "dissident" is fraught with historical baggage that Navalny and his closest associates don't want to carry. In their view, Navalny—who at the time of this writing is serving multiple sentences totaling thirty years in a high-security penal colony—bears enough other burdens.

More than anything, Navalny wants to be known as a politician and the undisputed leader of the Russian opposition.

During his nearly two-decade-long ascent to national prominence and worldwide fame, he has happily claimed an array of other titles: lawyer, blogger, grassroots political organizer, shareholder-rights activist, anti-corruption crusader, protest leader, mayoral candidate, political party chief, campaign and election strategist, presidential hopeful, enemy of crooks and thieves.

There are also terms that his critics have tried to slap him with—like "traitor," "foreign agent," "terrorist," and "extremist." These are absurd, given Navalny's obsessive, patriotic devotion to Russia, and would be laughable if not for their grave criminal implications. Then, there are other labels that Navalny has sought to finesse, or been forced to retreat from, over the years—pro-gun, anti-immigrant, ultranationalist, Russian imperialist—which were accurate or partly accurate until his views evolved.

"Dissident," however, is one moniker that he or his supporters do not embrace, even though they recognize it has international cachet.

"In Russian language, 'dissident' will have a connotation of those, like, eight brave people on the Red Square in 1968, right?" said Leonid Volkov, Navalny's longtime chief of staff and manager of his 2013 campaign for mayor of Moscow. "Those eight people in 1968, they were very brave. We admire them. But it was very clear for everyone that they were actually a minority among [an] enormous, vast, silent majority.

"These, like, great heroes of Soviet intelligentsia, those *Shestidesyatniki*, of those dissidents, like Sakharov and Bonner, and Marchenko and Gorbanevskaya and the rest, they were disconnected from the people," Volkov continued. "So, they played a very important historical role. We admire them a lot. But there was a dramatic difference between them and our movement because we don't want to be a minority and we are not."

Volkov, who was jailed himself numerous times and still faces serious criminal charges in Moscow, was sitting in a café in the Lithuanian capital of Vilnius, where he has lived in self-imposed exile since at least August 2019, and where, until stepping aside in 2023, he ran the Anti-corruption Foundation that continues Navalny's work.

In Lithuania, Volkov and the rest of Navalny's team were beyond the legal reach of the Russian government, which has cracked down mercilessly on all political dissent. But they were not beyond the reach of the Kremlin's assassins, who have undertaken brazen hit jobs abroad, including in Germany and Britain.

Like Navalny, Volkov is not known for pulling punches when he speaks. But talking about the legendary and revered *Shestidesyatniki*—the Sixtiers—he was being polite. What he really meant to say was that these brave dissidents were *losers*. Not losers in the colloquial sense—his admiration for their bravery and sacrifice is genuine—but losers in the very literal sense that they did not win their fight against the Soviet regime.

The lucky dissidents survived the gulags. Some even escaped and lived long enough to return to Russia and enjoy the early years of post-Soviet exuberance. But in the minds of many Russian citizens, the brave dissidents did not triumph over the repressive Communist regime—just as the United States did not defeat the Soviet Union but simply claimed victory when the USSR collapsed from its own, internal rotten mismanagement and corruption.

By some measures, these dissidents—generally members of a self-selecting intelligentsia—are also viewed as having suffered less than ordinary Russians, thanks to their prominence or infamy. Some like Natalya Gorbanevskaya were permitted by the Soviet authorities to emigrate, while others like Natan Sharansky were freed in prisoner exchanges. They were then welcomed as celebrities and moral authorities in the United States, Israel, and Europe; and avoided years of deprivation in Russia, especially in the early 1990s.

In a more global context, putting aside the sensitivity of the word for Russians, Navalny now is arguably the world's most recognizable dissident. He is in jail solely for his political views, for his stubborn, compulsive insistence on challenging Putin and the graft and criminality that surrounds and sustains the modern czar.

Separated from his beloved wife, Yulia, his college-age daughter, teenage son, and aging parents, Navalny communicates with the outside world mainly through handwritten notes, often scrawled on graph paper—known as *millimetrovka* in Russian—and ferried in and out of the penal colony by his lawyers.

In March 2022, Navalny was convicted of fraud and embezzlement and, in August 2023, of extremism. Those sentences total twenty-eight years, condemning him to remain behind bars until 2051 and preventing him from running in Russia's next five presidential elections. Changes to the Russian Constitution in 2021 allow Putin to run for two more six-year terms, in 2024 and 2030, potentially keeping him in power until 2036, when he will be eighty-three years old.

This leaves Navalny on the cusp of joining the ranks of Nelson Mandela, Lech Wałęsa, and other leaders, including Myanmar's Aung San Suu Kyi, who have battled authoritarian regimes and are indisputably regarded as dissidents. Some of them are also branded as revolutionaries, a label which in Russia is far more unsettling than "dissident," given the country's experiences of the early twentieth century.

For much of the world, especially the West, Navalny is the best hope for a post-Putin era in which Russia stops its war on Ukraine and rejoins the community of civilized nations. Other scenarios—the rise of another criminal strongman like Wagner mercenary boss Yevgeny Prigozhin; or Russia's breakup into a chaotic jumble of territories, some led by the likes of Chechnya's Ramzan Kadyrov—are more frightening than Putin. From that vantage point, an ideal outcome would be Navalny emerging from prison in the spirit of a modern Mandela, as a dissident-turned-president, to lead his nation through reconciliation and democratic reform.

Still, for all its moral authority, historical gravitas, and global cachet, the "dissident" label doesn't sit comfortably with Navalny or his most loyal confidants, collaborators, and loved ones—which explains why they had decidedly mixed emotions when the European Parliament announced in October 2021 that Navalny had been awarded the annual Sakharov Prize for Freedom of Thought—a prestigious honor but one named after Andrei Sakharov, arguably the most prominent of the dissident Sixtiers.

The Sakharov prize, which comes with an award of €50,000, was presented at the European Parliament in Strasbourg, France, in December 2021. Navalny's daughter, Darya Navalnaya, a student at Stanford University, flew in to accept it on his behalf.

Navalnaya, tall and blond like her mother, delivered a short but devastating speech, in which she accused Western and European leaders, including the members of Parliament, of being too timid in confronting Putin and his authoritarianism. She branded them "pragmatists" as if it were a slur and blamed them for not doing enough to free her dad and to end what she called her family's "nightmare."

Navalnaya stepped to the lectern holding a framed photograph of her father being arrested at a protest—the hands of police officers gripping at his arms and torso.

"It's a little frank and awkward," Navalnaya warned the Parliament, after initially charming them by saying how "terrified" she was about messing up her speech. Then, in a sweet voice, she accused them of issuing toothless statements, kowtowing to dictators, and inanely putting petty economic interests ahead of democratic ideals.

> You know, I've heard this many times, and I'm sure I will again, maybe even in the corridors after this ceremony: "You know, Dasha," they'll say to me, "I understand why you're feeling this way, because it concerns your family, and close ones, but in the real world, however, we have to be *more pragmatic*." And in those hallways, I'll nod my head and say, "Yes, of course." What else can I say? I'm a twenty-year-old college student, and I don't feel very comfortable arguing with experienced and responsible pragmatists.
>
> However, here today, taking advantage of the fact that I have the microphone . . . I would like to oppose that pragmatism. This is the Sakharov Prize and Andrei Sakharov was probably one of the most nonpragmatic people on the planet. I don't understand why those who advocate for pragmatic relations with dictators can't simply open the history books. It would be a very pragmatic act and having it done, it's very easy to understand the inescapable political law: the pacification of dictators and tyrants never works.

Indeed, pacification is not part of the Navalny playbook.

Navalny's politics are not violent. The rallies and demonstrations he has led have always been about messaging and mobilization, not destruction. But instinctively he is a fighter. His rhetoric often gets overheated, and he has ended up in more than his share of fistfights and brawls. He is driven by outrage, and what he has described as "hate"—a personal, visceral animus toward his opponents. He hates being lied to, hates feeling like he is being ripped off, hates being taken for a fool.

"I know this about myself," Navalny told Dud during their interview in Germany. "One of my flaws is that I'm prone to using certain epithets, that I should use less often or stay away from. I definitely get personal. It's part of my political strategy, if you will. Because I got into politics to criticize specific people, among other things . . . I fight corruption not as a phenomenon but as individual corrupt officials, crooks that I hate. I always call them [out] by their names. It's my principled stance. It obviously means a lot of emotional and personal language. Maybe it's a minus overall. I admit it. But it's a part of who I am."

In Strasbourg that day, Darya Navalnaya rebuked the West for trying to appease the Belarusian dictator, Alexander Lukashenko, for allowing Putin's special services to carry out assassinations with impunity, and for abandoning brave dissidents like her father.

"No matter how many people try to deceive themselves, hoping that another madman who clings to power will behave decently in response to concessions and flirtations, it will never happen," she said.

"The very essence of authoritarian power involves a constant increase in bets, an increase in aggression, and the search for new enemies," Navalnaya continued. She added:

> Another thing that pragmatists don't want to do for some reason . . . is simply to pick up a calculator and see how much their pragmatism costs, in particular to the European taxpayers.
>
> Years of flirting with Putin made it clear to him that to increase his ratings, he can start a war. How much will the war with Ukraine cost to Europe?

The speech took on an even more personal tone as Navalnaya described the murders and attempted murders of Russian opposition figures, including several attempts to poison her father. One such attempt, in July 2022, left her mother so ill that she could not stand up.

"One of the opposition leaders, Boris Nemtsov, is killed with shots in the back right by the Kremlin," Navalnaya told the Parliament. "And then comes the pragmatist and says, 'Well, we can't do much about it. Let's limit ourselves to a tough statement, and then continue the conversation.' And then they'll kill the second and the third, and the fourth will be killed in the center of Berlin, and the fifth in the UK. Then they also blow up some warehouses in Europe and then they start killing with chemical weapons."

She added, "A real terrorist group has been created inside Putin's special services, killing citizens of my country without a hearing or trial—without justice. They were close to killing my mother. They nearly killed my father. And no one will guarantee that tomorrow, European politicians won't start falling dead by simply touching a doorknob."

Members of Parliament loudly applauded her criticism of them—a surreal scene reminiscent of Gogol's *The Government Inspector*—the cutting satirical masterpiece about Russian public corruption, which is a favorite of Navalny's.

At a climactic point in the play, the protagonist, a humiliated governor, interrupts an absurd tirade at his underlings, turns to the audience, and breaks the fourth wall: "What are you laughing about?" he demands. "You are laughing about yourselves."

* * *

Unlike the intellectual Soviet dissidents—Sakharov himself was a nuclear physicist known as the father of Russia's "hydrogen bomb"—Navalny and his team see themselves as regular Russians, or at least as common members of Russia's modern, post-Soviet middle class.

"We are a political force that enjoys popular support in large cities and small cities, among high income and low-income people among educated and noneducated," Volkov said in Vilnius. "Like we have 10 million subscribers on social media. We have around 15 to 20 million subscribers, supporters in the country. We are able to organize like protest policy in 180 cities simultaneously. So, by all means: We are known."

Being a regular guy—and wanting to be known—have always been core to Navalny's persona, beginning as a kid, growing up on the outskirts of Moscow as a military brat, with a poster of Arnold Schwarzenegger, the Austrian-born bodybuilder, actor, and future governor of California, on his bedroom wall.

Heroes like Schwarzenegger are a big part of Navalny's life, fitting in well with his conviction that the world is filled with good guys and villains. Once, in 2010, long before he was assured of international fame, Navalny celebrated the idea that Schwarzenegger, then governor, must have seen an article about his anti-corruption efforts in the *Los Angeles Times*.

"Hooray. It's done," Navalny proclaimed on his blog. "Now he knows about me. The one that looked at me from the walls of my room for many years. Arnold Schwarzenegger... Should the governor of California read the state newspaper? He must. So, you read about me."

In his blog post, Navalny quoted a different line from Gogol's *The Government Inspector* in which one of the characters, Peter Bobchinsky says his only hope is for nobles in St. Petersburg to know of his existence. Navalny rewrote the line, crossing out Bobchinsky and inserting himself into the role. "[Schwarzenegger] probably sits and thinks ~~Peter Ivanovich Bobchinsky lives in such and a such a city~~ Alexey Anatolyevich Navalny lives in the city of Moscow," he wrote.

This hunger to be seen, to be known and acknowledged, drives many politicians, especially those like Navalny, who crave to be celebrated for helping people. But a craving for fame and attention is not Navalny's primary motivation, as some critics have asserted.

Navalny is also not particularly interested in getting rich. He has a capitalist instinct, and like many others in his generation, has often scouted out investment and business opportunities. His interest in money, however, has focused more on slamming greedy and corrupt officials who are obsessed with wealth and creature comforts—an obsession he never shared.

Understanding Navalny requires recognizing that he is instinctively a political animal. It is also crucial to know that he is a deeply patriotic, even nationalist Russian, that he harbors a visceral hate of liars and cheaters, and that he is animated by a keen sense of justice and outrage that often morphs into vigilantism. Perhaps most important, he views life as a series of contests between the forces of good and evil.

It is this worldview that has led him to portray Putin as the devil and to liken the Russian leader to the evil Voldemort of the Harry Potter series. Some of Navalny's close associates say that he even seems to think about himself and his team as corruption-fighting superheroes.

"He told me many times . . . to be with a group of good guys, he dreamed about it," said Ivan Zhdanov, the executive director of Navalny's Anti-corruption Foundation. "He dreamed about, like, you know, maybe comics—a comics group—and I don't know, heroes."

Zhdanov said that nothing angered or upset Navalny more than a sign of dishonesty or unfairness within his own team, because it was a betrayal of their noble mission. "It's not about only honesty," Zhdanov said. "It's about a group of people who, I don't know, have some secret, some secret between them about something and . . . they will save this world."

At times, Navalny even seems to think he and his team are characters in one of the animated TV shows he loves so much—the sitcom *Rick and Morty* perhaps being his favorite—moving from caper to caper, battling evil adversaries in one episode after another, despite the grave personal risks of imprisonment or even death.

One day they are exposing the ill-gotten wealth of a hypocritical politician; another day they are drawing attention to the shoddy construction of publicly financed housing; and another day they are tracking down the government assassins who tried to kill Navalny himself. Day after day, they come back—same time, same channel—to do it all again.

During another day of court proceedings in February 2021, a failed effort to appeal his parole-violation conviction and a separate hearing on absurd charges that he defamed an elderly military veteran, Navalny delivered two long statements, at times rambling but poignant, that touched on these themes of heroism and good vs. evil, and at the same time hammered home his central anti-Putin message.

The statements revealed a man wrestling with loneliness in the early weeks of a widely expected heavy prison sentence that somehow still seemed to have come as a shock—as if he had grown so accustomed to his cartoon-style cat-and-mouse hijinks with the Kremlin that he simply could not believe Putin was no longer willing to play.

"Certainly, I'm not really enjoying the place where I am, nevertheless I have no regrets about coming back, about what I'm doing," he said. "Because I did everything right. On the contrary, I feel, well, a kind of satisfaction."

Navalny insisted that he, and others like him, would not be broken by the authorities' attempts to isolate them.

"First it is important to intimidate, and then to prove that you are alone," he said, adding: "And this thing about being alone, it's very important, it's very important as a goal of power. Speaking of which, one of the great philosophers, Luna Lovegood, remember her in Harry Potter? And, talking to Harry Potter during difficult times, she told him: 'It's important not to feel lonely, because if I were Voldemort, I would really want you to feel lonely.' Certainly, our Voldemort in the Palace wants that, too."

Navalny also mocked Putin and Putin's cronies for trying to deny their fabulous wealth while most Russians remain impoverished. "Despite the fact that our country is now built on injustice... nevertheless we see that at the same time millions of people, tens of millions of people, they want the truth," Navalny said. "They want to achieve the truth and sooner or later they will achieve it."

Navalny urged the public not to be afraid of those calling for change in the country. "Because many people are afraid: 'Oh my God, what will happen, there will be a revolution, there will be nightmares and turmoil.' But think about how good life would be without constant lies, without these falsehoods," he said.

He then turned to the judge, asking wouldn't she prefer to work in an honest system. "Think how great it would be... you are a respected pillar of society and nobody can call you anywhere and give you directions on how to decide cases and you go to your children and grandchildren and tell them that yes, you're really an independent judge."

To the prosecutor, he added, "I mean it would be cool, just great, to be a prosecutor who actually acts in an adversarial system, runs an interesting kind of legal game, defends somebody or convicts some real villains. It's unlikely, I think, that people went to law school and became prosecutors so that they could then participate in fabricating criminal cases and forging signatures for somebody."

Then, he veered back to slamming his would-be assassins. "No one, not one person in the world, was a schoolboy with glowing eyes who said, 'I'll go to the FSB, and they'll send me to wash an oppositionist's underpants because someone put poison on them,'" Navalny intoned. "There are no such people! Nobody wants to do that! Everybody wants to be normal, respectable people, catch terrorists, bandits, spies, fight them all."

Navalny urged the public to join his cause, quoting the main character from his favorite show, *Rick and Morty*.

"It's very important to just not be afraid of the people who are pushing for the truth, and maybe even support them in some way," Navalny said. "Directly, indirectly, or just maybe not even to support, but at least not to contribute to this lie, not to make the world worse around us. There is a small risk in this, of course, but first, it is small, and second, as another prominent contemporary philosopher named Rick Sanchez said: 'Life is a risk. And if you don't take risks, then you're just an inert bunch of randomly assembled molecules drifting wherever the universe blows you.'"

It was at this moment, as he delivered the defendant's "last word," the closing statement to the court, that Alexey Navalny—activist, blogger, corruption fighter, opposition politician—seemed to metamorphose in front of everyone's eyes into a twenty-first-century dissident, calling out from captivity for Russians to overcome their authoritarian oppressors, and their centuries of misery.

"One last thing," Navalny said. "I'm getting a lot of letters right now. And every other letter ends with the phrase 'Russia will be free.' It's a great slogan, and I constantly repeat it, write it back, and chant it at rallies. But I keep thinking that there is something missing for me. That is, of course, I want Russia to be free; it is necessary, but it is not enough. This cannot be a goal in itself.

"I want Russia to be rich, which corresponds to its national wealth," he continued. "I want these national riches to be distributed more fairly, so that everyone gets their share of the oil-and-gas pie. I want us to be not only free, but also, you know, with decent health care. I want men to live to retirement age, because now half the men in Russia are not able to do so, and the women are not much better off. I want education to be good and for people to be able to study normally.

"I wish a lot of other things would happen in our country," he said. "We need to struggle not so much with the fact that Russia is not free, but with the fact that, on the whole, *it is miserable on all fronts.* We have everything, but nevertheless we are a miserable country. Open Russian literature, great Russian literature, my God, there are only descriptions of misery and suffering. We are a very unhappy country, and we cannot escape from this circle of unhappiness. But, of course, we want to. So, I propose we change the slogan and say that Russia must be not only free, but also happy. Russia will be happy."

* * *

Happiness has never been a reliable, let alone essential, currency in Russia. But Navalny's supporters are convinced that he can deliver such a national transformation—if he survives jail, if he is ever allowed to run for office, if he wins.

Yevgenia Albats, the longtime editor of *New Times* magazine who has served as a sort of political godmother to Navalny and other members of the political opposition from his generation, said that Navalny's imprisonment could well be one more, crucial step toward his destiny as a future leader of Russia.

"At least in my part of the world, you know, we are a country of prisoners," Albats said. "I wouldn't want him to have this experience, but that's a very important experience... it's also the experience of being deprived of all your rights. And, you know, he keeps his resistance even though in the penal colony."

Albats, who is close to Navalny's family and corresponds with him regularly, said that he remained defiant during daily roll calls, where he was expected to announce his presence by saying "Prisoner Navalny." Instead, according to Albats, he refers to himself as "the Illegally Imprisoned Navalny."

"In the Russian political culture, you know, all revolutionaries, they went through jails, whether it's Stalin or whether it's, you know, somebody better than that. Unfortunately, those who were educated but who chose not to be jailed, they never did anything."

For Albats, Navalny has proven to be nothing short of a revelation.

She has known him from the beginning, from when he was awkward, not particularly well-spoken, and certainly without benefit of an elite education, attending political salons on Tuesday evenings in her Moscow apartment in the mid-2000s. And she has witnessed his evolution into the charismatic leader of a national movement, able to command the rapt attention of giant throngs of people on the streets of Moscow and other cities—a politician who can relate to everyday citizens and speaks in language they understand.

"What is very important about him, that he is part of us, he is not above," Albats said. "He is not from outside. He's not somebody who's going to come from Switzerland, and you know, and teach Russians how to become happy. He is part of this people. Of the nation. And, you know, he is getting a very painful experience, as I said, you know, it's better not to have this experience. But I think it's very important."

Even by appearance, Navalny is "of the nation."

He, his wife, Yulia, and their children, Darya and Zakhar, look like they could be models in an advertisement depicting the stereotypical ideal of a Slavic, Russian family. So while Navalny has faced harsh criticism for some of his nationalist and anti-immigrant views and remarks, opponents cannot easily portray him as an outsider like so many of the Jewish dissidents, the refuseniks, were in Soviet times.

Volkov, Navalny's longtime deputy and chief strategist now living in exile in Vilnius, fits the old model: He is an observant Jew who adheres to kosher dietary laws. Volkov's successor as head of the Anti-corruption Foundation, Maria Pevchikh, can be portrayed as an outsider in another way: She has lived much of her life in Britain.

With Navalny in prison, and Putin presiding over a ferocious crackdown on political dissent following Russia's February 2022 invasion of Ukraine, Volkov, Pevchikh, and other lieutenants have shifted into survival mode, using their base in Lithuania to try to keep attention on Navalny's plight and keep the remnants of their political machine whirring, ready for the moment when he is free.

One of their goals has been to field as many candidates across the country as possible, following a strategy called "Smart voting" by which they aim to team up with anyone who is not part of Putin's United Russia party, which Navalny famously branded as the party of crooks and thieves. And it is precisely because they still hope to appeal to mainstream voters, Volkov said, that they want to be known as politicians, not dissidents.

"This means we actually, like, pretend to be the majority and, as we managed to prove during the Moscow mayoral campaign and then later during the presidential campaign, we are able to connect very different layers of the Russian society," Volkov said. "And in a fair and competitive election, well, maybe we wouldn't be the largest political force in the country, but definitely the second."

Albats, who is a generation older than Volkov and also an observant Jew, has a clearer recollection of Soviet times. She is willing to call Navalny a revolutionary but Navalny, she says, sees himself only as a politician.

"He's a politician," she said. "That's him, that's who he is. He's born... a political animal, and you know that's what he loves.

"He is thinking about himself as a future president of the Russian Federation," Albats said. "That's for sure. He is the future president of the Russian Federation. The whole question: Is it going to happen? I have no doubt. The guy—if he survives, if they fail to kill him in jail again—he will become the leader of Russia."

—1—

POISONING

"As the night wore on, it was those in the gray suits who gave the diagnosis."

—Leonid Volkov, Berlin, August 21, 2020

Alexey Navalny was sweating heavily and completely disoriented, unsure that he could walk the few steps from an airplane bathroom back to his seat. And yet, in that moment, he also understood, with terrifying clarity, that he was about to die.

"The closest analogy I found was the Dementors from Harry Potter," Navalny recalled about six weeks later, after waking up from a medically induced coma. "[J. K.] Rowling's description is a Dementor's kiss doesn't hurt, it just sucks life out of you. It didn't hurt at all, but the main overwhelming feeling is: I am about to die."

The forty-four-year-old political opposition leader was on an early-morning flight home to Moscow from the city of Tomsk in Siberia, where he campaigned for candidates in regional elections. After just a few minutes in the air, he felt perilously ill.

As his brain fogged up, and an awful feeling of dread began to spread through him, Navalny pleaded with his press secretary, Kira Yarmysh, who was seated next to him, to talk. When she did, he could see her mouth moving, but could not make sense of her words.

A flight attendant came by with bottles of water. At first, Navalny was going to ask for a drink, but decided to go to the bathroom and splash water on his face. He went in his socks, and after washing up, thought to sit there for a second and rest. Suddenly, however, he realized that he'd better get out of the locked bathroom while he still could. He had been inside for about twenty minutes, and a queue of passengers had formed.

"I came out and saw a bunch of unhappy faces, I thought: 'Maybe I've been in there for, like, ten minutes.'" Navalny told the Russian YouTuber and online journalist Yury Dud. "I realized that I should probably ask for help, because I didn't think I could walk back to my seat. To my own surprise, I turned to this flight attendant and said, 'I was poisoned. I am about to die.' And then I lay down in front of him."

Navalny described these events about one month after emerging from a medically induced coma, most of it spent at Charité Hospital in Berlin. And despite his difficult recovery, which was far from complete, his trademark humor had returned.

"The flight attendant looked at me with a little smirk like, 'What a nutjob!' Maybe he thought I got food poisoning from the tomato juice or macaroni," Navalny said. "I think he was about to tell me that they couldn't have poisoned me on the plane. but I wasn't listening, I had laid down on the floor, determined to die there and then."

In video posted online by passengers, Navalny could be heard wailing in agony. He himself would have no recollection of that, or of the emergency landing that saved him.

But Navalny's description of what he felt in those moments matched the experiences of others, including his own wife, Yulia, believed to have been poisoned with the same type of military-grade chemical weapon, an organophosphate acetylcholinesterase inhibitor from the Novichok family.

"It's your entire body is telling you: 'Alexey. It's time to say goodbye. You've done something to me that's 100 percent incompatible with life.'"

* * *

Navalny and his colleagues—Yarmysh and a project manager for the Anti-corruption Foundation, Ilya Pakhomov—had arrived at Bogashevo Airport in Tomsk comfortably early for their flight, S7 Airlines 2616, to Moscow-Domodedovo, the airport closest to Navalny's home in the capital.

Navalny, wearing a gray flowered T-shirt, posed for snapshots on the security line.

In the departure lounge, Navalny bought some candy for his two children. Then, the trio stopped by the airport's Vienna Café, where a display of clocks showed the time in Tomsk, Moscow, Crimea (which Russia had invaded and illegally annexed from Ukraine in 2014) and Surgut, a Siberian city to the northwest that is a major hub for energy businesses.

Navalny had not eaten breakfast, either at his hotel or in the airport. Airport surveillance cameras would show Pakhomov handing Navalny a cup of black tea.

On the shuttle bus from the gate to the aircraft, a Boeing 737-800 with S7's light green detailing on the wingtips, Navalny posed for more fan photos. He seemed perfectly fine. The plane departed at 8:06 a.m.

They were in the air for about ten minutes when he suddenly felt ill.

With Navalny lying on the floor in the crew area at the rear of the plane, a flight attendant made an announcement seeking passengers with medical expertise. One woman, a nurse, came forward. The flight attendants also asked the pilots to make an emergency landing, and shortly after there was an announcement that the flight was diverting to Omsk, where it landed at 9:01 local time, nearly two hours after takeoff.

In the roughly half hour between the emergency landing announcement and touchdown in Omsk, passengers would recall the ill man—most did not know his identity—wailing and screaming and, at one point, vomiting. The airline, S7, said that its flight crew had worked to keep Navalny conscious.

An ambulance crew was waiting, but the paramedics who boarded the plane quickly concluded that the case was too serious for them and called for a critical care ambulance. Video posted by local news sites showed Pakhomov standing near the back of the plane as the paramedics attached an intravenous drip. Other videos showed Navalny, unconscious, on a stretcher being loaded into an ambulance on the tarmac, and Pakhomov, with a knapsack slung over each shoulder, talking to paramedics.

Navalny's team suspected immediately that he was poisoned. It was not the first time he had fallen mysteriously ill. They also knew that they would soon be in an information war with the Kremlin, and that Navalny's survival could depend, in large part, on their ability to keep the world informed about his condition.

The events that morning would show the Navalny team fully activated in crisis mode, working across five time zones to fight for their fallen leader.

Yarmysh, the press secretary, put out the first word: "This morning Navalny was returning to Moscow from Tomsk," she tweeted. "In flight, he became ill. The plane made an emergency landing in Omsk. Alexey has toxic poisoning. Now we're going to the hospital in an ambulance." In a follow-up tweet, she registered suspicion of the Russian government. "A year ago, when Alexey was in a special detention center, he was poisoned," she wrote. "Apparently, they've done the same to him now."

Then, speaking live to the Ekho Moskvy radio station, Yarmysh drew a direct connection to the upcoming regional parliamentary elections and Navalny's political work in Siberia. "This is also connected with the election campaign," she said. "I think that the authorities proceed from some of their own ideas about when it is necessary to neutralize Alexey."

* * *

On that morning—August 20, 2020—Ivan Zhdanov, the director of Navalny's Anti-corruption Foundation, had just driven all night back to Moscow from Vilnius, where he had celebrated his thirty-second birthday, with his friend and boss, Leonid Volkov, Navalny's top aide.

It had been a smooth drive from the Lithuanian capital for Zhdanov and his wife, with their toddler daughter sleeping soundly in the back seat. They were about ten minutes from their home in the north of Moscow, when suddenly Zhdanov began getting urgent messages from Siberia.

"I see this message that he is in a coma, and that they stopped their flight in Minsk," Zhdanov recalled. He quickly reached out to Volkov in Vilnius and said he had messages that something was wrong, but the gravity of the situation wasn't clear. He initially told Volkov, "we should observe the situation and be in touch." The messages, however, kept coming and Zhdanov quickly called Vilnius again, telling Volkov: "I need a ticket to Omsk."

The only flight that day to Omsk was from Domodedovo Airport, a nearly two-hour drive at the opposite end of the city. Zhdanov began speeding there, blowing red lights. "I broke all the traffic rules," he said. "I really was out of any limits."

Navalny's wife, Yulia Navalnaya, was rushing for the same flight, though she lived much closer to the airport in the south of Moscow. Yarmysh had called and said their flight had been diverted to Tomsk. She did not provide details, but the emergency landing was enough to signal to Navalnaya that she should get to Omsk. She threw an assortment of clothes into a suitcase and left her apartment, not even waking up her children to say goodbye.

Navalnaya asked her taxi driver to rush, noting that she had just two hours to catch her flight. In fact, she had miscalculated and had an extra hour. Another airport. Another café. Yarmysh sent another message: Alexey is in a coma, on life support. "I got this message at the airport," Navalnaya told Yury Dud. "Now it was clear the situation was critical."

Sitting in the café at Domodedovo, she messaged a friend and started crying. The friend quickly texted back: "Do you have sunglasses with you?" "I said: 'What? Why? Sunglasses at the airport?' " Navalnaya recalled. "She said: 'Find a pair.' "

By chance, she had a pair of big sunglasses in her purse. She put them on, ordered a glass of whisky, and bawled. It was 8 a.m.

Zhdanov arrived at the airport in time. "I caught this flight with Yulia and she was really stressed," he recalled. "It was really important to fly with her because she was devastated absolutely."

At boarding, they realized they would be cut off from updates about Navalny's condition for the duration of the roughly four-hour flight to Siberia. The thought of being out of contact for that long, with her husband on the edge of death, was unbearable.

"I was flying with Vanya Zhdanov," Navalnaya would recall. "I can't say I'm a blabbermouth. But as I later learned, when asked about the flight after we landed, he said: "It was fine. Yulia talked for four hours without breaks. I told him about our kids, the one, the other, about our family and what we're up to as a family. I probably told him every secret. We haven't asked him yet about what I told him in those four hours. But I'm guessing he heard a lot.

"I was just scared of being left alone with my thoughts even for a second, so I had to talk to someone," she continued. "Landing was also scary. I said to Vanya: 'Is it okay if you read and I look at your reactions?' He was obviously nervous, too. He picked up the phone, scrolled through, and put it back down. I noticed the uneasy look on his face when he was scrolling. I even said to him then: 'Vanya, if it's really bad, tell me now.' I wanted to pull myself together on the plane to leave it composed. But he wouldn't tell me, and my guess was that he was afraid to tell me on the plane and instead wanted to talk in the airport, because he'd be able to get me a doctor in case I needed one. I kept saying: 'Tell me the truth. Tell me the truth.' "

Zhdanov remembers it differently. First, he was struggling to get a cell phone signal. Then, when he did, Navalnaya didn't believe him when he said that nothing had changed.

"It was really, so hard for us," Zhdanov said. "She really didn't believe me that everything is OK. When I tried to find a connection with the internet, several times she told me, 'You didn't want to tell me the truth yet.' "

* * *

As the ambulance raced to City Clinical Emergency Hospital No. 1 in Omsk with Navalny already comatose in the back, and while Navalnaya and Zhdanov were rushing to catch their flight in Moscow, the Navalny team still in Tomsk also kicked into gear.

At the Xander Hotel, Vladlen Los, a lawyer for the Anti-corruption Foundation, posted himself as a sentry outside Room 239, where Navalny had spent his nights in the city. He knew that crucial evidence was still in the room, and also that the Russian authorities would make no effort to investigate.

Los had been having breakfast at the hotel with two other longtime Navalny associates, Georgy Alburov and Maria Pevchikh. They had stayed behind to finish up work on the campaign video that Navalny had filmed in support of his party's local political candidates. At breakfast Alburov realized that Navalny's flight had been diverted to Omsk, and then heard from Yarmysh about the poisoning.

They pressed the hotel to let them into Room 239, which had not yet been cleaned. A desk clerk initially refused. The hotel also refused to turn over the video from the numerous surveillance cameras located on the property, including in the hallway just outside Navalny's room, which likely would have shown who had entered and planted the poison. Those videos later disappeared after being seized by the police, though the cameras had apparently been deactivated.

Los, Alburov, and Pevchikh were joined by Anton Timofeyev, a former detective in Tomsk who had become a lawyer and was working with the Navalny political network's local office.

Eventually, the hotel management relented and let them into Room 239, which they searched wearing rubber gloves while recording everything on video—footage that they would clip and put on social media and that would also feature later in the Oscar-winning documentary about Navalny's poisoning.

Among the items they found and carefully removed were bottles of Svyatoi Istochnik (Holy Spring) brand water—at least one of which would be determined by investigators to bear traces of Novichok, the military-grade chemical weapon developed in Russian laboratories. In hindsight, the search was dangerous, since the gloves provided little protection against the highly lethal nerve agent.

However, most of the poison, it would turn out, had been on Navalny's underwear.

* * *

Meanwhile, in Vilnius, Navalny's top aide, Leonid Volkov, had launched himself into figuring out medevac options that would get his stricken friend to Europe and away from Russia, where Navalny was still very much under the control of his would-be assassins.

The team of "good guys" that Navalny had dreamed of was now engaged in a full-court, multinational push to save his life.

Even if Russian doctors could save him, which was unclear, they were making no effort to figure out what—or, more important, *who*—had tried to murder him.

The prospect of an evacuation was complicated further by travel restrictions tied to the coronavirus pandemic. Volkov, nonetheless, developed several options of hospitals that could potentially handle Navalny's case. One was in Strasbourg. Three others were in Germany, including the Charité Hospital in Berlin, which two years earlier had treated Pyotr Verzilov, a member of Pussy Riot, the anti-Putin art collective and activist group, after what appeared to be a similar poisoning incident.

Verzilov, on Navalny's behalf, reached out to Jaka Bizilj, the head of the Cinema for Peace Foundation, which had helped arrange Verzilov's medical evacuation in 2018. Volkov was also in touch with Boris Zimin, a Russian-born business tycoon, philanthropist, and race car driver who had long been Navalny's financial patron, employing him on salary nominally for legal work. Zimin, whose father, Dmitry, founded the VimpleCom cell phone company, was also a founding benefactor of the Anti-corruption Foundation.

With no flights available to the German capital, Volkov set off in his car on the nearly twelve-hour drive to Berlin, hoping Navalny would soon be airlifted there.

In Russia, Navalny's personal doctors quickly began demanding the transfer.

"The doctors are not doing everything possible," Yaroslav Ashikhmin, a general practitioner and cardiologist who had treated Navalny, told the *Meduza* news site. "Navalny, of course, needs to be evacuated to Europe... There are very few institutions that can take a patient who is probably poisoned by some kind of toxin."

Ashikhmin stressed that treatment wasn't the only reason to send Navalny abroad.

"There is a second task: the search for a substance that may have caused the poisoning," he said. "It is in this particular situation that Western clinics could potentially have more experience."

* * *

In Omsk, the doctors resisted the idea of transferring Navalny. They also refused to let his wife see him, initially telling Yulia that her passport was not sufficient proof of marriage.

Navalnaya and Zhdanov arrived at City Clinical Emergency Hospital No. 1 in Omsk that evening. Navalnaya wore a black dress, a black Covid mask, and huge sunglasses. Zhdanov, wearing a white button-down and a gray plaid blazer, looked exhausted.

They immediately faced hostility from hospital, law enforcement, and security officials, who had gathered in surprising numbers, including local police, transport police, the Federal Security Service (FSB), and the Russian National Guard.

Another of Navalny's personal doctors, Anastasia Vasilyeva, had also rushed to Omsk but despite her medical credentials, she was flatly refused access to her patient.

"This is some kind of real madness and is simply inhuman and uncollegial," Vasilyeva tweeted. "Doctors all together in such a situation should forget about politics and do everything in the name of the patient's health. It is monstrous not to let me examine Alexey, not even listen to his history.

"I do not ask for much—to look at the fundus of the eye, reflexes, tell the anamnesis of past poisoning, show medical documentation to communicate and consult with foreign colleagues," she wrote. "No. They do not give. Argument—no right. Although the right to life is above all."

By late evening, Zhdanov posted an update, saying that Navalnaya had been granted an audience with the hospital's chief doctor but officials were stonewalling a transfer. "Perhaps she will be given more information as a wife," he wrote. "But they refuse to give any documents. They say transportation is not possible."

After the life-saving decision by the S7 pilots to make a fast emergency landing, the ambulance crew secured Navalny's chance of survival by administering atropine, a standard treatment in poisoning cases.

But at the hospital, the spinning and dissembling started almost immediately. Doctors said there was no sign of any toxin and began questioning Navalny's prior health and what he had eaten before the flight.

"So far, there is no certainty that poisoning was the reason for Navalny's hospitalization," Anatoly Kalinichenko, deputy chief physician, told reporters. "It is considered as one of the versions, but there are others."

Muddying the waters further, the chief doctor, Alexander Murakhovsky, said that Navalny had not been poisoned but was diagnosed with a metabolic disorder caused by low blood sugar.

News outlets close to the Kremlin quickly began reporting suspicions that Navalny had been drinking and suffered alcohol poisoning, despite everyone close to Navalny knowing that he was a very light drinker.

Within days a more sinister theory was spun out, alleging that Pevchikh, the Anti-corruption Foundation's chief of investigations, had actually poisoned Navalny and that she had been sleeping in his hotel room. This was even more outlandish than the allegation of alcoholism.

Navalny is not an idiot, and he had long taken precautions against getting ensnared in the sort of honey traps that pro-Putin forces ran against several opposition figures. A series of incidents in 2010 involved the same woman, Ekaterina Gerasimova, nicknamed Mumu, who tried to entrap her targets by recording videos of sexual escapades and drug use.

When asked about Navalny's situation, the Kremlin spokesman, Dmitry Peskov, said the president's office was aware he had fallen ill. Peskov said the Kremlin was even willing to help facilitate his transfer abroad—a seemingly magnanimous statement in Moscow, but one that did not quickly turn gears in Omsk. (Like his boss, Peskov often made great efforts not to utter Navalny's name.)

"Many Russian citizens these days, although the borders are closed, go abroad for treatment," Peskov said. "And of course, we will be ready to consider such appeals very promptly, if any."

The international stakes of Navalny's case also became apparent that first afternoon. French president Emmanuel Macron and German chancellor Angela Merkel weighed in, voicing concern for Navalny, offering to help with his medical treatment, and demanding an investigation.

"As for Mr. Navalny, we are of course very concerned and deeply regret his situation," Macron said during a news conference with Merkel at Fort de Brégançon, his official summer residence. "We fully support him, his family and loved ones... We are of course ready to provide any necessary support to Alexey Navalny and his family. This applies to the areas of health policy, asylum and protection.

"The facts that led to this situation must be analyzed," Macron said. "The causes must be determined and there must be an investigation. I think Mr. Navalny can be saved. We will also provide him with our support if requested."

Merkel, as usual, was more succinct but no less forceful. "As far as Mr. Navalny is concerned, we were of course also very upset in Germany today at the news that he is in hospital and, as we have heard, is in a very worrying condition. I certainly hope and wish that he will recover as soon as possible... What applies to France also applies to Germany, that of course we will also give him all the medical help in German hospitals," she said. "Of course, that has to be desired from there. It is now very, very important that it is urgently clarified how this situation came about. We will insist. Because what we have heard so far are very unfavorable circumstances. That has to be done very, very transparently."

* * *

There would be no investigation in Russia, of course. But Navalnaya sent a letter to Putin appealing directly to the Russian leader to allow her to take her husband abroad for treatment.

"He's not in a very good condition and we can't trust this hospital," Navalnaya told reporters outside the hospital the next morning. "We demand they release him to us so we can treat him in an independent hospital with doctors whom we trust."

Zhdanov told the journalists that a transport police official was overheard telling Murakhovsky, the chief doctor in Omsk, that a "very dangerous substance" had been found on Navalny, and that everybody involved in Navalny's case should be wearing protective gear. But Zhdanov said the officer and the doctor refused to divulge the name of the substance, and Murakhovsky insisted the information was not confirmed.

Vasilyeva, meanwhile, continued to rail against the local hospital officials for refusing to release Navalny, even after the air ambulance had been dispatched from Germany and was now waiting for him on the tarmac—with the German doctors having declared him fit for transport.

"If the diagnosis is just a 'metabolic disorder,' then why isn't Alexey allowed to go to Berlin," she tweeted scathingly, before answering her own question: "Because they wait three days so that there are no traces of poison in the body, and in Europe it would be impossible to establish this toxic substance."

Volkov, in Berlin, bluntly said politics were at play.

"Let me put it this way: there was an external factor that very suddenly put him in critical condition," he told *Der Spiegel*. "Initially, the doctors said unequivocally that it was poisoning. They did everything they could to stabilize his condition, put him in an induced coma and ventilated him. Suddenly, however, those in the white coats no longer had the floor. As the night wore on, it was those in the gray suits who gave the diagnosis."

Finally, later on Friday, after Putin's intervention, the doctors relented and discharged Navalny to the German transport team. "Hooray," Vasilyeva tweeted. "Everything has moved off the ground! I can't even believe that in some 2 hours Alexey will fly to Germany. And there they are most likely to cure him . . . Terribly glad."

Navalny was permitted to leave Siberia. Boris Zimin later confirmed that he had paid €72,000, or about $85,000, for the air ambulance. Three other Russian businessmen living outside of Russia—Yevgeny Chichvarkin; Sergei Aleksashenko, a former deputy chairman of the Russian Central Bank; and Roman Ivanov, an executive at Yandex, the internet company—confirmed to Reuters that they had contributed thousands of dollars for Navalny's medical care.

But while Navalny was cleared for medical evacuation, the clothing he was wearing on the day that he was poisoned was never returned to him. And his family, close friends, and colleagues still did not know if he would ever recover.

* * *

In Berlin, Navalny spent another fifteen days in a coma.

While he was unconscious and still connected to a ventilator, toxicologists at a German military laboratory confirmed that Navalny had been poisoned with a nerve agent banned under the international Chemical Weapons Convention, of which Russia is a signatory.

Merkel personally announced the findings at a news conference, underscoring the seriousness of the allegation. Only the Russian government had access to such a weapon.

"The special laboratory of the German Armed Forces has delivered a clear result," Merkel said. "Alexey Navalny was the victim of an attack with a chemical nerve agent from the Novichok group. This poison can be detected without any doubt in the samples.

"Thus, it is certain that Alexey Navalny was the victim of a crime," Merkel continued. "It was intended to silence him, and I condemn this in the strongest possible terms... Very serious questions now arise, which only the Russian government can and must answer."

In Russia, however, there were no answers, and there was no investigation—only dissembling and denials, and accusations against the West of an anti-Russian conspiracy.

When doctors finally brought Navalny out of his coma, he could not talk or walk. His hands shook uncontrollably and he experienced terrible hallucinations.

Some of these, he said, involved a Russian rap group called Krovostok. In another, his wife and Volkov told him that he had been in a terrible accident and that a Japanese professor would give him new legs and a new back.

Navalnaya and Volkov each had their moments when they realized

Navalny was getting back to his old self. In Volkov's case, it was when Navalny, who otherwise seemed in a near-catatonic state, looked up at one point and exclaimed: "What the fuck is going on here?" Volkov later told him, "That's when I knew you'd be OK."

For Navalnaya, the moment came when her husband was still not quite able to speak, but laughed when she showed him a report about Alexander Lukashenko, the Belarusian leader. Lukashenko claimed his security services had intercepted a phone call between a German intelligence agent, Nick, and a Polish operative, Mike, in which they asserted that Navalny's poisoning was a fraud.

In the hospital, Navalny also got a visit from Merkel, which was perhaps the highlight of his time in Berlin, though he sought to play it down.

Merkel started out by speaking to him in Russian, in which she is fluent. "It was a private conversation," Navalny told Yury Dud just days later. "Without delving into any details, nothing of importance came up.

"I was surprised by how detailed her understanding of current events in Russia was," he said. "Normally, you meet a foreign politician and go, 'Let me tell you what's *really* going on in Russia.' Because they live in an ivory tower. She knew current Russian events better than anyone, down to every detail. About Khabarovsk, about Belarus... Down to every detail, with full context, knows how things work, and in Russian, too!"

But pressed about whether there might be some political downside to the meeting because he could be portrayed as a stooge of the West, Navalny flashed a bit of the ego that has built over the years as his reputation has grown. He noted that Putin, Foreign Minister Sergey Lavrov, and other officials routinely meet Merkel.

"I don't mean it like I'm the second politician in the country, but I'm probably one of the key figures of the Russian political opposition," Navalny said. "So, I don't think there's anything wrong with me meeting with a foreign leader to discuss Russian or international affairs. I can discuss them as well as Putin can. I don't see a problem with that."

—2—

NAVALNY VS. PUTIN

"The United Russia party is the party of corruption. It's the party of crooks and thieves."

—*Alexey Navalny, Finam FM radio, February 2, 2011*

Navalny might not have seen any problem with the attention he was getting—not just from Merkel, of course, but from other world leaders, the international media, and, especially, from regular Russian voters.

However, Vladimir Putin and many of the people benefitting from his authoritarian leadership clearly did see a problem—enough of a problem that Navalny would be worth targeting with a deadly nerve agent.

According to an investigation led by *Bellingcat*, Navalny was followed to Siberia by a team of assassins from Russia's FSB. They followed him on and off for years, and this time planned to get rid of him for good.

The poisoning attack marked a threshold moment in a battle between Navalny and Putin that had been escalating for twenty years, in which each man underestimated the other.

Putin repeatedly failed to grasp Navalny's single-minded tenacity when it comes to his decades-long political aspirations. Navalny's status as a dissident—as a political prisoner now locked mostly in a solitary confinement "punishment" cell—resulted in many ways by default because Putin left him with no acceptable alternative in what remains, as Albats described it, "a nation of prisoners."

Navalny wants to live in a free and democratic Russia. He wants to be president of a free and democratic Russia. And he has made clear, time and again, that he is willing to risk his life and sacrifice his freedom in order to achieve it. In Navalny's view, Putin's Russia is a prison for everyone who lives there, not just those who are incarcerated.

Navalny, in turn, failed to grasp how far Putin was willing to go—not just to eliminate his political adversaries but to realize his revanchist Russian imperial fantasies. At rallies, Navalny and his supporters often chanted, "Putin is a thief." But Putin was, in fact, prepared to risk being indicted as a war criminal.

Navalny's close associates believe that the Kremlin has tried to kill him at least three times. In many ways, it was fitting that they had come closest in Tomsk, in the cold, frozen heart of middle Russia—where Navalny was demonstrating that he could pose a real threat to Putin's grip on power by reaching voters beyond the elite intellectual circles of Moscow.

* * *

On August 13, 2020, Navalny traveled to Siberia to campaign on behalf of candidates in local legislative elections scheduled to take place precisely a month later.

His first stop was Novosibirsk, Russia's third largest city, with just over 1.5 million people, about 1,750 miles from Moscow. Regarded as the capital of Siberia, Novosibirsk held a special fascination for Navalny because it embodied one of his core frustrations with Russia's political system and, especially, with the pervasive political apathy of many Russian citizens.

On a video recorded during that trip, which was released after his poisoning, Navalny framed the upcoming elections as the latest clash in a two-decade-long struggle against the political forces of Putin.

"They have always defeated us—for twenty years in a row," Navalny said. "And even if they lost, they would still declare victory with the help of deception and machinations. But we need to rise and go into battle again because, until we win, our country is doomed to slowly degrade."

Navalny understood that the Faustian bargain between Putin and the Russian elite was a deal forged in Moscow and St. Petersburg, the cosmopolitan centers of European Russia. Quality of life was always far better in the big cities than everywhere else—especially compared to smaller towns and villages, but even in comparison to large cities scattered across Russia's vast expanse, cities with good universities and educated citizens, but where the burgeoning middle class had never demanded more or better.

"I am now in the place where the most important political battle will take place—here, it's very hot in summer and very cold in winter," Navalny said on the video. "The number of people with higher education is abnormally high here. It could have been one of the most successful cities in the world, but instead became home to a Russian ghetto. Using the example of the third city of the country we will analyze how you can defeat this insatiable toad—the United Russia party."

To Navalny, Novosibirsk and cities like Khabarovsk in the Far East, where protests had broken out just a month earlier over Moscow's arrest of a popular governor, presented an opportunity—to awaken apathetic Russians, and turn "regular" Russia against Putin.

When he began preparing a potential campaign for president in 2018—an election in which he was technically barred from running because of a trumped-up criminal conviction—the first regional office Navalny and his team opened outside Moscow was in St. Petersburg. The second was in Novosibirsk.

At the official opening ceremony of the office, on February 18, 2017, Navalny explained why he had such hopes for Novosibirsk:

> We want the regions, cities, to participate more actively in the election campaign, because for twenty years now no city, except Moscow, has decided anything at all. Everything is determined in Moscow. We will fight this. We do not agree with this. We will change the situation in which only Moscow and the Moscow elite decide what the elections should look like. We are opening a headquarters to show that they don't think so in Novosibirsk, either.
>
> Perhaps Novosibirsk is the best demonstration of how the system of power in the country is now incorrectly arranged. Novosibirsk is the best demonstration of how a wonderful city, very rich, with huge potential, with a highly educated population, lives in quality

> much worse than it should. We will talk about this in this election campaign, about everything, ending with problems of housing and communal services.
>
> When I see rallies on the housing and communal services problem in Novosibirsk—in the cold, more than in Moscow, I understand—this problem... cannot be solved in any way, except for the presidential elections, except for the change of power in the country.

By August 2020, Navalny's network had nearly three dozen candidates running in the local elections in Novosibirsk, including the head of its own office, Sergei Boiko.

"Our plan was that we would drive through the cities of Russia and show you actual, real politics," Yarmysh, Navalny's press secretary, said later, "to show you that politics is not only the Kremlin, not only Putin, the State Duma, and famous ministers, but also dozens of regional parliaments, on which the lives of millions of Russians, all of us, depend every day.

"The United Russia deputies who sit in these parliaments are the actual backbone of Putin's entire regime," she said. "They are not cogs, but the foundation on which the ruling party, which has prevented us from living normally for twenty years, is built."

Her description of the regional politicians was an exaggeration, but it was in keeping with Navalny's tendency to regard whatever he happens to be working on at a particular moment—a mission, a political project, an exposé—as the one upon which Russia's entire future depends.

Navalny arrived in Novosibirsk on the evening of August 17, and spent the next two days shooting videos for an exposé on local corruption and its role in shoddy building construction. From there, he went to Tomsk.

Posting a photo of himself with supporters on Instagram, Navalny wrote: "People with long arms don't need selfie sticks. Tomsk is a great city, one of the most beautiful in our country.

"More volunteers are needed to beat United Russia candidates," he added. "The party in power has a lot of money, but we can only count on the help of good, honest people. If you live in Tomsk, then go to tomsk2020.ru and sign up as a volunteer. The swindlers won't kick themselves out of the City Duma!"

On September 13, while Navalny was recovering in Germany, Boiko, the head of Navalny's office in Novosibirsk, and Ksenia Fadeyeva, the head of his Tomsk office, each won seats in the legislative elections. Stunningly, Putin's party, United Russia, was stripped of its majority in both cities, as opposition candidates from other parties also won seats.

These were small victories, and with the repressions that were carried out in the run-up to the invasion of Ukraine, they would prove agonizingly temporary. Boiko fled the country, and Fadeyeva was arrested and charged with extremism. But at the time, it was precisely the kind of victory that Navalny had been striving toward for two decades.

* * *

Seven years earlier, in 2013, an interviewer asked Yulia Navalnaya if she could imagine her husband as president of the Russian Federation. "I imagine him as president, because I want a person who has overcome so much," she said. "I think he deserves it. Sharing his convictions, I imagine him as president.

"Myself I don't really imagine as first lady," she added. "I imagine myself as his wife, no matter what he is."

It was the kind of politically pitch-perfect answer that had even her mother-in-law cheering. And Navalnaya, of course, was not the only one who could imagine her husband as the president of Russia.

At 9 p.m. on February 2, 2011, Navalny appeared on the Finam FM radio station, on a program called *Dry Residue*—a nightly talk show that billed itself as analyzing politics, economics, and finance from the perspective of the stock market. The station had recently rebranded to focus on men aged twenty-five to forty-five with high discretionary income.

In other words, it was a perfect platform for Navalny, who had used his education and interest in finances and the stock market to launch a political career.

The plan was to talk about Navalny's fight against corruption in government procurement, which had set off shock waves throughout Russia. But the host, Yury Pronko, first wanted to talk politics, noting that numerous media outlets were reporting, "Well, it's time for Navalny to go to the presidential election."

Pronko also teased Navalny, saying it would be unforgivable if he didn't pull some "sensational" comments out of him: "You already know what journalists want."

Navalny, chuckling, said, "A few sensational statements." He sat in the studio wearing a white T-shirt and tight-fitting black cardigan, looking gangly and a bit geeky with his headset on.

Pronko dove in, noting that 97 percent of listeners said they supported the idea of Navalny as a presidential candidate. "You can put your hand over your heart, say honestly," Pronko said. "Are you connected in this way to politics? And do you have such far-reaching plans?"

Navalny began by thanking everyone for their support and confessing that he felt a "big responsibility" because people ask questions and they need to be answered.

But Navalny said he had a question of his own. "I would like to ask, including those who voted for me, this thing called presidential elections, what is this? We have in general in the country, a strange procedure in which [Central Election Commission chairman Vladimir] Churov sits there stroking his beard and fills in the blanks from his head, or [Kremlin adviser Vladislav] Surkov's head, or Putin's, and gives everyone results. This is an election. If there's at least one person who really assumes that the result of the presidential election is how people voted . . . I think there are very few such people. So, the question here is whether it is necessary to participate in the elections or is it necessary to participate in this strange procedure which is called elections in Russia."

Navalny's outrage was justified. Elections had been rigged in Russia at least since Boris Yeltsin ran for reelection in 1996. Putin was appointed as president, then won his first election in 2000 over the same systemic opponents, Gennady Zyuganov of the Communists and Vladimir Zhirinovsky of the far-right Liberal Democratic Party of Russia.

In 2004, Putin effectively ran unopposed. Then in 2008, after running up against constitutional term limits, he simply swapped jobs with Prime Minister Dmitry Medvedev, leaving Putin very much in charge. And four years later, Putin would orchestrate yet another switch, reclaiming the presidency and confirming that Navalny and millions of other Russians had every right to be jaded and cynical.

Navalny told Pronko and the Finam listeners that he was content in his role fighting corruption.

"Everyone should do their own thing," he said. "I like what I am doing right now and, apparently, I am not the only one who likes it, who thinks it is quite effective and useful. So to do this and work in a direction where I am useful rather than... dance and play a hamster running through a maze and Churov is standing over laughing cheerfully at these hamsters."

"How beautifully you ducked from answering," Pronko said, tweaking Navalny for not directly saying if he intended to run for president someday.

"I didn't duck," Navalny replied in a singsong.

"So, you don't have presidential ambitions," Pronko jabbed, still angling to make news.

Navalny, of course, did not want to commit, but also would not deny it, either. "My activity is without a doubt political," he replied. "I am not going to get nervous and say there's no politics in this. Without a doubt, corruption cases, which I am considering in general, are the country's biggest political issue."

Pronko observed, as many others had, that Navalny was largely carrying out the tasks of then president Dmitry Medvedev, who had professed to undertake a campaign against corruption but in fact had done little to impose any controls over Russia's vast kleptocracy.

"I am fulfilling the tasks of the multinational people of the Russian Federation, who have had enough of all this for a long time," Navalny said. "Therefore, my political activity, which I am engaged in, is important, much more important again, than running in the labyrinth built by the Central Election Commission and the crooks who run the Central Election Commission."

What Pronko didn't realize was that, totally unwittingly, he was about to get the sensational statement he had requested, one that would end up reshaping the political discourse in Russia forever. And it sprung from the simplest of questions: "So do you have your own political sympathies?" he asked Navalny. "I don't know how you feel about the United Russia party."

United Russia, the party of Putin and Medvedev, had been thwarting Navalny's democratic aspirations for Russia, and his own personal political ambitions, for a decade. And Navalny's investigations—first into state-owned companies as an activist shareholder, and later into public procurement—had painted a portrait of United Russia as a giant racketeering ring stretching across eleven time zones.

Navalny didn't hesitate in answering, and he spoke as calmly as if he was reporting what the weather was like outside the studio before he walked in.

"I have a very bad attitude toward the United Russia party," he said. "The United Russia party is the party of corruption. It is the party of crooks and thieves. And it is task of every patriot and citizen of our country to do everything in order to—"

Pronko, not grasping the electricity of the moment, interrupted him: "Are you a patriot?"

"Absolutely, I'm a patriot," Navalny said. He returned to his point about every patriot's duty, ". . . to do everything to ensure that this party is destroyed, not in the physical sense, I do not call for any extremism, but in the sense of . . . legal methods. I propose to make sure that United Russia and all similar formations, before it was Our Home Is Russia and so on, so they do not exist. Because this is the main pillar of corruption, of the lawlessness now happening in our country."

Pronko joked about Navalny's extremism disclaimer. "Yes, because after today's program there will be a headline: 'Alexey Navalny Proposes to Destroy United Russia.' "

In fact, after another decade of struggle against Putin and United Russia, after surviving the poisoning attack, Navalny would be in jail and under further prosecution, accused of running an extremist organization. His band of like-minded heroes, which by then had expanded across the country, would be smashed apart, the group itself and the individuals running it similarly labeled as extremist.

But at that moment, in February 2011, Navalny had just given birth to a phrase "the Party of Crooks and Thieves"—*Zhulikov i Vorov* in Russian—that would become the galvanizing mantra of the Russian political opposition. Something about it touched a nerve, spawning a meme that would spread from the European West to the Pacific Far East, and penetrate deep into the public consciousness. It was as if Russians had been searching for years for words to describe the culprits responsible for a national feeling of frustration and exasperation, and for the wall that the country had hit in its political and economic development. Suddenly, they all knew. Or as Pronko, the radio host, put it: "Alexey uttered a phrase that, in general, sunk into the soul of many."

Outraged members of United Russia professed to be deeply offended. Some quickly filed lawsuits accusing Navalny of slander and character defamation. Others went on radio and TV to proclaim their outrage, which only broadcast Navalny's message wider and wider.

Navalny could not have been more pleased with the way "Party of Crooks and Thieves" went viral. Two days after the Finam FM appearance, he posted the audio, video and the transcript on his blog, noting merrily: "The passage from 4:10 is trending on Twitter. It's about United Russia."

A week and a half later he posted again on LiveJournal: "United Russia is Suing Me."

Shota Gorgadze, who fashioned himself as something of a celebrity lawyer in Moscow, announced that he was suing the "famous blogger" Navalny, claiming, "Ordinary citizens turned to me, not public, not well-known and not officials, but members of the United Russia party with a request to protect their honest name. They are ordinary people earning an average salary, raising children, living in the country they love. And it is unpleasant for them when all over their country, just because they joined the United Russia party, they are accused on the air of a radio station, of being thieves and crooks."

Navalny, as usual, relished the idea of combat, and rather than waiting for the lawsuit to proceed, he pressed forward on his blog.

"I decided to conduct a survey in order to find out the attitude, so to speak, of the internet masses (also *ordinary citizens,* by the way)," he wrote. "For good representation, we would like at least 10,000 people take part in the survey."

The question was simple: "Is United Russia a party of crooks and thieves?"

In the end, 39,467 people responded. Of those, 96.6 percent—or 37,670—answered, "Yes, it is" while 3.4 percent, or 1,313 people, answered, "No, it is not."

The verdict was in, but Putin loyalists continued trying to fight back, mostly making themselves look silly.

One of those who tried to fight was Yevgeny Fyodorov, a United Russia member of the State Duma, Russia's lower house of parliament, and chairman of its Committee on Economic Policy and Entrepreneurship. Navalny had publicized Fyodorov's financial disclosure statement, available on the Duma website, showing that he owned five apartments and other assets that would be difficult to afford on his public salary.

Fyodorov agreed to go on Pronko's show and debate Navalny about whether it was accurate and justified to call United Russia a party of crooks and thieves.

Navalny quickly laid out a devastating case.

"My value judgment that the United Russia party is a party of crooks and thieves was made on the basis of those observations regarding the activities of the United Russia party, which I have been doing for many years," he said. "I study its work." He noted the results of his blog poll, in which 96 percent agreed with his assessment.

"All these people also consider the United Russia party to be a party of crooks and thieves," he said. "These people observe every day a situation in which every corrupt official in our country seeks to find the best cover for himself. At present, the United Russia party is the best refuge, which gives a political 'roof' and the opportunity for any corrupt official to escape punishment. And we see it every day."

Navalny began by asking why there had been no prosecution of Moscow's mayor, Yury Luzhkov, a longtime senior member of United Russia, whose wife, Yelena Baturina, had become a billionaire in construction development.

"This man was a member of the Supreme Council of the United Russia party, and he was absolutely unpunished. His wife earned billions," Navalny said. He also reminded listeners that Vladimir Resin, Luzhkov's longtime deputy in charge of construction, had been photographed wearing a $1 million watch, far beyond the means of his public salary—"a United Russia member with a million-dollar watch, a man who had never worked a day in commerce anywhere in his life, and so on."

Then, Navalny plucked out a list of current members of United Russia's Supreme Council—"Let's name names," he proclaimed—and he began laying out a list of alleged corruption schemes starting with Boris Gryzlov, the party leader and Duma chairman. Gryzlov had been pushing a plan for Russia to spend billions on water filtration, insisting it was needed to improve life expectancy. He was also co-owner of a patent for a water filtration system.

"The wonderful Clean Water program, which not even I, but the academicians of the Russian Academy of Sciences consider to be just a scam," Navalny said. "Here you have United Russia as a party of crooks and thieves, academics confirm the word 'crook.'"

Next, Navalny brought up Murtaza Rakhimov, the longtime head of Russia's Bashkortostan region. While Rakhimov, a United Russia member, was in office, a giant stake in the Bashneft oil company was "sold" by the region at cut-rate pricing to Rakhimov's son, who made a fortune off of it.

"The chairman of the Accounts Chamber called the situation when Mr. Rakhimov took the entire Bashkir fuel and energy complex, the Bashneft company, into the ownership of his son, 'the biggest theft in the history of Russia,'" Navalny said. "Can I find out why this man, who was at the same time the President of the Republic until the last moment, has not yet been punished?"

Then there was Alexander Tkachov, governor of Krasnodar, whose young niece, in her twenties, had pipe-building factories and a poultry farm registered in her name; and Alexander Misharin, governor of Sverdlovsk, whose eighteen-year-old daughter held numerous lucrative business interests.

"Can you find out why the wonderful entrepreneurial talents of children are manifested only in the children of members of United Russia?" Navalny asked. "How does it work? What business school do they go to?"

Navalny said he was describing the tip of the iceberg.

"This is only the list of the Supreme Council of the United Russia party," he said. "These people join the party, all such higher councils, in order to avoid responsibility for what they have done. And they want to snatch, this is the only motivation at the moment for which people join United Russia. They want to tear apart our country with impunity."

Such accusations, by Navalny and others, predictably met with a raft of denials. Baturina and Luzhkov had long denied that she received favorable treatment as the mayor's wife, but after Luzhkov was removed from office in 2010, her construction business quickly dried up, and they left Russia to live mostly in Vienna. Luzhkov died in 2019.

Gryzlov, the Duma speaker, insisted that the Clean Water Program had nothing to do with the patent that he co-owned with an investor named Viktor Petrik, and he lashed out at the experts who said he was just trying to get rich. "A few individual scientists don't have the right to claim that they are the authorities on truth," he told *Gazeta.ru*.

The Rakhimov ownership stake in Bashneft was a matter of public record.

Fyodorov tried to wave it all away and said Navalny was just hurling insults. "It is clear that the phrase...with which we started the conversation is just abuse," he said. "It can't even be described in any other way. And those alleged facts that have been voiced are, of course, not facts, but just chatter. There is no point in discussing any of them."

Instead, Fyodorov laid out a web of conspiracies, mainly describing Russia as a victim of the United States and other Western powers.

The U.S., he said, had created Russia's oligarchs, had nearly destroyed Russia in the 1990s, and was leading an international campaign to harm the country. "There is a gigantic and tangible open attack on Russia," he said, adding: "Here it is a cruel campaign aimed, of course, at destabilizing the situation in the country. It goes along with terrorist attacks. This is a campaign aimed at destroying the country."

Pronko seemed taken aback by the comparison to terrorists, though such outlandish allegations would become commonplace as Putin over the years grew increasingly insular, isolated, and paranoid.

"Yevgeny," the radio host said, "if I understand you correctly—I will interrupt you—that you compared your counterpart, Mr. Navalny, with terrorists."

"Of course," Fyodorov replied. "Do not forget that when United Russia was created, generally speaking, after the liquidation of the USSR, Russia was also almost liquidated. Don't forget that when we came with Putin, and that was ten years ago, Russia was at war in Chechnya."

Pronko urged Fyodorov to answer Navalny on the facts but he refused. "These facts do not exist," Fyodorov said. "This is some nonsense!" He insisted, unconvincingly, that if any member of United Russia did anything wrong, they would be prosecuted.

Navalny pointed to the oligarch Roman Abramovich living in London while also serving as the governor of Chukotka in Russia's Far East. He also mentioned Semyon Vainshtok, the former head of Transneft and a close ally of Putin, who was then living in Israel, and whom Navalny had implicated in an alleged $4 billion fraud tied to construction of an oil pipeline. "He left for London, now he lives in Israel, and he invests in real estate in the United States," Navalny said. "This is all precisely United Russia, which is the cover for all those who suck everything out of Russia."

Navalny in the mid-2000s had created and then moderated a hugely popular series of political debates in Moscow as part of a group called Democratic Alternative, or DA! (the word "yes" in Russian). And it was clear that he had learned a few things about rhetorical jousting. He thrashed Fyodorov, using Fyodorov's own words to point out that he and other Duma members and United Russia politicians had far more connections and business dealings in the West than Navalny.

"I just have to admit that my value judgment about United Russia has changed a bit," Navalny said, his sarcasm now coming to full force. "If earlier I thought that United Russia was a party of crooks and thieves, now I understand that United Russia is, apparently, a party of crooks, thieves, and CIA agents. Because it is United Russia that is responsible for everything Yevgeny tells us about."

He continued, "Because all the famous Yeltsin crooks who ruined the country, all of them, excuse me, migrated to United Russia. Who are the governors who declared independence for their Republics while inside the country?...All this Yeltsin gang. Without a doubt, there was a gang during Yeltsin's time. All this gang in its entirety is in United Russia. We have your great leader, Mr. Putin, who was? He was [St. Petersburg mayor Anatoly] Sobchak's assistant! He was in the [former prime minister Viktor] Chernomyrdin party."

Sobchak, a mentor of Putin, and Chernomyrdin, an ally of Yeltsin, were core members of United Russia's predecessor party, Our Home Is Russia.

Navalny was indignant, which is how he spends much of his waking hours.

"You tell me about some kind of geopolitics, terrorist attacks, about financing, and so on. But everything was financed through some people who now absolutely all remained in power," he said. "You have had a qualified majority in the State Duma for ten years. United Russia can push through any issue, any one! And for some reason you are talking about some entrepreneurs of foreign jurisdiction. So, what's the problem? Well, change these laws! For ten years you can do everything in the country: You control the courts, you control the prosecutor's office, you control the central election commissions—you control everything in the world. TV, radio—everything! Everything but the internet..."

Navalny took a moment to slam Fyodorov about his own personal assets, but there was little point. The debate was done. Pronko's listeners were asked to call in and vote; 99 percent said Navalny won.

* * *

In a short amount of time, Navalny would no longer have to write out United Russia in his blog posts. It would be recognized instantly merely as Zh-V, the Russian initials for "Crooks and Thieves."

The phrase had sticking power. Nine months later, Navalny appeared on the cover of Russian *Esquire* magazine with the headline: "About Crooks and Thieves."

In the *Esquire* interview, Navalny explained how the phrase came out inadvertently. "This is absolutely an accident," he said. "No creativity. Tell me come up with a slogan and I will never come up with it in my life."

What was not an accident, or a random, impulsive utterance was his dismay over the system being led by Putin.

"When he started, he was anti-Putin from the very beginning, that I remember very well," said Maria Gaidar, the daughter of former acting Russian prime minister, Yegor Gaidar. She was a friend of Navalny's and was herself active in prodemocracy Russian political circles during the 2000s.

In those days, Navalny was part of the progressive liberal party Yabloko. Gaidar was a prominent member of the Union of Right Forces, a small liberal party associated with free market reforms, which was founded by her father, by Boris Nemtsov, and by Anatoly Chubais, Russia's privatization guru, among others.

"Most people met Navalny—for them he started to exist in 2010, 2011," Gaidar said. "But he had a long political history before that, and he was changing and maturing as a politician or finding his way, also in reaction to what was going on, in the regime.

"In 1999, Navalny joined Yabloko because it was the only political party that was against Putin," Gaidar said. "For me, for example, it wasn't obvious that Putin was so bad. I didn't belong to the generation of wise people like, you know, Zhenia Albats and many other people who said, 'OK, he's KGB. You cannot trust him. It's going to be bad.' "

In the *Esquire* interview, Navalny insisted that corruption was at the root of Russia's political stagnation. "Russia's main problem is that the state has turned into a mafia—in the very Italian sense of the word, when everyone is tied to each other," he said. "The only difference is that there is no place in Moscow where they all gather at once."

He complained that the country's leadership was squandering the opportunities afforded by soaring commodities prices that had improved quality of life, especially by expanding the middle class in Moscow and St. Petersburg.

"Right now, Russia is the richest in its history and the freest," Navalny said. "The huge amount of money that is currently pouring into the country gives us a chance for grandiose changes, but this chance, apparently, will not be used."

He predicted that change would come. "Revolution is inevitable," he said. "Simply because most people understand that this system is wrong. When you sit in a party of officials, most of the talk is about who stole everything, why nothing works, and how terrible everything is."

And Navalny insisted, "Everyone is ready to live honestly. Look at Georgia. If twenty people—those who are at the very top—begin to follow the rules and laws, they will force everyone else to follow the rules and laws."

The comments on Georgia were striking, given that not even three years earlier Navalny had cheered the Russian war in Georgia, and even suggested expelling all Georgians from Russia, calling Georgians "rodents." He later apologized for this. What Navalny had come to realize was that Georgia—at least at that point in 2011—appeared to have broken free of its Soviet past, thanks to aggressive reforms led by President Mikheil Saakashvili, who had come to power in the Rose Revolution of 2003.

* * *

Saying that revolution is inevitable and threatening to actually lead a revolution are two very different things, of course. But Putin, as an ex-KGB officer, has never shown much patience for nuance on that subject.

Profiles and biographies of Russia's supreme leader have often focused on the night in Dresden, East Germany, in December 1989 when crowds stormed the headquarters of the Stasi, the secret police, and threatened to lay siege to the local KGB building across the street. Putin, then stationed there, called for military help but was told that nothing could be done without orders from Moscow. "And Moscow is silent," Putin was told.

Putin has long made it clear that Moscow would not stay silent in the face of a revolutionary threat if he has anything to say about it.

Navalny's own theory is that Putin's fear of public opinion intensified after one of his first major crises as president—when an accident destroyed the Russian nuclear submarine *Kursk*, killing all 118 on board, on August 12, 2000. Putin realized how much was outside his control.

"The first changes in his character occurred in the wake of the *Kursk* tragedy," Navalny told the Polish historian Adam Michnik. "That's when he saw the power of public opinion and it frightened him. Everything seems to be going OK, it's all under control, but then some random accident happens, there's some black swan event, and suddenly it's out of your hands. People don't like you anymore and ask questions you struggle to answer."

Navalny believes Putin's push to control the Russian media, notably television, began then, culminating with the takeover by Gazprom of the independent channel NTV in 2001. Putin was shaken again by Ukraine's Orange Revolution of 2003–2004, during which mass crowds rallied on Maidan Nezalezhnosti—Independence Square—in Kyiv. Maidan was also the site of Ukraine's Revolution of Dignity in 2013–2014, making its name synonymous with popular uprising.

"Putin's worst nightmare is a Maidan on Red Square," Michnik told

Navalny in a conversation in 2015 that they turned into a book. Michnik also noted Putin's fury over the prosecution of Egypt's Hosni Mubarak, and especially over the killing of Libya's Muammar Gaddafi. Putin, in public comments, confirmed this anger.

The first public signs that Navalny had come to Putin's attention as a political threat emerged in 2007, the same year that Navalny was expelled from the progressive liberal political party Yabloko and became a cofounder of a nationalist political group, the National Russian Liberation Movement. Its Russian acronym spelled NAROD, or "People."

Before that, the Kremlin seemed largely preoccupied by a potential threat from Russia's oligarchs, which was effectively dealt with when Mikhail Khodorkovsky, the head of the Yukos oil company, was arrested in 2003. Stanislav Belkovsky, a political analyst and operative, was widely credited with having publicized the prospect of an oligarchic takeover of the government with Khodorkovsky as ringleader.

The goal of NAROD was to be a supraparty network uniting politicians from across the ideological spectrum, politicians who shared a Russian nationalist streak that, at least in the minds of the chief organizers, would not veer into extremism.

Navalny that year had auditioned for and won a job as host of a new debate program on the TV Centre television channel, which was controlled by the government. The program would have meant giant exposure for Navalny, and the organizers were quickly ordered not to let him go on air. Because he was instrumental to the project, Navalny was named editor in chief of the program, an off-camera role.

But after two episodes, despite apparently successful ratings, the show was cancelled.

Navalny and his close associates believed that Putin's media adviser, Vladislav Surkov, personally gave the order for the show to be shut down. In any case, it was the beginning of a long crusade by Putin, his media manipulators and political technologists to ban Navalny from the federal channels.

Later in the fall of 2007, Sergei Markov, a political scientist tied to

United Russia who also worked as an adviser to Putin, unexpectedly backed out of a plan to attend a public debate with Maria Gaidar, moderated by Navalny. Instead, hooligans were sent to disrupt the event—a sign of the Kremlin's intent to ice out opposition voices before the December elections to the State Duma.

Gaidar was running in those elections on the list of the Union of Right Forces party. As part of that campaign, Navalny worked with her to produce an anti-Putin video called "Devil." The tongue-in-cheek attack ad used horror movie narration, ominous music, images of Putin surrounded by flames, and dubious numerology to suggest the president was evil. It noted he became head of the KGB in 1998, which was 666 × 3, and that he was appointed acting prime minister on August 9, 1999—here the video showed three 9s on-screen, which then inverted to become another 666. The ad accused Putin, among other things, of dismantling Russia's last independent federal television station. It ended by urging voters to the polls for the December 2 parliamentary election. "Is this man the antichrist? Decide for yourself," the ad said. "Don't make yourself an idol. Make the right choice. December 2, 2007."

Russian politics had never before experienced that form of attack advertising, and the video caused a small sensation.

Over the years, while trying to deny Navalny any attention, Putin's forces in and outside government would bring numerous investigations and prosecutions against him and would subject Navalny to repeated searches of his apartment, arrests, lawsuits brought by proxies, and ultimately the poisoning attempt. If Navalny got any attention on the most-watched federal television channels, it was for smear campaigns, in which he was accused of corruption schemes or of being an operative for Russia's enemies in the West.

Putin adopted the practice of never uttering Navalny's name, referring to him instead as: "The citizen." "The defendant." "This gentleman." "This person." "The Berlin clinic patient."

Putin's press secretary, Dmitry Peskov, said it was easy to come up with labels for Navalny—"detention center inmate," "convict," "defendant for insulting a veteran." Asked why Putin was reluctant to utter his leading critic's name, Peskov said it was obvious.

"Apparently, this is due to the attitude towards this person, which the president did not hide," Peskov told Life News.

Putin is known to have said Navalny's name in public only once, when the American journalist Alec Luhn asked Putin at a reception in 2013 if refusing to say Navalny's name was intentional. "No, why?" Putin replied. "Alexey Navalny is one of the leaders of the opposition movement."

Navalny's name has also rarely appeared in official Kremlin statements. One notable exception was in a readout of a meeting between Putin and Merkel in August 2021 in Moscow, the chancellor's last visit to Russia before her retirement from politics. During the meeting, she pressed for Navalny's release from prison.

On that occasion and nearly all others, Putin avoided saying Navalny's name even while fielding direct questions about him at press conferences or other events.

Perhaps the most revealing of these was his annual news conference in December 2017, where Putin was confronted with a question by Ksenia Sobchak, the daughter of Putin's onetime mentor, the late St. Petersburg mayor, Anatoly Sobchak.

Two months earlier, Sobchak, a TV presenter and onetime Russian "It Girl," had announced plans to run for president in 2018, mounting a challenge that some, including Navalny, believed was a Kremlin-backed scheme to split the opposition. Sobchak, in any case, used her question to press Putin about the restrictions on the political opposition including Navalny.

She opened her question by pointing out her own plans to run against Putin, prompting him to suggest that she had deceived everyone and attended the news conference as a candidate. "I didn't deceive," Sobchak replied. "I came here as a journalist with TV channel Rain because unfortunately, at the moment, it is the only opportunity to ask you a question, since you are not participating in debates."

"Please," Putin invited her to continue.

Sobchak complained that Putin's press secretary, Dmitry Peskov, who was sitting there on the dais, had said that Russia's political opposition had yet to mature. Sobchak disputed this, saying there were candidates who had been preparing for a long time.

"For example, there is a candidate, Alexey Navalny," she said, who was already campaigning but had been blocked from participating by "fictitious criminal cases created against him." She noted that the European Court of Human Rights had found the convictions to be politically motivated and invalid. "As you know, the Russian Federation recognizes the European court," Sobchak told Putin. She complained that for her own campaign, no one wanted to do business with her—making it difficult even to rent a meeting hall.

"It's all connected just with fear," she said. "People understand that to be in the opposition in Russia, this means that either you will be killed, or you will be imprisoned or something else will happen. In this spirit my question is: Why is this happening? Is the government afraid of honest competition?"

Putin said he wanted to address the questions about the opposition and about competition separately, and started by insisting that political opponents have an obligation to put forward a positive agenda. He chastised Sobchak for her own slogan. "You go under the slogan 'Against all,'" Putin rebuked her. "Is this a positive program?"

Then he turned his attention to Navalny, whom of course he would not name, and made clear that Navalny, in his view, had no right to political expression or activism because he was a potentially dangerous revolutionary.

"About the characters named, we've already had questions about Ukraine here. Do you want here dozens of these para—sorry, Sakaashvilis running around the squares here?" The audience laughed at his near reference to parasites.

Putin continued, "Those whom you have named, this is Saakashvili, only the Russian version. And do you want that such a Saakashvili destabilizes the situation in the country? Do you want us to worry about one

Maidan to another, so that we have attempted coups? We went through all of this. Do you want to return to this? I'm sure that the vast majority of Russian citizens don't want it, and we won't allow it."

In a flat-out lie, Putin insisted that of course "there should be competition and without doubt there will be." But, he said, "the question is radicalism."

The Russian leader then turned to his favorite pastime of whataboutism likening the squashing of Navalny to the disappearance of the Occupy Wall Street movement in the United States. "Where are they now? They are gone," he said. "Is this democracy or not? Let's ask ourselves.

"I assure you the authorities aren't afraid and won't be afraid of anything," Putin said. "But the authorities should not be like a man lazily picking cabbage out of his beard, and watching as the state turns into a muddy puddle from which the oligarchs can pick and catch golden fish for themselves as in the 1990s.

"We do not want to be the second edition of today's Ukraine," Putin said. "And we won't allow it."

* * *

At the same news conference three years later, Putin was confronted with a different question about Navalny: Why had the Russian government not opened an investigation into his poisoning?

Putin pivoted and laid out a conspiracy blaming the United States. He dismissed an investigation by *Bellingcat* and other news outlets that identified the FSB poisoning team, even though Clarissa Ward of CNN visited the home of one of its alleged leaders, Oleg Tayakin, who slammed the door in her face.

Referring to Navalny as "the Berlin clinic patient," Putin said *Bellingcat*'s report was based on "materials from the American special services." He insisted that Russian agents knew better than to get tracked using their mobile phones.

"It means that this patient of the Berlin clinic is supported by the special services of the United States," Putin said. "And if this is correct, then it's interesting, then the special services, of course, should look after him. But this does not mean at all that it is necessary to poison him."

Putin noted that he had personally given the "command" allowing Navalny to go to Germany for treatment, and he expressed annoyance at all of the fuss over someone he considered an unworthy rival, part of a group of opposition figures who had never proven their ability to lead anything.

"The trick is to attack the top officials, and in this way pull themselves up to a certain level, and say . . . 'I am the same caliber person,' " Putin said. "In my opinion these are not tricks that should be used in order to achieve respect and recognition from people. You need to prove your worth."

Overall, Putin tried to portray Navalny as not worth the trouble, even though the Russian government had taken extraordinary measures over the years to block Navalny's political aspirations and generally make him miserable. Chillingly, he also insisted that if the Russian special services wanted Navalny dead, he would be dead.

"Who needs him?" Putin asked the hall full of journalists, chuckling aloud. "If they really wanted to, they probably would have finished it."

—3—

REVENGE

"I believe he deliberately decided to get arrested. He did what he wanted to do. So, what is there to be discussed?"

—Russian President Vladimir Putin, Geneva, June 16, 2021

Hi, it's Navalny. I know who wanted to kill me," he says, sounding chipper as he looks directly into the camera. "I know where they live. I know where they work. I know their real names. I know their fake names. I have their photos."

In fact, the photos are in Navalny's right hand as he introduces the first of several blockbuster videos about investigations led by *Bellingcat*, the forensic-investigative news site, and its partner organizations, including the *Insider*, a Russian outlet.

Those investigations revealed the identities of the assassins who put a nerve agent in Navalny's underwear in Siberia, as well as the identities of their bosses. They also exposed a Russian government hit squad and provided evidence implicating the Federal Security Service, the FSB, in several murders and attempted murders.

"This is a story about a secret group of murderers from the FSB that includes doctors and chemists, about how they tried to murder me multiple times and almost killed my wife," Navalny says. "They definitely won't tell you that on TV, considering that this group receives orders directly from Vladimir Putin."

For many years, interviewers had asked Navalny why he wasn't already dead. After poking so many of Russia's biggest bears—"with a sharp stick," as Navalny himself liked to say—how was it possible that no one had tried to kill him? Navalny on many occasions complained that he was bored of the question. "Why are you still alive?"

"I don't know," Navalny told the U.S. news program *60 Minutes* for an episode that aired in December 2017. Then, he was mounting a symbolic campaign for president of Russia, even though he was technically barred from appearing on the ballot because of his convictions in trumped-up criminal cases.

"Maybe they missed the good timing for it, when I was less famous... actually I am trying not to think about it a lot because if you start to think what kind of risks I have, you cannot do anything," he said.

Navalny at various points had tried to suggest that there were unspoken rules, that assassinations were reserved for ex-spies like Alexander Litvinenko, who was killed with radioactive polonium in his tea in 2006, and Sergei Skripal, who was poisoned with Novichok in 2018.

In fact, there was no logical basis for Navalny's assertion.

Boris Nemtsov, a longtime leader of the Russian political opposition, was shot to death on a bridge near the Kremlin in 2015. Verzilov, the Pussy Riot member, had been poisoned. So had Vladimir Kara-Murza, an opposition activist who, recognizing the danger, had his wife and children living in the United States.

There were other cases of political violence that Navalny surely knew about. In 1994, the college-age son of Grigory Yavlinsky, the leader of Yabloko—Navalny's first political party—was attacked at Moscow State University. His son, Mikhail, was a piano player; the attackers mangled his hands, and a note was stuffed in his pocket warning his father to get out of politics. Yavlinsky rarely discussed the incident. A party spokeswoman, confirming it, told the *Moscow Times*, "Luckily they were able to sew his fingers back on." Mikhail Yavlinsky, and a younger son, Alexey, then a teenager, were sent to live in Britain.

And in 2004, Ivan Rybkin, a former chairman of the State Duma who was running for president against Vladimir Putin, mysteriously disappeared for four days. Later he said he was kidnapped and drugged, and that his attackers had made a compromising video of him that they threatened to release if he continued his campaign.

Rybkin was running as the nominee of the Liberal Party, backed by the oligarch Boris Berezovsky, a rival of Putin. In the campaign, Rybkin had leveled many of the same allegations that Navalny makes today, including that Putin was involved in shady business dealings. In a full-page ad published in the *Kommersant* newspaper, which Berezovsky owned, Rybkin accused Putin of being "the main oligarch in Russia."

"Power and money go hand in hand in dictatorial regimes," the ad stated. "Putin is no exception." Before his poisoning death, Alexander Litvinenko said that when he was working in the FSB, he and other officers had been ordered to assassinate Berezovsky.

For Navalny to think that he was too famous to be targeted was sheer hubris. The FSB killers were often sloppy, as the investigations revealed, but they acted on orders, and those giving the orders had long stopped caring about the rest of the world's opinion.

Under murky circumstances, the Russian public would likely accept Navalny's death as the inevitable fate of a guy who had pushed the envelope for far too long in a country where there has never been much tolerance for dissent. And the rest of the world, at least the Western world, already thought the worst of Russia.

* * *

Contrary to Navalny's hypothesis, the FSB killers had not missed their chance. They were waiting for the order, and sometime in the first half of 2020, with the regional elections approaching in the fall, the order was apparently given.

Indeed, for much of that year, according to the investigation by *Bellingcat*, Navalny was tailed by a team of agents who were experts in working with poisonous substances.

That crew included two medical doctors, Alexey Alexandrov and Ivan Osipov, and a third man, Vladimir Panyaev. They are believed to be the would-be assassins who followed Navalny to Tomsk, snuck into his hotel room while he was out for a swim, and deployed the nerve agent in his underwear.

Christo Grozev, *Bellingcat*'s lead Russia investigator, who had previously identified the FSB officers who attacked Skripal, had decided to figure out who tried to kill Navalny. He had reached out previously to Navalny to say he thought he had identified the assassins. As the investigation neared its conclusion, Grozev traveled to the rural town of Ibach—in the Black Forest of southeast Germany, near the borders of France and Switzerland—where Navalny was recovering, to work directly with him and Maria Pevchikh, the Anti-corruption Foundation's chief of investigations.

As in the Skripal case, Grozev used vast stores of cell phone metadata and airline passenger information purchased on the black market in Russia, then crosschecked that information with the locations of different FSB offices, including its criminalistics unit, as well as with Navalny's own travel in recent years. After hitting on remarkable matches, Grozev and his collaborators said they had identified the kill team.

The core seven members of the FSB unit were all born between 1976 and 1981, making them part of Navalny's own generation that came of age as the Soviet Union was falling apart. They had been tracking Navalny at least since 2017, following him on nearly all of his trips outside of Moscow.

One of the investigation's most chilling conclusions was that the poisoning in Omsk wasn't their first try. More than a month before the Siberia trip, in July 2020, Navalny and his wife had gone for a few days of vacation in Kaliningrad, the seaside Russian exclave, north of Poland.

On July 6, the fourth morning of their trip, after taking a walk on the beach, Navalnaya suddenly felt terribly ill. She and Navalny went to a café planning to have lunch but she felt so sick she did not order any food. She struggled to get back to her hotel room, stopping to rest on benches, even though it was a short walk. She had trouble describing what was wrong. After a while she fell asleep until the next day, when suddenly, as mysteriously as she had fallen ill, she felt better.

Two of the three FSB agents who later went to Siberia had followed the Navalnys to Kaliningrad—Alexandrov, traveling under the alias Frolov, and Panyaev, along with a third officer, Mikhail Shvets. "What a coincidence," Navalny said, describing the overlapping journeys for the video. "What does this mean? Are these men not just secret agents but secret members of my family?"

The video, *Who Poisoned Alexey Navalny?*, which Navalny proclaimed a real-life "Hollywood thriller," first aired in mid-December 2020. It was quickly viewed more than 20 million times.

Never missing an opportunity to tweak United Russia, Navalny started his introduction to the video by first thanking Grozev and *Bellingcat*. Then he thanked Irina Yarovaya, the deputy chairwoman of the State Duma. In 2016, she pushed through legislation vastly expanding the Russian government's surveillance capabilities. The law required mobile telephone companies to store the contents of voice and data calls and messages for six months, and cell phone metadata for three years. It also obligated them to make such information available to the authorities upon request.

Yarovaya's law, Navalny pointed out, had created an expansive black market for data, in which corrupt Russian officers profited by selling such information to anybody willing to pay. This made it possible, he said, to identify his attackers.

On the video, Navalnaya recounted not being able to describe what ailed her in Kaliningrad. And Navalny said that after his own brush with death, he understood.

"Just imagine," he said. "Someone tells you that he feels really sick and can't take it anymore. You ask them: 'Where does it hurt? Is it a heart attack? Should I call an ambulance?' But they tell you that there's no pain. Now that I've gone through it myself, I understand how bad it can feel and how impossible it is to explain what's going on."

The initial investigation used the phone data to reveal that the men following Navalny were part of a unit from the FSB's Institute of

Criminalistics, reporting to Col. Stanislav Makshakov, and that from 2017 to 2020 Navalny took at least thirty-six trips in which members of the team were trailing him. Navalny also recalled briefly feeling symptoms similar to his poisoning while on a flight in the summer of 2019, suggesting that the FSB agents had tried to poison him at least three times.

More explosive revelations came in subsequent videos. Armed with the identities of his would-be killers, Navalny and Grozev launched a sting operation, phoning the FSB officers to get them to talk about the case. Most refused and hung up quickly, but one agent, Konstantin Kudryavtsev, a chemical specialist, took the bait.

The team disguised the caller ID of the phone Navalny was using, to make it seem as if he was calling from a main FSB line. When Kudryavtsev picked up, Navalny identified himself as an aide to Nikolay Patrushev, the head of Russia's national security council. Kudryavtsev said he was home in Covid quarantine, but it was not clear if he was ill.

During the forty-nine-minute recorded phone call, Kudryavtsev described the attempted assassination. He said he had treated Navalny's clothing, particularly his underwear, to remove traces of the poison.

The call took place early on the morning of December 14, 2020, the same day that *Bellingcat* and Navalny planned to publish the results of their initial investigation.

But Kudryavtsev's confession was so electric that they decided to delay revealing it so they could verify the details and consider its full ramifications. They also debated the ethics of Navalny lying and posing as a high-ranking security official but ultimately concluded that it was justified.

"Navalny was not working on behalf of any police or security service, nor was he conducting a traditional journalistic investigation—rather, he was in the unique position of investigating his own assassination attempt at a time when no law enforcement agency is willing to do so," *Bellingcat* said when the bombshell disclosure was published a week later. "To our knowledge, it is without precedent that a target of a political assassination is able to chat for nearly an hour with one of the men on the team that tried to kill him and later cover up the evidence." The news outlet added: "The information provided by Kudryavtsev is credible and has led to new investigative leads we had not previously discovered."

During the phone call, Kudryavtsev blamed the failure of the assassination on the swift emergency landing by the S7 pilots.

"Well, they landed, and the situation developed in a way that... not in our favor, I think," Kudryavtsev said. "If it had been a little longer, I think the situation could have gone differently."

Navalny pushed to make sure he understood. "A little longer what, Konstantin Borisovich?"

"Flying," the FSB officer said.

"If he had flown longer?"

"Well, possibly, yes, if he had flown a little longer and they hadn't landed it so quickly, it all could have gone differently. That is, if it hadn't been for the prompt work of the medics, the paramedics on the landing strip, and so on."

Navalny suggested that maybe the officers had failed to apply the proper dose of poison: "You can't say the plane landed instantly. You miscalculated the dose, or probabilities. Why?"

Kudryavtsev then got defensive. "Well, that I can't say why. How to say this? My understanding is that we added a bit extra."

Video footage of the call, which later appears in the Oscar-winning documentary *Navalny*, shows Grozev pumping his fists in the air with a thumbs-up as Kudryavtsev admits having traveled to Omsk for the cleanup. "We applied a solution... so no traces could be found." Pevchikh, stunned, puts her hands over her mouth.

Navalny asks Kudryavtsev to sum up, saying, "According to your opinion, the subject survived because the plane landed too soon?"

"Yes, it seems to me yes... everything could have ended differently."

The second factor, Kudryavtsev said, was the quick action of paramedics. "They gave him first aid, looked at his condition, gave him some sort of antidote." He also went over the details of the cleanup, describing the blue color of Navalny's underpants and how he had focused on the seams of the "fly area."

Navalny's own assessment of his survival was quite similar to that of Kudryavtsev.

"The beauty of the situation is that they did their jobs perfectly according to protocol," Navalny told Yury Dud. "The pilots were told that a passenger was about to kick the bucket, they instantly landed the plane. The paramedics were told the guy's out, they confirmed it and injected atropine... They did everything the protocol required perfectly. But you know how Russia is. When everything goes according to protocol, it is a series of lucky accidents. Sadly."

At the end of the remarkable video of his call with Kudryavtsev, Navalny described his own near-death experience as further evidence of the Russian regime's criminality.

"As you can see, everything that I said... about the complete degradation of the law enforcement system is confirmed," he said. "They're acting like bandits, not government agents. Look how many people are already involved: from doctors and police officers to the local FSB."

Remarkably for someone who often seethes with fury at his adversaries, Navalny expressed little public anger at the FSB assassination team—as if the reality and gravity of the situation had not fully sunk in. Or as if this was all just another episode of the animated adventure cartoon in which he is crusading against the evil forces of Vladimir Putin.

In an interview on Ekho Moskvy radio after his attackers had been unmasked, Navalny was asked how he felt when he saw their faces.

"This is an excellent question. Everyone asked me about it. Nothing," he said. "I myself tried to understand. You look into the face of the person who tried to kill you—do you feel something or do you not feel it? Actually, nothing."

However, he clearly had pondered the question and had made up his mind about what happened even if there would be no formal investigation, prosecution, or trial.

"Alexandrov, this dude with a mustache—this can be considered a direct killer, along with Osipov, who was there," Navalny said. "It is clear they are all a group of murderers, but this mustachioed comrade with glasses, he is literally the one whose face you need to peer into... I don't feel anything."

* * *

After Navalny's arrest, his team and *Bellingcat* continued to investigate the poisoning attack, the FSB unit, and the government cover-up. Six months later, Navalny's team posted a new video, narrated by Pevchikh, in which she described how Navalny's medical records had been falsified in an attempt to hide blood test results that offered near-certain proof that he was attacked with an organophosphate poison.

For months, Navalny's lawyers had demanded the return of the clothing he was wearing on the day he fell ill, and his full medical records from the hospital in Omsk. Their demands were refused.

Finally in November, Zhdanov, the director of the Anti-corruption Foundation, and another Navalny lawyer, Vyacheslav Gimadi, went to the hospital in Omsk to request the records in person. They took a selfie outside the hospital, and talked to the management, which sought to stall, saying they would need to wait a week for the records to be retrieved from the hospital archive.

"The effect of surprise was supplemented by the famous effect of bungling and carelessness," Pevchikh explained on the video.

The two lawyers then simply went to the hospital archive office and requested the records, saying everything had been agreed with the management. "Thanks to that magic phrase," Pevchikh said, "they were allowed to photocopy everything that was in the archives that day."

A month later, they received the reply to their official request for the records, but the two sets of documents turned out to have key differences. Most important, according to Pevchikh, one key record was missing—the biochemical blood test of Navalny from the N. V. Sklifosovsky Research Institute for Emergency Medicine in Moscow.

"Crooks simply threw it out, hid it from us, as if it had never existed,"

Pevchikh said. "But it did. And it recorded a critical decrease in the level of cholinesterase. That, together with other symptoms described in the medical card, confirms the diagnosis of poisoning with cholinesterase inhibitors in 100 percent of cases. Here is this document. The test date is August 25, 2020. That is, after Alexey was discharged and the next day after the Charité clinic announced that Navalny had been poisoned, Russian specialists conducted exactly the same study–and they found the same things."

On the video, Pevchikh disclosed that Grozev had identified an additional key suspect—an agent who had trailed Navalny more than any other, Valery Sukharev. In the weeks before the poisoning, Sukharev spoke on the phone constantly with members of the alleged kill team. Grozev discovered that Sukharev, under the pseudonym Gorokhov, traveled with Navalny fifteen times in 2007. Grozev also noted that the original *Bellingcat* investigation had not fully deciphered how the FSB operations were organized.

One part of the team, it turned out, was from the Institute of Criminalistics, including scientists and doctors—"people who can poison and hide their tracks," Grozev said. The others, including Sukharev, he explained, were from the FSB's Second Service, which includes a Department for the Protection of the Constitutional Structure. This department is dedicated to fighting terrorists, extremists, and radicals who pose a threat to the Russian state.

Pevchikh, however, alleged, "They are fighting threats not for Russia but for Putin personally and his regime."

In the video, Grozev said, "These are the people who actually follow those who are deemed undesirable by the president himself, and there is no other logic that would somehow connect this with ideology or the terrorist threat. They simply prepare lists of people who aren't allowed to exist."

The Second Service, Grozev explained, were the bosses, following political targets, and deciding when to strike them and how. "People from the Second Service are always present, on every trip, where they monitor the object of future poisoning, and sometimes 'contractors' from the Institute of Criminalistics join them," Grozev said.

But he added, "You need to understand this is not the only tool in their arsenal... they always travel, and sometimes they don't involve these poisoners at all. They involve others. For example, assassins with nothing but a pistol. This also happens."

Grozev said he had managed to link the same FSB assassins to other cases, including Kara-Murza, who was apparently poisoned twice, in 2015 and 2017, and fell into a coma each time. Kara-Murza survived those attacks but after the invasion of Ukraine was jailed and sentenced to twenty-five years in prison for treason. According to *Bellingcat*'s investigation, the same FSB officers, including Alexandrov, Osipov and Kudryavtsev were involved in both attacks on Kara-Murza.

Grozev also connected the unit to Nikita Isaev, another political opposition figure who died of a heart attack in 2019 just days after his forty-first birthday. "Our friends from the Second Service followed him seven times," Grozev said.

The investigation linked the same group of FSB chemical weapons specialists to a Russian poet, Dmitry Bykov, who mysteriously fell gravely ill in April 2019 on a flight to the Russian city of Ufa.

In the video, Pevchikh brought everything back to their central question: "Who tried to kill Navalny?"

Grozev said there could be no doubt. "This is a government institution, which must demand consent or receive instructions from a higher person for every such attempt." Even Alexander Bortnikov, the head of the FSB, Grozev said, could not make such decisions on his own. "I am personally convinced as an analyst," Grozev said, "that all these decisions were made at the level of Putin himself."

* * *

Putin has literally laughed off such accusations, and during an interview with the NBC television network ahead of a summit meeting with President Joe Biden in Geneva in June 2021, he flatly denied the allegations.

"Did you order Alexey Navalny's assassination?" Keir Simmons, NBC's senior international correspondent, asked.

"Of course not," Putin replied. "We don't have this kind of habit of assassinating anybody, that's first."

Putin then tried to turn the tables by demanding explanations for the response by American authorities to the January 6 storming of the U.S. Capitol. "I want to ask you: Did you order the assassination of the woman who walked into the Congress and who was shot and killed by a policeman?" the Russian leader said to Simmons. "Do you know that 450 individuals were arrested after entering the Congress and they didn't go there to steal a laptop? They came with political demands."

Simmons is British, not American, but no matter.

Putin over the years has often made clear that he makes all key decisions in Russia, despite his press secretary, Peskov, constantly deflecting by saying that various matters are not the president's purview or concern. Verdicts in the legal cases brought against Navalny are a matter for prosecutors and the courts, according to Peskov, even though it is widely known that the Russian judicial system is highly politicized. Navalny's treatment in prison is the responsibility of the Federal Penitentiary Service.

And yet, when the imprisoned oligarch Mikhail Khodorkovsky was released from prison in 2013, Putin, announced to a cluster of journalists after his annual news conference that he had granted a pardon. And Putin similarly took personal credit for the "command" that allowed Navalny to leave Russia for treatment in Berlin.

The meeting between Putin and Biden in June 2021 occurred at a tense moment. Russia had massed some one hundred thousand troops on Ukraine's borders, setting off a wave of anxiety in the West. Relations between Moscow and Washington were abysmal. Despite Putin's success in manipulating Donald Trump—notably at a joint press conference in Helsinki where Trump said he trusted Putin over the U.S. intelligence services—the Trump presidency had not improved relations with Russia. On the contrary, allegations of Russia's meddling in the U.S. elections and continuing fallout from Russia's Olympic doping scandal only worsened perceptions of Russia in the United States.

Meanwhile, the 2018 poisoning attack on Skripal in Salisbury, England,

and the brazen murder of Zelimkhan Khangoshvili, a former Chechen platoon commander shot to death by an FSB operative in Berlin's Kleiner Tiergarten park, infuriated London and Berlin.

The Geneva meeting yielded virtually no tangible results, but at a news conference afterward, Putin was asked about Navalny. He said that in his view, Navalny had willingly chosen to go to jail. Of course, he did not utter Navalny's name.

"With regard to our nonsystemic opposition and the citizen you mentioned," Putin said, "first, this person knew that he was breaking applicable Russian law. He needed to check in with the authorities as someone who was twice sentenced to a suspended prison term.

"Fully cognizant of what he was doing, I want to emphasize this, and disregarding this legal requirement, this gentleman went abroad for medical treatment and the authorities did not ask him to check in while he was in treatment," Putin continued. "As soon as he left the hospital and posted his videos online, the requirements were reinstated. He did not appear. He disregarded the law—and was put on the wanted list. He knew that going back to Russia. I believe he deliberately decided to get arrested. He did what he wanted to do. So, what is there to be discussed?"

Putin also used the question to gripe about the U.S. meddling in Russia's affairs, complaining that "the United States declared Russia an enemy and an adversary."

"Now let's ask a question," Putin continued. "If Russia is an enemy, what kind of organizations will the United States support in Russia? I think not the ones that make the Russian Federation stronger but the ones that hold it back, since this is the goal of the United States.

"How should we feel about this?" he added. "I think we should be wary."

For more than a decade, Putin and his subordinates had tried to paint a picture of Navalny as an agent of the United States, but it was a far-fetched claim. It was obvious to Russians that Navalny was not only a patriot but also that he had a Russian nationalist streak. As Navalny said on the radio in 2011: "I am absolutely a patriot."

What Navalny absolutely refused to do was get in line and accept the Russian state's corruption. He had undertaken shareholder activism in 2007, around the same time that the Russian political analyst Stanislav Belkovsky told the German newspaper *Die Welt* and other outlets that Putin controlled a vast fortune, including major stakes in Surgutneftegas, Gazprom, and the giant oil transport firm Gunvor. Navalny immediately targeted these companies, seeking to uncover information about their ownership and operations. At the time, Belkovsky, in an interview with the *Guardian*'s Luke Harding, suggested that Putin was worth at least $40 billion. Harding would later be expelled from Russia, the first British journalist to be banished since the Cold War.

* * *

Over the years, Navalny's investigations largely avoided going after Putin directly. He focused instead on the breathtaking corruption committed by those getting rich off of Putin's rule, with the clear implication that Putin was the ultimate beneficiary. Whatever they were stealing, Putin no doubt was stealing more—probably much more.

But two days after Navalny's arrest, his team responded with a full-scale frontal attack on the Russian leader: a nearly two-hour documentary alleging vast corruption by Putin, beginning from his earliest days serving as a KGB officer in Germany, that would ultimately make him, according to Navalny, "probably the richest man in the world."

Called *A Palace for Putin: History of the World's Largest Bribe*, the film pulled together an array of long-known information about how Putin enriched himself and his family, friends, and cronies primarily at the expense of Russian citizens, while adding an array of salacious new details about the huge residence that was allegedly built for Putin on the Black Sea.

"Hi, it's Navalny," he began with his signature chipper opening. "We came up with this investigation when I was in intensive care, but we immediately agreed that we would release it when I returned home to Russia, to Moscow, because we do not want the main character of this film to think that we are afraid of him and that I will tell about his worst secret while abroad.

"This is not only an investigation," Navalny continued, "but also in a sense a psychological portrait. I really want to understand how an ordinary Soviet officer turned into a madman who's obsessed with money and luxury and literally ready to destroy the country and kill for the sake of his chests of gold."

The documentary was also, in its purest form, revenge. Revenge for trying to murder Navalny with a chemical weapon; revenge for nearly killing his wife in a botched earlier poisoning attempt; revenge for thwarting Navalny's political ambitions; revenge for more than a decade of harassment, jailings, and legal prosecutions, including a three-year imprisonment of Navalny's younger brother, Oleg.

Most of all, it was revenge on behalf of the Russian people—the generation of Navalny's parents, his own generation, and his children's—who had been denied democratic freedom and prosperity in a country with vast natural resources and energy wealth.

The Kremlin has denied that Putin is the owner of the extravagant property in Gelendzhik, a beautiful resort town on the Black Sea with a famous safari park. But Navalny assured his viewers that his investigation had debunked these denials.

"The only real owner of this famous place from the very beginning to the present day was Vladimir Vladimirovich Putin, and . . . looking inside you will understand that the president of Russia is mentally ill," Navalny said, seated at a wooden table, his fingers knit together, with a glass of water nearby. "He's obsessed with wealth and luxury."

The existence of the palace and the vast corruption scheme that financed it were actually revealed more than a decade earlier by Sergei Kolesnikov, a close business associate of Putin's and a partner of Nikolai Shamalov, one of Putin's closest friends.

In December 2010, in an open letter to President Dmitry Medvedev, Kolesnikov wrote: "Dear Mr. President, A palace is being built on the Black Sea for the personal use of the Prime Minister of Russia. To date this palace costs over $1 billion U.S. mainly through a combination of corruption, bribery and theft. This unpleasant tale of illegal payments, with threats, and with rampant corruption portends poorly for our beloved nation as we struggle to improve the lives of all Russians and be a full partner in the global community of nations that ascribes to the rule of law."

At the time, Navalny wrote about Putin's Palace on his LiveJournal blog under the heading "Mikhail Ivanovich," and he pointed to an article written by Yevgenia Albats, Navalny's political mentor, for *New Times* magazine. In the article, Kolesnikov described how he, Shamalov, and others secretly managing Putin's personal money had taken to calling Putin "Mikhail Ivanovich."

It appeared to be a tongue-in-cheek reference to dialogue in a famous Soviet movie, *The Diamond Arm*, in which a character says, "I need to speak to the chief, to the boss... to Mikhail Ivanovich."

In his blog post, Navalny offered only a brief comment. "And so it is known that those in power in the country, by chance, turned out to be ordinary, mid-tier St. Petersburg swindler-schemers," he wrote. "But the documentary evidence is amazing every time. Read and pass on to others."

Kolesnikov, in his open letter, expressed a hope that Medvedev was sincerely committed to fighting corruption, as he had professed during his campaign for president: "I address you openly, rather than privately, because I have been inspired by your public speeches highlighting corruption as a main cause of crisis in our country."

* * *

Kolesnikov's hopes, of course, were terribly misplaced—as were the hopes of President Barack Obama, his secretary of state, Hillary Clinton, and an array of other U.S. officials who made a terribly false bet on carrying out a "reset" with Russia during Medvedev's presidency.

Not only would Medvedev do nothing to put a stop to Putin's vast corruption schemes but he would follow in Putin's footsteps. According to Navalny, Medvedev allegedly set up his own fraudulent graft through dummy charities to accumulate his own extravagant portfolio of real estate and other assets both in Russia and abroad.

And instead of the president of Russia mustering a charge against corruption, that fight would be led instead by Navalny.

In March 2017, Navalny and his team published the results of an investigation into Medvedev. After swapping roles from 2008 to 2012 to keep Putin in place as the country's supreme leader—an arrangement known as "the tandem"—Medvedev was back in his old job as Russian prime minister.

Navalny alternated over the years between ridiculing Medvedev for his ineffectiveness and applauding whenever Medvedev rolled out some change in legislation or regulation that, at least in theory, might help fight corruption. But in the end, it was clear that Medvedev was little more than a Putin puppet, and not a particularly effective one at that.

Medvedev was often teased in the Russian press for being a bit of a geek. In a land of hockey and soccer fanatics, Medvedev was shown on a leaked video playing badminton. It was a stark contrast from Putin, who was shown bare-chested on horseback and in other macho wildlife settings. Since the start of the invasion of Ukraine, however, Medvedev has become better known for threatening nuclear strikes against Russia's enemies—a transformation from lapdog to attack dog, but subservient to Putin nonetheless.

The 2017 Anti-corruption Foundation investigation of Medvedev was actually a follow-up to an earlier look at just one of the luxury properties allegedly used by Medvedev—a huge vacation home sitting on two hundred acres and surrounded by a twenty-foot-tall fence in the town of Plyos, about a four-hour drive north of Moscow.

Medvedev's connection to the estate was quite well-known. In 2011, after Kolesnikov's disclosure about Putin's palace on the Black Sea, Roman Anin, an investigative journalist then working for the *Novaya Gazeta* newspaper, wrote about Medvedev's luxury properties.

But Navalny's team revived the outrage with a slick video, including aerial footage, which allowed viewers to peek behind the giant fence. Among the revelations was a pond with a small structure in the middle that Navalny identified as a "duck house." Rubber ducks quickly became an internet meme among Navalny supporters.

Navalny estimated the value of the property in Plyos at $300 million to $400 million. "The chic residence for the leader of the United Russia was paid for by gas magnates from the Novatek company, transferring this money as 'charity,'" he said.

The new video, titled *Don't Call Him Dimon*, demonstrated the Navalny team's flare for focusing on viewer-friendly, human details—in this case, Medvedev's love of designer sneakers. This detail was used to confirm that a stash of hacked emails released by the group Anonymous International contained genuine messages from Medvedev's account.

Navalny's team matched the internet orders of distinctive, colorful pairs of Nike footwear and some shirts, to photos of the prime minister. Then, they looked more closely at the orders, and the name and address on the shipments.

The information led to a web of corporate entities and charitable organizations, one named Sotsgosproekt, which stands for the Fund for Socially Significant State Projects, and another called the Dar Foundation, headed by a friend and university classmate of Medvedev's named Ilya Yeliseev. These organizations owned giant estates and other assets that, according to Navalny, actually belonged to Medvedev.

"You would never take this man for some kind of a villain or an underground billionaire," Navalny says at the start of the fifty-minute video. "He's a smartphone and gadget enthusiast, a ridiculous simpleton, who falls asleep during important events. The internet calls him Dimon."

The film then cuts to a clip of Medvedev's longtime press secretary chastising a Russian journalist for referring to him by that nickname: "He is not Dimon to you."

"Dmitry Medvedev, prime minister and former president of Russia, is crazy about money and elite real estate," Navalny says, picking up the story.

Shot with a drone—one of the Navalny team's favorite tools for surveying the ill-gotten wealth of Russian officials—the video shows a thirty-thousand-square-foot house, with a swimming pool, a giant pond, and numerous outbuildings, including a guesthouse and several gazebos. The property is located in an area close to Moscow favored by senior government officials and wealthy business executives.

Navalny estimated the value of the property at about $85.5 million, and in the video wondered aloud how the Sotsgosproekt had that kind of money to buy such property. "Here's the answer," Navalny says. "It didn't buy the estate. It received it as a gift. And here we come to the description of the felony. Because you know who made this gift? Here's who: Russia's richest oligarch, Alisher Usmanov. The owner of a giant fortune built on the remains of the Soviet mining industry. A tax resident of Switzerland. He simply gave an estate, worth $85.5 million, as a gift to the foundation with very close ties to the prime minister."

"What is that called?" Navalny asks. "That's right—a bribe. A real bribe. A classic one. And both Usmanov and Medvedev understand this, which is why the gift was registered to the foundation, which is managed by one of Medvedev's classmates, and chaired by another." Medvedev and Usmanov vociferously denied Navalny's claims, as did the foundations and Medvedev's friends who managed them.

On Sunday March 26, 2017, three weeks after the release of the video, thousands of people in cities across Russia answered Navalny's call for a day of anti-corruption protests. Despite stern warnings from the police that demonstrators would be arrested, sizable actions took place from St. Petersburg in the West to Vladivostok in the Far East. Hundreds were arrested across the country—including Navalny, who was detained in Moscow. He was sentenced to fifteen days in prison and fined about $350.

A few days later Usmanov sued Navalny for defamation, and the following month the oligarch attempted to hit back using Navalny's own methods. Usmanov released two videos, in which he lambasted Navalny. The first one ended with Usmanov saying, "I spit on you."

"Out of the two of us, you're the criminal," Usmanov said, referring to

Navalny's conviction in an embezzlement case, in which the charges were widely viewed as trumped-up for political retribution.

In May 2017, Usmanov won his defamation lawsuit, and the court ordered Navalny to delete sections of the video accusing Usmanov of bribing Medvedev. That September, Sotsgosproekt won a similar defamation lawsuit against the Anti-corruption Foundation. Navalny refused to comply with the court orders to edit the videos and publicly recant the bribery allegations.

Usmanov was hardly the only Russian business executive to sue Navalny. He has been targeted repeatedly. Others who have taken Navalny to court include Roman Abramovich, Oleg Deripaska, Viktor Vekselberg, Kirill Shamalov, Gennady Timchenko, Arkady Rotenberg, Yury Kovalchuk, and Yevgeny Prigozhin.

At one point, in 2013, Navalny took aim at Vladimir Yakunin, the longtime head of Russian Railways, and launched a website headlined "The Adventures of Piglet Yakunin." Presented in the form of a graphic novel, the site documented extensive real estate holdings abroad and a chain of hotels connecting to rail stations, which allegedly helped the railway chief accumulate vast wealth. "Over the course of 10 years, the head of Russian Railways and old friend of Putin's has achieved consistently high ticket prices, amassed hundreds of millions of dollars and sent his children to live abroad," the site declared.

In 2018, an exposé by Navalny about corruption in the Russian National Guard found that the government was vastly overpaying for food served to guard troops. That led the head of the National Guard, Viktor Zolotov, who was Putin's former head of security, to deny the accusations and challenge Navalny to a duel.

"You have made me the subject of insulting, defamatory remarks. It is not customary among officers simply to forgive," Zolotov said. "From time immemorial, scoundrels have had their faces smashed and been called to duels." He added, "I simply challenge you to a duel—in the ring, on the judo mat, wherever, and I promise to make good, juicy steak of you."

A 2019 investigation accused Medvedev of appropriating a private jet controlled by a subsidiary of VTB, the government-controlled bank, for his wife's personal use. In the same investigation, Navalny accused Andrei Kostin, the head of VTB, of similarly making a company-connected plane available for the use of his lover, the television journalist Nailya Asker-Zade. VTB denied the allegations and said the airplanes had been sold.

But an investigation by the Russian news outlet, the *Bell*, confirmed that the planes were owned by VTB subsidiaries before being transferred to another company called Skyline Aviation SRL, registered in San Marino, and that another Skyline plane was used by Patriarch Kirill, the head of the Russian Orthodox Church. Navalny's investigation showed that Kostin's chief of staff at VTB had connections to companies that operated the planes before and after the sales. "They steal, hide and lie," Navalny said in a video laying out the details. "They constantly lie in our faces." One of Navalny's strangest investigations was set off after a group of scantily clad women burst into the Anti-corruption Foundation's offices, followed by a crew from the Kremlin-connected Life News television channel, which filmed the women. The group turned out to have staged a protest, naked, outside the U.S. embassy in Moscow in support of the disgraced American film producer Harvey Weinstein.

Another woman connected to the group posted a video in which she personally threatened Navalny, vowing that one of them would have sex with him and release a video of it. Randomly, she added: "Because of you and those like you, people keep fighting wars now."

That threat prompted further investigation. Navalny's team found that the woman called herself Nastya Rybka, but her real name was Anastasia Vashukevich. She was a Belarusian-born escort who had traveled with the oligarch Deripaska on his yacht and written a how-to book about seducing billionaires.

Video of Rybka and Deripaska on the boat, posted by Rybka on Instagram, showed another man on board with them: Deputy Prime Minister Sergei Prikhodko, a former senior aide to Putin, allegedly in the company of prostitutes. At one point on the video, Deripaska can be heard discussing relations between Russia and the United States and referring, perhaps sarcastically, to Victoria Nuland, a high-level State Department official, as Prikhodko's "friend."

Navalny compiled all of his investigative findings into a video, released in February 2018, in which he repeatedly expressed disbelief at how Rybka had laid out so many details, which Navalny's team easily confirmed by tracking the movements of Deripaska's yacht, Elden. Navalny alleged that Prikhodko's trip on the yacht, as well as the services of the women on board, amounted to bribes paid to the deputy prime minister by Deripaska.

"I never in my life thought I would say such words, let alone in front of an audience of a million viewers, but there is no choice," Navalny said. "The deputy prime minister, head of Medvedev's office, spends his vacation on an oligarch's yacht, in the company of this oligarch, excuse me, and several prostitutes. Yes, there were several."

But the investigation didn't stop with these salacious details. Navalny pressed on, using widely reported business connections between Deripaska and Paul Manafort, Donald Trump's disgraced campaign manager, to declare that the Anti-corruption Foundation had essentially cracked the case of Russia's alleged meddling in the 2020 U.S. presidential election.

Navalny, claiming to have put all the puzzle pieces together, accused Manafort of trying to pay off his financial debts to Deripaska by giving briefings on U.S. politics to the oligarch who, in turn, passed the information to Prikhodko, for the benefit of Putin and the Russian government. The video did not remotely offer conclusive proof of election meddling, which Russia has denied repeatedly, if not quite convincingly.

Rybka ended up arrested on solicitation charges in Thailand, where she and some associates were conducting "sex workshops." From prison, she made an unsuccessful pitch for political asylum by offering the U.S. consul information about Trump and Russia.

Deripaska issued a statement denying the allegations, and successfully sued Rybka for invasion of privacy. Prikhodko also denied the allegations. In a statement to Russia's RBC newspaper, Prikhodko called Navalny a "political loser" who "once again tried to arrange a provocation... chaotically mixing everything possible and impossible."

Prikhodko acknowledged that Deripaska was a friend but denied knowing Manafort. But in a cabinet reshuffle following the Russian presidential election later that year, Prikhodko was left without a post. He died in 2021.

In one head-spinning investigation in 2015, Navalny linked the sons of Russia's general prosecutor, Yuri Chaika, to a vast business empire, including a luxury hotel in Greece co-owned by one of the sons, Artem Chaika, and Olga Lopatina, the former wife of Gennady Lopatin, Russia's deputy prosecutor general. The investigation alleged business ties to one of Russia's most notorious criminal gangs and documented an array of raids carried out on businesses around the country with the help of prosecutors abusing the power of their office. The raided businesses ended up controlled by the Chaika family, according to registration documents.

In any other country, the allegations would be jaw-dropping. According to Navalny and his team, Russia's justice system was a racketeering operation, and the chief prosecutor was a mafia don.

Chaika forcefully denied Navalny's allegations and alleged that someone else had paid Navalny to publish the false accusations. "The information presented is deliberately false and has no basis," Chaika told the Interfax news agency.

Lopatina, the ex-wife of Chaika's deputy, also denied Navalny's charges and threatened a lawsuit, insisting she had no connection to the Tsapkov criminal gang. However, *Vedomosti*, Russia's leading business daily, reported that business ownership records confirmed connections.

It's no wonder then that Navalny for years was asked why he was still alive. Navalny insisted on provoking the most powerful people in the country, people who considered themselves untouchable. Chaika did not need to feel above the law; he *was* the law. Russia's criminal justice system, according to Navalny, was a tool not for justice but for the enrichment of Chaika and his family.

This was part of Navalny's point. Russia, he believed, was run by a bunch of greedy, murderous gangsters. They were bandits, no different from the corrupt and greedy Communist Party bosses who exploited the Soviet system and led it to ruin.

Through his investigations, Navalny was effectively building a wide-ranging case against Putin and Putin's entire system of government. This case almost certainly would never reach a courtroom, but Navalny held out hope that it could win in the court of public opinion, that he could persuade voters that for Russia to develop, Putin had to go. It wasn't just the prosecutor's office. The entire system was rotten.

When Navalny first started digging into Gazprom as an activist shareholder, he was warned that people get killed for digging up this kind of dirt. But his hunch was that the criminals robbing Gazprom shareholders of dividends and asset value were the same criminals robbing Russian citizens of their tax money, and robbing Russia of its future as a normal European country.

Navalny felt personally affronted by it all. They were robbing him, robbing his parents. Navalny believed that someone needed to bring these crooks and thieves to justice. And for reasons that even he and his family would struggle to explain, Navalny, a military brat who grew up with a poster of Arnold Schwarzenegger on his bedroom wall, decided he would be the one to mete out justice and extract revenge.

He also refused to be afraid. By nature or nurture, he was incapable of backing down from a fight, and repeatedly urged his followers to show the same fearlessness. "We are the power," he would tell them from the stage of mass protests, a statement that Putin and his riot police would prove false again and again by repeatedly tossing Navalny into prison.

And yet, Navalny refused to bend a knee to the regime, generating fascination and consternation in Russia. Who was this Navalny who insisted on taunting the Kremlin and baiting fate? Where did he come from? Who or what made him like this?

—4—

EARLY YEARS

"My main hero was, and still is, Arnold Schwarzenegger."

—*Alexey Navalny,* Esquire, *December 2011*

Even as a child, Navalny was indignant, righteous, dubious of authority, and unbending in his principles.

"His character manifested itself very quickly," his mother, Lyudmila Navalnaya, told an interviewer. "To parent him was impossible; it was impossible to say 'no' to him. I remember he was once scolded for something by a teacher, so he refused to go to school the next day [saying]: 'I don't want to be forced to study.' Nothing can be forced upon him."

But if righteous indignation and stubborn relentlessness are among Navalny's defining character traits, what has always made him especially confounding to his opponents, and so infuriating and threatening to Putin, is his ordinary, Slavic Russianness.

Russia, historically, is hypersensitive to ethnic distinctions. The word for a Russian citizen—*Rossiyanin*—is different than the word for an ethnic Russian—*Russkiy.* Being a Jew or a Georgian or a Tatar, or any of Russia's more than one hundred other ethnicities, signals minority status. And despite Communism's aspiration to maintain an egalitarian society, acute differences were also noted between those in the party *nomenklatura*, the Chekhists in the security services, the intelligentsia, and the creative classes.

Navalny—with Russian and Ukrainian ancestry, a military family, classic good looks—does not stand out in any way that could be criticized as subversive or dangerous to Russia and Russianness. His family history, childhood upbringing, education, love life, and early career are so utterly mainstream, majoritarian, and normal—initially so Soviet, then so Russian, and all along, so Slavic—as to make it ridiculous, if not impossible, to try to paint him with "otherness." He is a guy who spent a half year on a fellowship at Yale University and later said he realized he could not live in America because he missed black bread.

Of course, in a country with a long tradition of real and imagined conspiracy theories, suspicions, and betrayals, that has hardly stopped critics and opponents from trying to portray him as an outsider and a threat, to brand him as an "extremist" and a "foreign agent." Yet, Navalny's personal biography at its core is a Slavic-Russian one.

"He considers himself a simple, common, even mediocre Russian guy," Konstantin Voronkov, a friend, colleague and supporter of Navalny's, wrote in a 2011 authorized biography, *Threat to Crooks and Thieves*.

For some of Navalny's supporters, the more crucially important point is what he is not—not a Jew; not an oligarch; not from the intelligentsia, or the Soviet *nomenklatura*. Rather, he comes from an Orthodox Christian military family, whose ancestors fought for the Red Army in World War II, which the Russians call the Great Patriotic War.

"Finally," one of Navalny's closest supporters said, voice dropping to a whisper. "Finally, we have a Russian guy."

To call him Russian, however, is not entirely precise, at least not in the Russian way of thinking about ethnicity. Navalny's mother is Russian. His father was born in Ukraine, in a village, Zalissia, just fifteen miles from the future site of the Chernobyl nuclear power plant. The town was abandoned after the nuclear disaster in 1986, and all its residents, including Navalny's grandparents, uncles, and other relatives, were eventually forced to evacuate and relocate.

As Navalny once told the novelist Boris Akunin, swatting back an assertion that he harbored ethnic prejudices: "I myself am half Russian, half Ukrainian. And I do not want to feel a bit like a second-class person."

In fact, Navalny's Ukrainian background served only to bolster his street cred as a man of modern Russia. His own family history is tied up not only in the Chernobyl catastrophe but also in Russia's more recent aggressions against Ukraine, in Crimea and Donbas in 2014, and, ultimately, the full-scale war that began in February 2022.

Navalny's Russian nationalism and his initially ambiguous public statements about the annexation of Crimea in 2014 have made him suspect, or even hated, by many Ukrainians, some of whom are unaware of his Ukrainian roots and regard him as a Russian imperialist.

But in Russia, Navalny's personal narrative is so unremarkable as to be inherently patriotic. His physical appearance, and that of his blond, blue-eyed wife and children, is so classically Russian that this alone often seems to undermine, if not neutralize, efforts by Putin and other critics to portray him as a treacherous Western agent.

In 2018, on Victory Day, which Russians observe on May 9 with far more reverence than Americans mark Memorial Day or Veterans Day, Navalny posted photos of his grandparents' military medals on Facebook and noted that while he had never met his grandfather, he had grown up asking his grandmother: "How many fascists did you kill?" Like so many who served, he said, she preferred not to talk about the war.

And once, thwacking a critic on Twitter, Navalny compared his family's military service to that of the country's senior political leaders, and some of Russian television's most famous commentator-propagandists. He singled out Putin; longtime defense minister Sergei Shoigu; Medvedev; the editor in chief of the propagandist RT channel, Maria Simonyan; and the bombastic talk show host Vladimir Solovyov.

"I'm alive thanks to my parents," Navalny tweeted. "And they're alive thanks to my grandparents. Grandfather fought and was wounded. Grandmother ended the war in Berlin. But neither Putin, nor Shoigu, nor Medvedev, nor Simonyan and Solovyov, nor the crazy propagandists with ribbons have anything to do with this."

Indeed, the police officers and security agents sent to search Navalny's home and office, to stalk him, or guard him under house arrest, have often privately conceded feeling at least some solidarity with Navalny and his close associates, sometimes even warning them of raids in advance, at other times quietly telling them: "We know you are good guys."

* * *

Butyn, a tiny, former military outpost in the southwest of Moscow region, where Navalny lived until he was six years old, is often cited as Navalny's birthplace. But in fact, Alexey Anatolyevich Navalny entered the world on June 4, 1976, at a hospital in Solnechnogorsk, a town on the northwest fringe of the capital region.

Solnechnogorsk is located on the road from Moscow to St. Petersburg, just outside of the fabled Golden Ring comprised of some of Russia's most picturesque and historic cities, and a bit more than a half-hour drive northwest of Zelenograd, where a pregnant Lyudmila Navalnaya was living with her own mother.

Her husband, Anatoly Ivanovich Navalny, was an officer in the missile forces stationed at a garrison in Butyn. Though they had married the year prior, in 1975, the couple lived apart during the week. Lyudmila Navalnaya worked in a lab at the Soviet Center for Microelectronics during the day, and in the evenings she took classes in economics at the Moscow Institute of Management, which today is Russia's premier business school, the State University of Management. In 1975, however, it was named, ironically enough, after Sergo Ordzhonikidze, a Bolshevik revolutionary who later served as a senior Politburo official and was a close confidante of Stalin, whom he first met when they shared a prison cell in Baku in 1907.

On the morning that Lyudmila Navalnaya went into labor, the hospital in Zelenograd was closed for reconstruction.

Navalnaya and her mother hitched a ride on a truck heading north, and Navalny was born in Solnechnogorsk in the early afternoon. According to his mother, he weighed about eight pounds, two and a half ounces, and he was twenty-four inches long. That put him in the 99.9 percentile for height, in what would turn out to be an accurate predictor of his lanky, six-foot-two-inch frame as an adult.

The year of Navalny's birth, 1976, was a generally uneventful one in the Soviet Union. Elsewhere, exciting things were happening. In Poland, that same month, a plan to raise prices for many basic commodities set off violent protests that ultimately led to the dismissal of Prime Minister Piotr Jaroszewicz.

In Montreal, the following month, a fourteen-year-old Romanian gymnast, Nadia Comăneci, was awarded the first-ever perfect score of 10.0 in gymnastics at the Summer Olympic Games; she would go on to win three gold medals. And in the United States, President Gerald Ford stumbled during a campaign debate by insisting that there was no Soviet domination in eastern Europe, one of numerous missteps that led to his defeat by the Democratic governor of Georgia, Jimmy Carter.

In the Soviet Union, however, it was literally the same-old, same-old as the aging Communist Party elite sought to maintain stability and their own grip on power.

Leonid Brezhnev, already the Soviet leader for a dozen years, was reappointed in March 1976 as general secretary of the Communist Party, insuring a continuation of his policy of détente with the West. The one surprise at the Party Congress was the ouster of the agriculture minister, Dmitry Polyansky, as punishment for the failure of the 1975 grain harvest—a foreshadow of the far more severe food shortages and logistical breakdowns that would contribute to the Soviet Union's collapse.

Navalny was born into a relatively nondescript period of stasis, in which some aspects of the Soviet project were calcifying and others beginning to rot. It was virtually the midpoint between the apex of Soviet glory—Yuri Gagarin becoming the first human to journey into space in 1961—and the Communist superpower's dissolution and demise in 1991.

This meant some inherent contradictions. As a boy, he felt innocent patriotism.

"I am a guy from the Soviet Union," he told an American interviewer. "I was very proud that my father is guarding Mother Russia from evil Americans with their bombs and missiles."

But some of Navalny's earliest memories were also of the Soviet Union entering a pitiable state, and by the time he was a teenager, momentous events were beginning to unfold.

It was in his Soviet childhood that Navalny also developed an early and enduring disdain for government dysfunction, ineptitude, and the corruption, whether petty or on a grand scale, that pervades Russian life.

When chatting about his upbringing, Navalny has said that one of his defining childhood recollections is of standing in line, to get milk for his brother, Oleg—a seemingly endless queue each day after school.

"Main childhood memory—I stand in line for milk," he told his friend, Voronkov. "All the time I stand in line for milk. When I was seven years old, my brother was born. And when he was little, he needed a lot of milk. And for him, all the time I went to stand in line. It was necessary to arrive at two p.m., when this milk was delivered, and every time I would return from school, and stand."

Navalny's other childhood chore was returning glass bottles on which Soviet consumers paid a relatively steep deposit of twenty kopecks. But when the young Navalny arrived at the collection point, he and others were invariably told that the bottles could not be accepted because there were no storage containers available—a maddening and absurd process that was designed to get people to toss the bottles in frustration, or to accept reimbursement at cut rates.

"This nonsense was a truly nationwide problem," Navalny told Voronkov. "And the realization of the meaninglessness of the economic order, uselessness and chaos happened through this."

* * *

The absurdity of the bottle redemption process, and the unhappy memories of the queues for milk, and of his parents lining up before dawn to buy meat, were just two factors that shaped Navalny's clear-eyed, unromantic, and scathing opinion of Soviet Russia.

Like others in his generation, he viewed Gagarin as a national hero, but he never bought into the Soviet myths, and he recognized the ineptitude of Soviet officials as a national embarrassment.

"When now some people, especially young people who didn't experience the Soviet Union, begin to tell me stories about how wonderful it was there, I don't need them to tell me this," Navalny said. "I stood [in line] for this milk. My mother and father still remember how at five in the morning they had to go to get in line for meat. And this was in a military town, where there was a good supply. I do not think that the Soviet Union should be cursed in some indiscriminate way, but now we definitely live better than then, and I have no nostalgia for it. And there was nothing to eat in the Soviet Union. We brought buckwheat from Moscow to Ukraine, where this buckwheat is grown."

Carrying packages of buckwheat, among the most basic staples of a Russian diet, on visits to your grandparents' village, is the sort of detail that becomes imprinted in a child's mind. And it wasn't just buckwheat. Navalny's aunt and uncle would recall their Moscow relatives also bringing sugar, oranges, and other basic goods during times of deprivation. In exchange, they would send them home with local fish and mushrooms.

Navalny's childhood trips to Ukraine, where he spent virtually every summer with his paternal grandmother until he was eight years old, were a journey into a natural paradise.

He would live during those months in his grandparents' white cement house, with green-and-white wooden shutters, on October Street—surrounded by other children, swimming in the Uzh River, fishing, picking cherries, eating poppy-seed pies and the Ukrainian crescent-shaped dumplings called *vareniky*.

"My most vivid childhood memory is the Uzh River, which flows into the Pripyat—a high precipice and swallows' nests," Navalny once told Russian *Esquire* magazine. "I keep trying to get this swallow, I stick my hand in there, but I can't get it."

It was also in Ukraine that Navalny's grandmother took him, secretly at age three, to be baptized in the Orthodox Church. "When I was three years old my grandmother took me to be baptized among relatives in Ukraine, secretly from my father, because he was a Communist. They were afraid that he would be expelled from the Communist Party," Navalny told the Polish historian and public intellectual Adam Michnik.

Relatives recalled the young Alexey as a friendly, well-behaved, outgoing kid, who didn't complain, and notably didn't cry or whine, who blended in easily and, by the end of each summer, could converse comfortably in the local Ukrainian dialect, which has a bit of Belarusian mixed in.

Navalny's father, Anatoly, was the second of three sons of Ivan Tarasovich Navalny, and Tatyana Danilovna Navalnaya, both of whom worked on the local *kolkhoz*, or collective farm. Ivan Tarasovich was also a carpenter. A monument to fallen soldiers listed a half-dozen with the surname of Navalny who died in World War II.

Today, Zalissia is a ghost town, the abandoned houses and other buildings crumbling back into nature, as is the case throughout the Chernobyl exclusion zone. A sign at the entrance of the village notes that Zalissia had "2849 inhabitants before the Chernobyl disaster" and notes the evacuation date: May 4, 1986—eight days after the explosion and meltdown in the power plant's reactor No. 4.

For Navalny and his family, the disaster was deeply personal. Navalny has frequently remarked that if the reactor explosion had happened just a few weeks later in June, after the start of school holidays, he would have been there. And in the years since, he has visited the exclusion zone countless times.

Most crucially, though, the tragedy of Chernobyl impressed on Navalny at a young age the very real life-and-death consequences of government lies, disinformation, and incompetence. In tones of fury, he has described how the Soviet government delayed evacuations of families, while trying to hide the magnitude of the disaster.

"In order not to raise panic, the collective farmers—and our relatives too—were sent to [plant] potatoes, digging in the radioactive dust," he said. "It was a real universal catastrophe, in which my family and I were victims."

After HBO released its hugely popular *Chernobyl* miniseries in 2019, Navalny took to YouTube to angrily denounce Russian television commentators who criticized the show as inaccurate and alleged purposeful misrepresentations of history by its Western creators.

"What happened in Chernobyl was really a monstruous catastrophe, in which guilt lay precisely with the constant lie, the disgusting, ugly lie told by these people, all these Soviet bosses sitting in Moscow and Kyiv," Navalny said. "I am a bit emotional speaking about this because in a sense this is the story of my family. All the relatives from my father's side are from Chernobyl.

"I know perfectly well from my relatives about this whole story of endless lies," he added. "The power station blew up, but nevertheless they were silent, and drove them out there to plant... potatoes for the collective farm. Here they were digging with their own hands, with the radioactive dust falling and receiving a huge dose of radiation."

As an adult, Navalny has returned to the area numerous times, generally in May when permits are issued allowing family visits on Victory Day and on the anniversary of the Chernobyl disaster itself later in May. He has described seeing a coat on the floor of his grandmother's abandoned house that he had worn during his summer visits.

Navalny's connections to Ukraine and to the Chernobyl disaster are not merely a matter of boyhood memories and old ancestral ties. They also cemented some of his defining personal and political beliefs. One of those convictions was that the Soviet Union was a debacle. Its leaders and authorities were alternatively cruel and inept and—even more infuriating to Navalny—a bunch of greedy, hypocritical liars.

Another of those core beliefs was an inherently racist one, though Navalny himself would describe it as realism, not racism: that Russians, Ukrainians, and Belarusians formed "brother" nations, bound together by their white, Slavic ethnicity and by Russian culture. This perspective was part of a larger equation in which Navalny would insist that there were core cultural differences between these "Russian" people and people from the North or South Caucasus (even those in Russia), or from Central Asia.

"Of course, it would be great if now we lived in one country with Ukraine and Belarus, but I think that sooner or later it will happen anyway," Navalny told Voronkov. "The common cultural and linguistic space has been preserved, and it will exist for the foreseeable future. Russian culture is the only thing that truly united that country and continues to unite the Russian Federation. Why is the talk now that the Caucasus may secede so real? Because there are no Russians there."

Navalny's view about the brother nations would be shattered, at least as far as millions of Ukrainians were concerned, by Putin's full-scale invasion of Ukraine in February 2022. But during his two decades in public activism and politics this Russian-centric outlook—which critics would brand as chauvinism or worse—would fuel a flirtation with nationalist ideologies and political forces. This put him at odds with some of his allies in liberal political circles and would end up staining his reputation at home and abroad. It would also create an agonizing tension between Navalny's aspiration to be a "good guy" and his desire to be populist enough to have a chance at winning elective office.

In the late 1980s and early 1990s, however, as the Soviet Union moved toward its inevitable collapse, and Russia experienced seismic political and cultural shifts, the teenage Navalny's outlook was defined by his childhood experiences, by the visits with his grandparents and relatives in Ukraine, by conversations about politics around the kitchen table with his parents, and by his firsthand observations of other military families he lived with on the outskirts of Moscow.

Growing up with military brats meant more than a few fistfights for Navalny. Kids in those military towns would also take leftover ammunition cartridges from firing ranges and fashion fireworks out of them, sometimes with disastrous, disfiguring results.

In 1988, the year that Navalny turned twelve, the Austrian-American bodybuilder and actor Arnold Schwarzenegger visited Moscow for four days of filming for the movie *Red Heat*, in which Schwarzenegger plays a Soviet policeman, Ivan Danko. Schwarzenegger, as a champion weightlifter and star of the 1984 hit *The Terminator*, was already a giant celebrity in Russia. The trip to Moscow would only the fuel the adoration. In addition to filming some takes in Red Square for the movie (which was mostly shot in Hungary) Schwarzenegger insisted on meeting his own childhood idol, the champion Soviet bodybuilder Yury Vlasov.

Under these circumstances, it's hardly surprising that a poster of Schwarzenegger would end up on the wall of Navalny's childhood bedroom. But while Navalny is no muscleman, it turned out that his idol and his idol's idol were also captivated by politics. Vlasov was elected to the Congress of People's Deputies in 1989, at the tail end of the Soviet Union, and to the State Duma of the Russian Federation in 1993. Initially, he was a supporter of democratic reforms and was part of the interregional group of deputies that included Andrei Sakharov, Anatoly Sobchak, the future mayor of St. Petersburg, and Boris Yeltsin. Vlasov would even go on to run for president as an independent candidate in 1996.

Schwarzenegger, of course, would later be elected governor of California. Navalny would continue to follow his career with childlike admiration, telling Russian *Esquire* magazine in 2011: "My main hero was, and still is, Arnold Schwarzenegger."

As a teenager, Navalny's passions were politics and music, and they came together on a television show *Vzglyad*, or "Outlook," which was a current events talk show that also featured foreign music videos. He would watch it with his mother. "At first everything was about politics, and then about music," Lyudmila Navalnaya told *New Times* in an interview. "Here Alyosha watched with me," she said, using the diminutive nickname for Alexey. "He was waiting for music."

Navalny was also a big newspaper reader as a teenager. One day, browsing through the large-circulation daily *Moskovsky Komsomolets* when he was in the eighth grade, he learned about a high school that trained young economists called the Plekhanov Institute. He passed the six-hour entrance examination, and for two years commuted into the center of Moscow to study there.

* * *

Navalny has spoken often about the special nature of his particular mixed-breed generation—those born between 1976 and 1982. That six-year bracket was not Navalny's invention but was actually an online community of LiveJournal, the hugely popular blogging platform where Navalny himself rose to internet fame.

"This is the Moscow baby boom and it has come of age," Navalny said in an interview with *Time* magazine published in January 2012. "The name 76-82 comes from an insanely popular community on LiveJournal, called 76-82, where people write short memories that they share with people from this generation. Things like, I don't know, chewing gum, movies, a very specific type of Communist youth camp from the end of the Soviet Union, in the late '70s and '80s."

Like other generations defined by a unique moment in history, the 76-82 Russians shared experiences and jokes that resonated deeply only within their cohort. They had been Communist Young Pioneers as kids, wearing red ties and forced to march and sing patriotic songs, but they changed the lyrics to insert crude vulgarities. They listened to a mix of Soviet and Western rock music.

Voronkov summed up Navalny's view of his in-between generation as follows: "We got a full dose of radiation from the Soviet Union, but adulthood began in another country... the new world was built by those who were slightly older, and those who were slightly younger fit into this world perfectly because they did not know otherwise. We, on the other hand, were left standing on our backs, witnessing interesting times but gaining nothing from them and not knowing how to apply ourselves."

Navalny put it in harsher terms. He would later describe himself as disgusted by the lies and hypocrisy of the Soviet state, and he would try to define himself as the antithesis of a *Sovok*—the pejorative label for a person with a conformist, Soviet mentality.

"It was clear that this whole shitty system was built on deception, and all these agitators and propagandists, who lived here and told the tale of their Party, dreamed only of getting a trip to Bulgaria, buying a watch here, exchanging it there for some perfume and two tape recorders," Navalny told Voronkov. "Everybody wanted to go abroad. And the only people who went abroad were those who told us how wonderful the Soviet Union and the Soviet system was. The realization of this, plus the *Vzglyad* program and rock music, made me a fierce, infernal democrat and liberal.

"You had to be a child to feel all the abnormality of the reality around us—Soviet hypocrisy reigned, which adults hardly noticed any more. It is hard to say whether we managed to free ourselves from it," he continued. "But the outward manifestations of 'Sovokism' are definitely still alive."

Navalny admits that as the Soviet Union collapsed, he joined in the national denigration of Mikhail Gorbachev and was a huge supporter of Boris Yeltsin and of his team of reformers, including the main proponent of privatization, Anatoly Chubais. Navalny would later say this position was naïve and mistaken.

"I have to admit over the past few years I've reevaluated the events of the late '80s and early '90s," Navalny told Michnik, the Polish historian, in 2015. "Back then I was a massive fan of Yeltsin's, but Gorbachev seems a far more appealing figure to me now. I understand what scenarios he could have put into effect—anything from bloodshed to stratospheric personal enrichment. He could have done everything Putin's doing now but didn't. He was detested by the whole country then, Communists and liberals alike."

But Navalny in his exuberant youth was a strident democrat, influenced in large part by his anti-Communist parents but also driven by his own fierce indignation.

In 1993, he enrolled in the law faculty at People's Friendship University in Moscow, a second-tier school, having missed admission to the more prestigious Moscow State University by a single point. That same year, he helped his parents start a wicker and basket-weaving business in the town of Kobyakovo, southwest of Moscow, where his father was last stationed in the military. Navalny, his brother, Oleg, and their parents each owned 25 percent of the company.

Navalny began working even as he was still in school, initially taking a position at Aeroflot Bank. But in January 1997, the Central Bank revoked its license. Shortly after, Navalny took a job in the legal department of ST Group, a Moscow real estate development company owned by two brothers, Shalva and Alexander Chigirinsky.

Years later, appearing on a talk show with Ksenia Sobchak on TV Rain, Alexander Chigirinsky would admit that he had no idea Navalny had been his employee. "I just didn't even know that he worked for us," Chigirinsky said, laughing.

Sobchak, the daughter of the former St. Petersburg governor, pressed him for details: What was he like? Was he a good worker?

Chigirinsky had zero to offer. "And when the press reported it," he said, "the most interesting thing is this, that it seemed to me that the press was lying, that it wasn't true."

He said that he called one of his managers, to confirm: "Is it true, Navalny worked for us?" he asked. "Navalny came in 1998 on the basis of an advertisement," Gennady Melkumyan, who headed the company's legal department, told *Vedomosti*. "We considered several candidates, settled on him: He is smart, catches on quickly."

While working at ST Group, Navalny learned how to process property deal approvals through the Federal Anti-monopoly Service and realized he could make good money this way on his own.

In those years, Navalny registered several businesses. One, created in 1997, was called Allekt, which he would later use as a vehicle for political consulting work among other ventures.

Another, called Nesna, was to be dedicated to hairdressing, according to the corporate filings. Later, he established N.N. Securities with a school friend, Ivan Nesterenko, as a vehicle for trading on the stock market. Another was called Eurasian Transport Systems. The flurry of entrepreneurialism reflected Navalny's effort, common among many in his generation, to catch a bit of the capitalist wave after having missed out on the privatization frenzy that followed the Soviet collapse.

* * *

While on vacation in Turkey during the summer of 1998, Navalny met his match. Yulia Abrosimova, tall and blond, was not only a member of the 76-82 club, she was born in Moscow just seven weeks after he was, on July 24, 1976.

Fate? Destiny? Inevitability? Navalny has never hidden his disdain for people who are dumb or, even worse, disengaged and indifferent. "When a person tells me they are not interested in politics, I just think they are stupid," he told Voronkov. "Or it's an excuse to swim with the current, to explain his laziness or meanness."

Yulia, strikingly pretty, might have caught Navalny's eye anyway. But he was immediately smitten for other reasons. She had a degree in economics. She was a democrat and, like Navalny, a member of Yabloko, the center-left, liberal-minded political party founded by the free-market economist Grigory Yavlinsky. She was up on current affairs, for instance, and could name all of Russia's governmental ministers.

For Russians of their generation and demographic, holiday romance at a Turkish resort was almost comically typical. In fact, the Russian press, which would become obsessed with the country's best-known blogger and the "first lady of the Russian opposition," later noted that what was atypical was that they managed to sustain the offshore summer romance back home in Moscow.

But looking at any photograph of them together—on vacation, with their children, in endless courtrooms—there is no doubt that this is a handsome, Russian, and specifically modern, middle-class Muscovite couple. Navalny—tall, often joking and smiling, and posting openly on social media about his family—offered a stark contrast to Putin, who exudes the paranoia of an ex-spy, refusing to ever speak about his family (or families) and even having his two acknowledged daughters use different surnames. This was—and still is—a core pillar of Navalny's political appeal and helps explain why he has always posed a very different sort of threat to Putin than the so-called systemic opposition.

Where Yavlinsky, born to Jewish parents in Lviv in Western Ukraine, represented the tweedy intelligentsia that historically had never gained any political traction in Russia, and Gennady Zyuganov, the general secretary of Russia's Communist Party since 1993, represented the failed apparatchiks of yore, Navalny offered something new and different—a modern, telegenic family man.

Convincing mainstream Russia to endorse that new, different profile would become Navalny's personal and professional challenge for the next decades. Moscow is not Russia, just as New York is not the United States. Most of Russia is not middle class but abjectly poor, and the overwhelming majority of Russian voters are not part of the modern, urban professionals, hipsters, or creatives found in the capital or St. Petersburg, the country's second city.

Alexey and Yulia were married in August 2000 and, in keeping with their typical profile, followed in the path of other typical Russian newlyweds in their early twenties: They began making babies. A daughter, Darya—Dasha—was born in 2001. A son, Zakhar, was born in 2008, matching the seven-year difference between Navalny and his brother, Oleg.

Navalnaya has always maintained a protective shell around herself and her children, stressing that Navalny is the politician. Nonetheless, she is unquestionably a driving force behind him and everything he does. In her first TV interview, in 2013, Yulia Navalnaya told Leonid Parfenov on TV Rain: "I didn't marry a promising lawyer, and I didn't marry an opposition leader. I married a young man named Alexey. I married a man with whom it was clear from the very beginning that sharp turns were possible, so nothing unexpected happened to me."

Parfenov, intrigued, pressed the point about sharp turns. "He has always been very active," Navalnaya said of her husband, "with a very active citizenship."

Yevgenia Albats, Navalny's political godmother, has frequently said that she believes Navalny will spend his life striving to prove that he is worthy of such a smart, beautiful partner.

Albats interviewed Navalny's mother, Lyudmila, for *New Times* magazine, and asked her what the Navalnys thought of their daughter-in-law.

"We have always liked her very much—a rare combination of intelligence and beauty," Lyudmila Navalnaya replied.

"Didn't you fear that Yulia is so beautiful that Alyosha will have to conquer her all his life, to prove that he is worth it?" Albats asked.

"What," Lyudmila shot back, "my son is ugly?"

—5—

MAKING OF A POLITICIAN

"He's totally a political person, totally, as people say, a political animal."

—Maria Gaidar, August 2021

When Navalny was a boy, his father used to rail against the Soviet Communists so loudly that his mother, Lyudmila, said she would shut the windows for fear that neighbors living nearby would hear him and it would cause her husband, a career military man, problems at work.

Beginning with the Russian legislative elections of 1993, Navalny's parents had always supported the democratic alliance of Grigory Yavlinsky, Yury Boldyrev, and Vladimir Lukin, which would later become the center-left political party Yabloko, whose name means "Apple."

Ideologically, Navalny was also a supporter of the social-minded democrats. But in 1996, Boris Yeltsin, then sixty-five years old and in ill health after a series of heart attacks, was suddenly locked in a tight race against a Communist, Gennady Zyuganov.

Navalny, like many in his generation, had been caught up in the euphoria of the Soviet collapse. Fearing a slide back toward Communist misery, Navalny—with the exuberant self-assuredness of having turned twenty years old just two weeks before the election—told his parents to vote for Yeltsin.

"In 1996, his dad and I timidly said that Yeltsin was not very good for us," Lyudmila Navalnaya recalled in an interview with *New Times* magazine. "But Alyosha told us to go and vote for Yeltsin. There was a choice—either for him or for Zyuganov."

Yeltsin won, in an election largely perceived as marred by fraud. But he would end up resigning before the end of his term and handpicking a successor; Vladimir Putin, the prime minister and former head of the KGB. Putin's selection was part of a deal that would shield Yeltsin and his family from vengeful prosecution.

Navalny eventually concluded that he was wrong about Yeltsin, and that he had failed to recognize the threats to democracy posed by the disrespect for rule of law, and the circumventing of constitutional controls that eventually brought Putin to power.

A first inkling of those misgivings emerged when talk began in Russian government circles about plans to raise the so-called "percentage barrier"—the threshold for parties to enter as a faction into the lower house of parliament, the State Duma.

Democracy advocates often recommend a threshold of 3.5 percent. Russia in its parliamentary elections of 1993, 1995, and 1999 had a threshold of 5 percent. But chatter soon started about raising the threshold to 7 percent, or even 12.5 percent. This would have killed the chances of minority parties, which were still developing in Russia's young, rough-and-tumble democracy, and were in fact struggling to gain any footing against the governing coalition, given the country's strong presidential system.

Yabloko had worked in coalition with Yeltsin, mainly to counter the Communists, and Yavlinsky, the Yabloko party chairman, had even voted in the State Duma to confirm Putin when Yeltsin named him as prime minister in 1999. But Yavlinsky was in the minority and had even asked his party's governing board for permission to cast his vote for Putin—knowing it would be controversial. Most of the party's Duma members voted against Putin.

Navalny was among a new generation that was drawn to Yabloko because it was the one decidedly anti-Kremlin party. Another Yabloko member of that generation was Ilya Yashin, who joined shortly after Navalny and became a longtime ally. "When we went to Yabloko, we all had the same motivation," Yashin told *Afisha* magazine. "We have seen threats to the democratic structure of our country."

Navalny said he was motivated to prevent the raising of the electoral threshold and to preserve the possibility for opposition movements in Russia to win seats in government. But when he first walked into Yabloko's offices on Moscow's New Arbat Avenue, he hardly seemed like a guy who would attract much notice.

Navalny, with a young career and a serious girlfriend who shared his political leanings, was drawn to the progressive party and eager to get involved, but he was also a bit reticent, and in those days seemed a bit shy.

He gamely took a back seat to others who had taken on more proactive roles in Yabloko, including Daniel Meshcheryakov, a veteran human rights activist who was a director of the Moscow Helsinki Group, and Timofei Nizhegorodtsev, who had headed a firm called the People's Opinion Agency for Economic and Political Consulting. Nizhegorodtsev, who was from the Siberian city of Irkutsk, was just three years older than Navalny, yet Navalny considered him a political mentor.

"First of all, he wasn't famous," Maria Gaidar said. "Second, he wasn't leader of anything. Third of all, he would, like, happily and effectively work in second positions, or third positions. He would help for example, [Sergei] Mitrokhin, who was in Yabloko. He was helping me. He was helping Ilya Yashin. And so, he was helping."

* * *

Navalny's work in Yabloko, initially as an unpaid lawyer, was less than scintillating. And what he discovered when he first got a look inside the party's operations left him less than impressed. "I came, looked around and realized that no one was doing anything," he told *New Times* magazine in 2010. "It was a hellish mess, and it was clear that Yabloko would not get even 5 percent."

It actually was not clear, or not clear enough. And what Navalny did not fully grasp then, in 2000, was that Yabloko, and in fact democracy in the Russian Federation, had already peaked, at least in terms of party politics and representation in the State Duma.

In 1993, in the first Duma elections after the Soviet collapse, the Yavlinsky-Boldyrev-Lukin, which would become Yabloko, won more than 4.2 million votes, notching 7.86 percent and winning 20 of the 225 seats allotted by party list. It won seven more seats in voting for individual constituencies, for a total of 27 out of 450 seats in the chamber.

In 1995, Yabloko won nearly 4.8 million votes, or 7.02 percent, to snag 31 of the 225 seats awarded proportionally, and another 14 individual district seats, for a total of 45 seats, a gain of 18 seats. That left the party holding 10 percent of Duma seats overall.

But in 1999, the party won 3.9 million votes, or 6.05 percent, and while it met the threshold to have a faction in parliament, it lost more than half of its seats, emerging with 16 from the party list and 4 from individual constituencies. And in 2003, the first elections in which Navalny helped on the party's campaign, Yabloko won just 2.6 million votes for its party list. At 4.37 percent, it failed to meet the 5 percent threshold—the party with the most votes to fall short of the barrier.

For that election, Putin's forces had coalesced into the United Russia party, which finished first with more than 38 percent of the party list votes, and a total of 223 seats, just short of the 226 needed for an outright majority. That year marked the end of free, democratic parliamentary politics in Russia. At Yabloko, Navalny had joined a dying organization.

In 2010, a decade after he officially joined the party and three years after being expelled from it, he would claim to have known this all along. But in fact Navalny, when he started at Yabloko, knew almost nothing about politics.

He instinctively did not like Putin, and he was drawn to the idea of being active and involved, but his own ideological views were not formed. Friends and supporters would later say that he was always a "political animal," but if so, in those days he was more a political neophyte.

Navalny's years in Yabloko might be described as one long journey of self-education on political organizing, electoral campaigning, and community activism.

"When I met him for the first time in 2004, you know, he was one of those guys, young guys, who were playing politics, with very little knowledge about grassroot politics," Albats said. At that time, she had recently returned to Moscow from getting a graduate degree at Harvard University and was hosting a group of politically active young people at her apartment every Tuesday evening.

"My whole idea was to try not to teach but to learn with these young kids how to do this grassroot politics without big money," she said. "Let's try and learn how to knock the doors, how to speak to people, how to do everything out of our own pocket—no oligarchs, no huge expensive rallies."

Navalny's time in Yabloko was a depressing and frustrating education in losing. But, by all accounts including his own, he had a lot of fun.

His greatest satisfaction in those early years came from the creation of an organization called the Committee to Protect Muscovites, technically a project outside of Yabloko, but one that the party helped coordinate.

The Russian capital was experiencing an extraordinary construction boom—and it was rife with abuses. Residents were often furious, and sporadic protests would erupt. Yelena Baturina, whose husband, Yury Luzhkov, was Moscow's mayor from 1992 to 2010, became Russia's first woman billionaire by working as a construction developer.

So in June 2004, with Putin tightening control over national politics, the democratic opposition forces focused locally. The purpose of the new Committee to Protect Muscovites, according to a Yabloko press release, was "to unite scattered groups, which currently number more than 200... into a single powerful organization that defends the interests of Muscovites in the field of urban planning."

Sergei Mitrokhin, the head of Yabloko's Moscow branch and Navalny's boss in the party, was named chairman of the group. Navalny became the executive secretary and did most of the work. "Don't think that we are helpless! We have different ways of putting pressure on the government," Mitrokhin said.

The stated goals of the new group also bore a hallmark of Navalny's acute sense of justice, which has always entailed a keen desire to cast blame and level punishment. "The Committee plans to seek the resignation of officials who make illegal urban planning decisions and who are guilty of red tape when considering complaints from citizens," the press release said.

Within the committee, its organizers created a "Conflict Commission," intended to resolve any disputes between residents, developers, and city officials. Navalny was named the coordinator of that commission. "All meetings of the Conflict Commission will be held as publicly as possible, with the involvement of representatives of the public and the media," Navalny said in the press release.

In an interview with the newspaper *Izvestia*, Navalny said his goal was to start a conversation between residents, city officials and developers before anyone put a shovel in the ground. "Let's reserve a place in these newspapers and websites where we will publish projects and discussions of these projects—moreover, at the stage of pre-project study," he said. "When a bulldozer drives into the yard, it's too late to talk to people."

The Committee to Protect Muscovites jumped into the fray and began opposing some of the most high-profile construction and development projects underway in Moscow.

These included a plan by the television personality Vladimir Pozner to construct a media studies school over a landmark-protected building on Malaya Dmitrovka Street, a proposal to replace the demolished historic Hotel Moskva overlooking the Kremlin, and a plan for a giant highway and tunnel in the capital's Krylatskoye District, connecting the Ring Road with the city center.

Another major target was the Don-Stroy development company, whose projects in residential neighborhoods had set off a chorus of public outcry in the city. There were repeated complaints that the company was putting up buildings with more floors, or more overall square footage, than were approved.

Initially, the committee boasted some quick successes. The Federal Antimonopoly Service temporarily blocked the highway project, and Don-Stroy agreed during a mediation meeting to help finance a citizen information center and to conduct briefings for local residents about its projects.

In 2006, Navalny expressed special outrage over a project that involved the expansion of a car dealership, taking over part of a public space and playground. "I am used to hearing about the 'construction pranks' of our authorities," Navalny wrote on LiveJournal, "but still I sat and listened and lost my mind."

After the car dealership twice tried to get permission and was refused to take over the public space, suddenly "dudes" from a government-controlled agency showed up and declared that there was radioactive contamination. The area was fenced off, trees began to be cut down.

According to Navalny, the Ministry of Emergency Situations said there was no radiation detected and the fence was deemed illegal. Residents wanted to tear it down but were being blocked by private security guards stationed by the developer.

These were the sorts of fights that Navalny took on, arming himself with the details of building regulations, environmental statutes, and rules on competitive bidding and tenders. It was the start of what would become his seemingly never-ending crusade against Russian corruption in all forms.

At this point, it was anchored in his political work, trying to channel citizen anger into support at the polls—and the results, if any, were difficult to quantify.

Navalny, however, later boasted to Voronkov that it was a major success, bringing media attention to Yabloko even as party officials were denied access to state-controlled TV channels. "We felt that we were feared; we were really creating problems for this corrupt Luzhkov government," Navalny said. "It was a real political activity. But, again, it was very hard, both physically and organizationally."

Critics, though, accused Navalny and Yabloko of opportunism and of failing to follow through with their initial efforts to block projects. The real goal, the critics said, was to use the Committee to Protect Muscovites as a publicity and vote-manufacturing machine for Yabloko, in particular with a bid to get Mitrokhin reelected to the State Duma from a district in Moscow where there was a special election to fill a vacancy.

If that was the goal, however, it did not work. Putin's United Russia had more effective dirty tricks than helping constituents with their complaints. By running a candidate with the identical name of the Duma member who had resigned, they made sure no candidate met the necessary threshold to win and the special election was declared invalid, allowing a replacement to be appointed.

Navalny, in any case, defended the overall approach and said that if there were political benefits to Yabloko's activism, it was a good thing.

"We did not take these votes from scratch," he told *Izvestia*. "We really helped people... Yes, we also received political dividends, but what's wrong with that? Let other parties conduct their policies this way. We cannot make this topic exclusive. Recently, the Motherland Party held a protest action to stop the construction of a concrete plant in Novoperedelkino. And it's wonderful."

* * *

The Committee to Protect Muscovites was not Navalny's only side project.

In 2005, Navalny teamed up with Maria Gaidar to create the Democratic Alternative movement, abbreviated as DA! (which means "Yes!" in Russian). DA!'s other cofounders were Natalia Morar, an investigative journalist with *New Times* magazine, and Oleg Kozyrev, a blogger, activist, and man of letters.

The goal was to bring together like-minded young political activists, including from different parties, under a single umbrella. "The Democratic Alternative Movement is part of civil society. We don't fight enemies. We want to solve specific problems that concern us in our country," the group posted on its website. "Our task is to show citizens that they have enough means in their hands to participate in determining the path of development of their country."

They described DA! as a "nonpartisan youth organization," adding: "We focus on thinking young people, on those who believe in the possibility of changing something in Russia."

"We believe that people with active citizenship can really change lives for the better through legal and nonviolent means," it said on the website.

"Nobody will do it for them. This is our alternative to extremism, idleness, whining, and complaints."

DA! was designed with a horizontal structure and, therefore, no leader. "Each is responsible for [his or her] own part of the project, voluntarily undertaken to lead. Anyone can become a coordinator of their own project, which is consistent with the main principles of DA!"

The group added, "Members of DA! are good, active and purposeful people. We are not fanatics and not city madmen, we study and work. We are not building a revolutionary group and do not want to overthrow anyone. We just want to live in a free and democratic country and force the government to do what it is instructed to do."

It was a sign of the political climate in Moscow in those days, that the fledgling group also felt compelled to deny—repeatedly—any revolutionary tendencies. On the "About" page of its website, the group's founders included a question they had been asked on Ekho Moskvy radio: "Do you import Ukrainian revolution? Is it true that you are being helped by political technologists who made the Orange Revolution?" They replied:

> The Ukrainian revolution was "made" by ordinary Ukrainians, not by technologists. Anyone who was in Kyiv in those days, and did not watch what was happening on Russian TV channels, understands perfectly well that without conscious citizens, political technologies would have turned into a farce (as happened with the Kremlin PR people).
>
> The government understands that the main threat to it is active citizens who are not silent when they see corruption, incompetence, gagging of independent journalists, and arbitrariness. Therefore, it is interested in our passivity, and imposes on the Russians a cynical attitude towards manifestations of civic activity.
>
> No, we are not revolutionaries, and we are not going to overthrow anyone. We are holding and will continue to hold peaceful civic actions. The safety of our supporters is very important to us, so we will do everything to avoid clashes with the police. We just want the

authorities to respect our right. All we demand is the implementation of the Constitution, which was adopted by the Russians themselves.

Over time, DA! undertook four core projects: a volunteerism initiative focused on helping the neediest in society, led by Kozyrev; a media freedom program led by Gaidar; a police watchdog component led by Navalny; and an anti-corruption-in-universities campaign led by Morar.

The movement ended up with branches in at least eight cities, including St. Petersburg, Novosibirsk, and Perm. But DA! became most famous for a series of live political debates, with Navalny acting as the emcee. The first took place on February 28, 2006, in a packed club, and featured Nikita Belykh, leader of the Union of Right Forces political party, and Maxim Kononenko, a well-known online journalist, on the topic of fascism.

Among a certain slice of Moscow's hip, young, political elite, the debates were a sensation, and seemed to fill a vacuum for genuine, public discourse, and engagement. In the Soviet Union, such open debate wasn't allowed. By the 2000s there was debate, but it was all in the virtual reality of the internet.

At the time, the LiveJournal blogging platform was the hub of political conversation in Moscow, and for the members of the audience who crowded into the Apshu Klub that night it was almost an out-of-body experience to see everyone in person.

"LiveJournal has entered the real world," Rimma Polyak wrote for "Russian Nights"—the nightlife section of the *Russian Journal* online magazine. "An impressive part of Moscow's LiveJournal users gathered at the Apshu Klub for a debate on one of the key issues of our day: Where are the fascists?

"The hall, filled with faces familiar from user-pics, seemed like family, welcoming remarks poured in from everywhere, shining with smiles of recognition," Polyak wrote. "Everyone clearly felt good, almost like at home in front of their favorite computer with a user-feed on the monitor."

She added, "The smartest users managed to catch a waitress on the way and order beer or branded mint tea. Stronger drinks have not yet been successful."

Navalny was a presence on LiveJournal at the time but not yet a celebrity.

A panel of judges scoring the debate voted narrowly in favor of Belykh, the crowd for Kononenko. The specific arguments, in hindsight, were less important than the mere fact that a public conversation was underway. The second debate featured a face-off between leaders of the pro-Putin Nashi ("Our") youth movement, and the youth wing of Yabloko. For the third one, the writer Viktor Shenderovich and journalist Oleg Kashin, centered on the question: "Where are the honest journalists?"

With each appearance, Navalny grew more comfortable in his role as master of ceremonies, referee, and sportscaster. In a rave review after the third debate, Polyak wrote: "Navalny is certainly a talented showman (even if, God forbid, something happens to Yabloko, he will definitely not be left without work now)."

"Respect to Navalny," another viewer posted on LiveJournal after the third event. "He leads the debates better and better."

One debate even had the opposition politician Boris Nemtsov, who years later was shot to death outside the Kremlin, square off against Dmitry Rogozin, a right-wing, pro-Putin member of parliament who would go on to become Russia's ambassador to NATO and a deputy prime minister known for issuing blustery threats against the West.

But in those days, Gaidar recalled, neither she nor Navalny nor others in the DA! movement or in opposition circles had given up entirely on engaging with the government.

Rather, she said, Navalny was working out his own politics and looking for openings to push Russia in a different, democratic direction. "He was trying to find [his] place when he was a young man... active with a lot of ideas with a lot of energy," she said. "He was trying to find different ways... to put his political passion into work."

The first debate of the 2007 political season, on October 30, at Gogol, a bar in the center of Moscow, promised the most provocative topic yet: "Putin's Plan or Putin's Clan?" And it was supposed to feature Gaidar crossing rhetorical swords with Sergei Markov, a political scientist and adviser to Putin, who was also a United Russia candidate in the upcoming Duma elections, which were scheduled for early December.

That evening, however, things quickly went sideways. Barely an hour before start time, Markov's assistant called and said he had to leave on an urgent business trip. The organizers scrambled and persuaded Eduard Bagirov, a writer who had published a popular novel, *Guest Worker*, to stand in. Bagirov was not a member of United Russia, but he generally supported Putin's policies and agreed to argue the position.

Replacing Markov, however, was only the start of the problems that night. A group of rowdy hooligans arrived early, took seats toward the front, and from the outset began disrupting things.

One guy approached the stage with flowers, which he handed to Gaidar while bestowing loud and solicitous compliments. "I want to congratulate all those present on the upcoming New Year, 2008," he said, "you, Maria Gaidar on your victory in the presidential elections, or whichever ones you are planning. I don't remember."

Navalny tried to shoo the man away, but he persisted. "Your hairstyle is charming; your blouse, too," the heckler told Gaidar. "Everyone goodbye! Vote for United Russia!"

Bagirov, who had argued "I am not for Putin, I am for Putin's course," won the debate, according to the jury, although two of five judges abstained. But within moments a brawl broke out. A bottle was thrown and cracked over someone's head.

Yashin recounted the events on LiveJournal, where he described the rabble-rousers as *gopniks*, a derogatory Russian term for low-class hoodlums. "The dudes took turns shouting insults at Navalny and Gaidar and tried to snatch the microphone," Yashin wrote. "In fact, the entire discussion took place against the backdrop of the drunken yelling of these *gopniks*. In the end, they grappled with the audience, during the scuffle they broke a bottle on someone's head. In addition, the club's security guard was injured. Finally, the guards led the provocateurs out into the street."

Navalny was enraged.

"I stood next to the stage," Yashin recalled. "Navalny came down with furious eyes." Navalny followed the men onto the street. Yashin followed Navalny, trying to enlist other supporters in case of a fight. Outside the club, Yashin suddenly noticed the grip of a handgun sticking out of Navalny's pocket.

The hooligans saw it, too, backed away, and scurried off. One heckler, though, had been held inside. The man, Timur Teziev, a twenty-three-year-old car mechanic, now emerged and made a charge at Navalny. They fought. Navalny, stepping back, pulled out the pistol, an air gun, and fired several shots. The police soon arrived, and Navalny was arrested.

At the police station, Teziev lodged a complaint against Navalny, accusing him of causing bodily harm. He later dropped the allegation, *Nezavisimaya Gazeta* reported, "in view of the awareness of the provocative nature of his behavior."

Yashin and others, including Nikita Belykh, the head of the Union of Right Forces party, provided witness statements, and there was ample video evidence. The case, however, provided a convenient way to hassle Navalny, and it dragged on for six months before it was finally closed without any charges against him.

Many years later, Kremlin propaganda outlets would continue to revisit the incident. In 2013, the RT television network reported: "A fight outside a nightclub in the center of Moscow, shooting at point-blank range and the bloody face of a victim offended over his nationality: RT publishes unique materials about how Alexey Navalny managed to avoid trial for hooliganism with a weapon in 2007."

That was the end of the DA! debate series, as it was clear they would face continuing harassment. "We realized that we could not guarantee security," Navalny recounted later. "We didn't have money for security, but what if next time they send someone to stab or break a head?"

Yashin said it was obvious that the hooligans were part of a premeditated assault on the political opposition.

"What we do know for sure is that these guys are connected to one of the pro-Kremlin youth organizations and have cover in the presidential administration," he wrote on LiveJournal. "There is no doubt that the provocation was invented by the Kremlin specialists in the fight against the 'orange infection'... In addition, there is every reason to believe that United Russia's Sergei Markov knew in advance about the impending provocation, and that is why he refused to participate at the last moment."

What Gaidar recalls most vividly about those days is Navalny's passion for politics.

"He just loved politics. He wanted to do politics, no matter what, no matter what his position was," she said. "So, he's totally a political person, totally, as people say, a political animal." Later, after he achieved some fame, Navalny developed a reputation for demanding to be front and center. But in those days, Gaidar said she never experienced that. "I only know that for him, he always wanted to do politics and be in politics. And I remember times when he wasn't successful in politics, and it wasn't giving much reward to him in any way."

* * *

In the fall of 2006, Navalny was furious to learn that the Moscow authorities had cooked up a plan to demolish seven buildings in the city center that had served as vocational schools and turn the lots over to a private developer, called Stalitsa-Zapad, which of course had won the deal without any competition.

The schools were to be replaced by a big new vocational campus on the far southwestern edge of the capital—far beyond a reasonable commute for most families.

The Committee to Protect Muscovites quickly took up the cause and began organizing protests.

"By order of the Moscow government... seven Moscow vocational schools located in the sweetest places for investors in the city... will be destroyed," Navalny wrote on LiveJournal. "And in their place (how unoriginal) office buildings will be built. As 'compensation' one hefty vocational school will be built. But in South Butovo... where to get to, as you know, is two hours one way from any place in Moscow, except for the far South-West."

Flashing his outrage, Navalny wrote: "It is clear that many consider students of technical schools and vocational schools worthless cattle."

But there was another aspect of Navalny's response that hinted at a very different part of his continuing political evolution: his own instinctive Russian nationalist streak, and his flirtation with far right and xenophobic political movements to see if there was any ground on which they might be able to build common cause.

"Vocational schools are needed; not everyone is able to go to college. The country is in direct need of skilled workers," Navalny wrote on his blog, adding in bold for emphasis: "Migrants, by the way, are attracted for this."

Navalny, by all indication, has always harbored anti-immigrant views. He seemed to regard some degree of xenophobia or racism to be normal, and mainstream. And, in his own statements, he has admitted viewing certain people—those from the Caucasus, for instance—as different from Slavic Russians like himself. Like many xenophobes, Navalny at times has tried to couch his views as mainly an economic position. In pushing for visa regimes that would limit immigration to Russia, Navalny has professed concern for the well-being of migrant workers, who inevitably face harsher discrimination and mistreatment when they are undocumented, and are therefore vulnerable to extortionary abuse.

In any case, Navalny recognized the political potency of anti-immigrant sentiment and, in search of a political formula that would offer a viable alternative to Putin, he began entertaining the possibility of reaching out to nationalist and right-wing forces despite the deeply unsavory elements. In this regard, he had the encouragement of Albats, his mentor, who is Jewish and keeps a kosher home.

Together with Albats, Navalny had begun attending the Russian March, an annual gathering of nationalist and right-wing groups that included the most extreme elements of Russian nationalism, including neo-Nazis and fascists. Albats likes to point out that she walked with Navalny at these marches wearing a large Star of David.

In 2007, Navalny became a cofounder of a new political project, called the National Russian Liberation Movement. Its acronym in Russian is spelled NAROD, which means "People."

Where DA! was designed as a civic movement, independent of political parties, NAROD was created as a supraparty coalition, a movement of like-minded thinkers who could potentially bring together groups with different ideological leanings under a shared call for reviving the Russian nation.

Among the financial backers of NAROD was the political technologist and commentator Stanislav Belkovsky, who was closely associated with the anti-Putin oligarch Boris Berezovsky. Belkovsky has said he donated several tens of thousands of dollars to help launch NAROD.

The movement's manifesto, which Navalny signed, proclaimed:

> Russia is facing a national catastrophe. In peacetime, in a favorable economic situation, in the richest country in natural resources and territory, the population is rapidly degrading and dying out.
>
> The lack of an adequate reaction of society to an unprecedented level of corruption, to official lies, to widespread bribery and theft, to bureaucratic lawlessness and a cynical attitude of the authorities towards the people, allows this handful of people who have usurped power in the state to prolong the days of snickering and detachment from society.
>
> The main attributes of democracy—the principle of separation of powers, the institution of free elections, the federal structure, local self-government, the independence of the courts, and much more—have been virtually eliminated. They were replaced by the power vertical—a set of commercial clans that usurped the functions and powers of the state...
>
> If Russia does not acquire a national program for the future, then the country will disintegrate and disappear from the political map of the world.

In connection with the launch of NAROD, Navalny made two videos, posted on YouTube, that documented his virulently anti-immigrant views with racist and even violent overtones.

In the first video, Navalny, identifying himself as a "certified nationalist," promoted his support for legalizing gun ownership. "Hello, today we are going to talk about pest control," Navalny declares in the same chipper tone that he would later make famous in his anti-corruption exposés. He is standing behind a table, and arrayed in front of him are a slipper, a flyswatter, and a handgun. "None of us is immune from a cockroach crawling into our house, or a fly coming in through a window," Navalny says, as animated images of a cockroach and a fly appear on a screen next to him.

"Everybody knows that a flyswatter is great help against a fly and a slipper against a cockroach. But what happens when the cockroach is too big or the fly too aggressive?" On the screen, a photo appears of three men who look to be ethnic minorities, under the caption "Borderless Homo sapiens." Suddenly, a ghoulish intruder runs into the room completely covered in a black cloak, seeming to shout, "Allahu Akbar!"

"But in this case," Navalny intones, taking the gun from the table in front of him and shooting the intruder, "I recommend a pistol." The video ends with the message: "Firearms should be permitted" printed on the screen.

In the second video, Navalny, dressed up as a dentist, talks about how fascism can be prevented by deporting migrants from Russia. "Our society is corroding," Navalny says as images of skinheads and Asian immigrants flash on the screen.

"The clinical picture is clear even to a nonspecialist," Navalny says. "There is no need to beat anyone. Everything that interferes with us should be carefully but firmly removed by deportation.

"Only someone with calcium in their head thinks that nationalism is violence," Navalny proclaims. "A tooth without a root is called dead. A nationalist is someone who does not want them to remove the Russian root from the word 'Russia.' We have the right to be Russian in Russia and we will protect this right." The video ends with a tagline: "Think about the future. Become nationalist."

The videos were amateurish and bizarre. Over the years, Navalny struggled to defend himself against accusations of ethno-nationalism, in part because of his anti-immigration statements and policy positions, but also because he had made unmistakably racist comments. He apologized for some of these; others he simply tried to deny.

A fellow member of Yabloko, Saadat Kadyrova, who is of Azerbaijani descent, had once lodged a complaint against Navalny for using crude, racist language in front of her while working in one of the party's offices and then insulting her directly when she challenged him.

According to Kadyrova, who has recounted the story many times, the incident began when Navalny asked why she was going to so much trouble to invite a Chechen Duma deputy, Aslambek Aslakhanov, to speak at an event. Navalny, she said, referred to Aslakhanov with the phrase "black ass," a derogatory term referring to people from the Caucasus or Central Asia. She suggested she call Aslakhanov's office and dared Navalny to say it directly.

At that point, she said, he turned the epithet on her, calling her "a black ass who had come down from the mountain." When Kadyrova shot back, "And what are you?" according to her account, Navalny replied, "I am the affectionate representative of God's chosen nation."

Navalny has denied the incident ever took place, but Kadyrova's account has remained consistent over the years and was corroborated by documents showing she filed a complaint with Yabloko's leadership, though nothing was done.

When Russia fought a brief war against Georgia in 2008, Navalny's reaction bordered on extreme. He called for "a complete blockade of Georgia" and to "expel all Georgian citizens on our territory from the Russian Federation." Even worse, he referred to Georgians as "rodents." He later apologized for the rodent remark.

The suspicions of Navalny's nationalist leanings have never dissipated and later would be fanned by Ukrainian anger over Navalny's statements about annexed Crimea.

In an exchange in 2012 with the Russian novelist Boris Akunin, the writer noted that many of his acquaintances had mixed feelings about Navalny and he asked if he could start with a "childlike" question.

"If I understand correctly, you are a supporter of the idea of a 'national Russian state,'" Akunin wrote. "What is that in a federation where a hundred different nationalities live, and in large cities the 'mestizo' population almost predominates? Should all ethnically non-Russians or semi-Russians feel like second-class people in your Russia?"

Navalny immediately took grave offense, or at least feigned it. "To be honest, I did not expect such questions from you or from the democratic intelligentsia from your circle," he replied. "The democratic intelligentsia should, in theory, read the newspaper, and if they are even slightly interested in my activities, they should have a basic understanding of my political views. Know about the Yabloko party, about the Democratic Alternative movement, about current activities.

"Your question is not childlike but offensive. You work, you work, and then the 'democratic intelligentsia' is interested in whether I consider someone as second-class people," Navalny shot back. "There are no second-class people, and if someone thinks so, then he is a dangerous lunatic who needs to be reeducated, treated, or isolated from society. In principle, there can be no question of any restriction of the rights of citizens on the basis of ethnicity. By the way, I myself am half-Russian, half-Ukrainian, and I don't want to feel like a second-class person."

Navalny has made efforts to show he opposes discrimination or racial aggression of any kind. But his own evident unconscious biases, and his willingness to forgive more virulent expressions of nationalism in search of electoral support, have raised questions that will follow him for as long as he is a public figure with political ambition.

In another conversation with Adam Michnik, the Polish historian, Navalny again sought to clarify himself. "My thinking is that we need to communicate with nationalists and conduct explanatory work among them. By no means are all nationalists in Russia driven by a clear-cut ideology," he said. "They just identify some general injustice or other, and respond to it by directing aggression against people of a different color and/or eye shape. I believe it's essential to explain to them that the problem of illegal migration is going to be solved not by violence against migrants but by other means entirely, democratic methods."

Navalny conceded that Putin's brand of neo-imperialist nationalism had won the day, leaving no space for the civic-minded nationalism that Navalny himself envisioned. "So far admittedly, I've accomplished nothing but damage to my own image," Navalny told Michnik. "I'm branded a nationalist by liberals and a liberal by nationalists. And everyone has me down as a fifth columnist."

But even two years after his conversation with Michnik, in July 2017, Navalny remained willing to risk his reputation to engage with nationalists. That summer, he agreed to a public debate with Igor Girkin, a former Russian security officer, who had been involved in the military annexation of Crimea and would later be convicted of murder by a Netherlands court in connection with the downing of Malaysia Airlines Flight 17, which was shot down over eastern Ukraine.

Girkin had publicly challenged Navalny to the debate, and Navalny, never one to back down from a fight, agreed. It was livestreamed on Navalny's website and drew criticism that Navalny had merely provided a platform for a war criminal.

Girkin, who also goes by the nom de guerre "Strelkov," was also believed to be responsible for at least three extrajudicial killings in Russian-controlled areas of Donbas. When Navalny was asked during the debate if he believed Girkin was a war criminal, he said it was up to a court to decide.

The court in the Netherlands did just that, a little more than five years later, convicting Girkin in absentia and sentencing him to life in prison for the MH-17 killings.

Yevgeny Feldman, a photographer who traveled extensively with Navalny to document his presidential campaign in 2017, was among those to criticize him for engaging Strelkov. "I can understand holding a discussion with politicians who have even the craziest of views," Feldman tweeted. "I can't understand someone who executes the unarmed."

Navalny, however, had never given up on the idea that he could somehow engage even the most militant of Russian nationalists.

Vladimir Tor, an organizer of the Russian March, described meeting Navalny in 2006, when authorities were threatening to ban the annual event. "Alexey and I spent hundreds of man-hours discussing our cases," Tor told *Afisha* magazine. "There may be liberal nationalists, democratic nationalists, conservative nationalists, traditionalist nationalists. Navalny, probably, can be ranked in the line of a moderate national democrat." Tor said that Navalny's nationalist views were pragmatic and smart for a politician. "A politician who seeks the sympathy of the majority in Russia, in fact, should take national problems seriously. Because it is the Russians who are his voters," Tor said.

Interviewed for the same article, Ivan Bolshakov, another member of Yabloko, said: "Navalny believed that there was nothing contradictory between democrats and nationalists, he said that many nationalists, speaking out against the regime of Vladimir Putin, are also in favor of the democratic structure of the state. This means that you need to join with them. Of course, he is not a fascist. But he's an ethnic nationalist, and the official position of Yabloko was that we saw this as a danger."

Oleg Kozyrev, Navalny's collaborator on DA! and a fellow regular at Albats's Tuesday night gatherings, said that he had no trouble reassuring those with doubts about Navalny, who asked "What if he becomes a dictator?" and he would simply tell them about Navalny's love for animated comedies. "I usually say, 'Guys, he has a great sense of humor. How can a person who loves *Futurama* become a dictator?' "

Kozyrev said that he and Navalny were bound together by a desire to use civic activism to improve the world. "There was a time when we all tried to create a healthy environment, built not just on protest or criticism, but on the defense of understandable ideas. Kozyrev told *Afisha*, "We wanted to help where the government does not help, to protect where it does not protect."

On the issue of the vocational schools, at least, they succeeded. "We launched a vigorous action: pickets, leaflets, called the mayor's office. And in the end, the court took our side," Kozyrev said.

Navalny proclaimed victory on LiveJournal: "The punishing hands of the Committee to Protect Muscovites and the 'DA' movement have finally reached out to the Government of Moscow!!!!"

* * *

Navalny's clash with Yabloko reached its decisive climax in December 2007 when the party leadership called a meeting to consider Navalny's expulsion. The decision, of course, was already made and Navalny knew it. But he was not about to go quietly, and he used the meeting to vent seven years of pent-up frustration and fury with Russia's failed liberals.

Navalny's speech that afternoon was arguably his most important public statement yet as an aspiring politician, and it was a virtuoso performance—oozing with trademark Navalny scorn and sarcasm. At the very start, he noted that his personal status was up for discussion "at the first meeting after the very dramatic failure of the Duma elections."

"This suggests," Navalny said archly, "that the issue of my expulsion is seen as a key political issue and the most important stage of Yabloko's exit from the crisis. I'm a little embarrassed by this attention but thank you anyway."

In his speech, Navalny expressed pride in his work since 2002, especially in helping to organize street actions, and mobilize the party's youth wing. And he voiced special satisfaction over creating the Committee to Protect Muscovites, which he called "the most successful human rights organization in Moscow."

Navalny asserted that the youth wing, and the Moscow division of Yabloko, of which he had become deputy head, kept the party alive from 2003 to 2005 during its toughest years. "We in the Moscow Yabloko were the first to organize a system for collecting donations, which was later adopted by the federal Yabloko," Navalny boasted. He crowed about the success of the local press operation, and gave a big shout-out to Sergei Mitrokhin, the head of the Moscow branch.

"So, I know the value of my work, and my comrades know the value of my work," Navalny declared in his speech, which he posted in full on his blog.

But then, Navalny tore into Yavlinsky, the party's cofounder and patriarch, who ran unsuccessfully for president of Russia in 2000 and 2004. Navalny complained that he was once told, "your problem is that you don't love Grigory Alexeyevich [Yavlinsky] sincerely."

"Yes," Navalny now exclaimed, "I respect him for some of his past service, but I don't like him one bit."

Navalny since then has griped repeatedly that Yabloko had become a cult of personality around Yavlinsky, who had never led the party to any serious electoral success. In his speech, Navalny excoriated Yabloko's leadership for not recognizing the need to broaden support and for condemning his alleged nationalist views rather than endorsing his call for a big-tent coalition.

"The suggested reason for my expulsion: public propaganda of nationalistic ideas," Navalny said. "Yes, indeed, I argue that only by abandoning the dead-end, narrow-minded left-liberal ideology and moving toward the creation of a national-democratic movement can the dem-movement be revived. The experience of many neighboring countries proves this."

He offered Serbia as an example, pointing out that the warmongering Communist strongman, Slobodan Milošević, was ultimately defeated by Vojislav Koštunica, a nationalist who led a broad coalition of democratic forces.

"Milošević's wild, insane, totalitarian nationalism was crushed not by the pathetic liberal opposition, but by Koštunica's national-democratic movement, which gained mass support from voters," Navalny said. "I argue that the endless equation between nationalism and fascism comes simply from primitive thinking and simple political illiteracy."

Navalny's comparison was over-simplified. But it illustrated how in 2007, more than a decade and a half after the Soviet Union's collapse, politically engaged Russians were still struggling to find a framework for democracy, which had never fully taken hold.

Attacking Yavlinsky, however, was not Navalny's main purpose nor his main concern. His main complaint was that Yavlinsky and Yabloko were losers, and that party leaders persisted in making excuses for their electoral failures while refusing to change.

The 2007 legislative elections had been disastrous, with Yabloko receiving just 1.61 percent of the vote, or about 1.1 million votes out of nearly 69 million cast. The party lost all four of its seats in the State Duma.

Navalny said he was being targeted because he refused to join his fellow party leaders in a la-la land of excuses and rationalization. "The real reason for my exclusion is that I openly state: 'Yabloko has completely failed in this election.' And I'm not satisfied with the sweet syrupy talk about how they stole the victory from us.

"Spreading this untruth is humiliating for the party and for all of us," Navalny continued. "We already went through this in 2003... It was a lie."

Navalny accused Yavlinsky of putting his self-interests and desire for attention ahead of the party. "The main reason for the current collapse is that Yabloko has become a dried-up, closed sect," he said. "We demand that everyone be democrats, but we don't want to be... And the worse the results are, the stronger is the position of the leadership. The more tightly we must rally our ranks around it."

Navalny's criticism was brutal, scathing and spot-on. Yashin, who would end up expelled from Yabloko himself a year later, said that Yavlinsky and the party were simply unwilling to accommodate talent and success.

"There are a lot of talkers in politics and few people capable of organizing something," Yashin told *Afisha* magazine. "A person that can also connect two words is generally a rarity. In this sense, Navalny was a very valuable functionary for Yabloko. But as soon as you start claiming to really influence the politics of this party, your career ends there. You are either expelled or squeezed out."

Navalny, in his final farewell remarks, urged Yabloko to throw off the cloak of failure and self-deceit. "Since this may be my last speech as a member of Yabloko, I appeal to you to stop the self-delusion on the topic of our high results, on the topic of possible vote theft," he said. "Stop lying about it." He demanded that Yavlinsky and the entire party leadership resign.

"To the members of the Bureau who are about to vote, I want to say that the power is in the truth, and the truth will still win," Navalny said. Then, jabbing his sarcastic dagger at them one last time, he threw his arm up in a Nazi salute, shouting "Glory to Russia!" and walked out.

The vote to expel Navalny from Yabloko was nearly unanimous. Only Yashin took Navalny's side. Valery Borshchev, a veteran human rights activist, abstained.

The experience in Yabloko would prove a bitter lesson, and many years later, after emerging from his coma, Navalny would cite it as one of his biggest mistakes.

"I've made a million mistakes. I make thirty mistakes a day like any other human being. I don't have a problem admitting my mistakes," Navalny told Yury Dud, in his first major interview after surviving the poisoning attack. "But every decision we make, we think through very thoroughly."

"What were three most recent mistakes?" Dud asked.

"Staying with Yabloko too long," Navalny replied.

—6—

ANTI-CORRUPTION CRUSADER

"There's only one effective way to vanquish corruption and that's to build a democracy."

—Alexey Navalny, 2015

At the end of April, spring is typically in the air in Moscow, and early May brings holidays—Labor Day on May 1, and Victory Day on May 9, which celebrates the triumph over Germany in the Great Patriotic War. Many Russians head off on vacation.

But instead of going to the beach, Navalny, in 2008, organized a different type of exploratory trip—to the Western Siberian city of Surgut, home to the drab, sprawling headquarters of Surgutneftegas, one of Russia's major energy companies, and where the Kremlin-connected management was holding their annual shareholder meeting.

"Some go to May barbecues, some on tours abroad (there are these), and I went to the city of Surgut," Navalny wrote on his LiveJournal blog. He also complained about the cold weather—temperatures in the low thirties and snow. "When will they fix the weather situation in this country?" he asked. "It would be about time."

Navalny wasn't sightseeing. Rather, he was taking the first big, public step in a new role—that of shareholder activist—which would transform him into a celebrity and propel his career from gadfly and obscure democracy advocate to the most recognizable leader of the Russian political opposition and Putin's foremost nemesis.

The post-Soviet privatization frenzy in Russia had created an abundance of publicly traded but majority state-owned companies, many under the management—or mismanagement—of former government officials, or cronies of current officials. The Kremlin maintained large stakes in these corporations, especially in the energy and banking sectors, but exerted little oversight while the managers made fortunes.

Corruption was rampant. At the same time, corporate governance was virtually unheard of. "We have shareholders but they don't know their rights," Gennadi Gerasimov, a former spokesman for Mikhail Gorbachev, the last Soviet leader, told the *Washington Post* in 2003. Gerasimov, who was also a journalist, had befriended one of the leading shareholder-rights advocates in the United States, Evelyn Y. Davis, and had even written an article about her. "I thought it was important for Russians to know that even if you're the owner of only two or three shares, you can raise hell," he said.

Navalny wasn't the first person in Russia to take up the cause of shareholder rights. Bill Browder, the founder of Hermitage Capital Management, who at one point was the largest foreign investor in Russia, had made shareholder activism a core component of an investment strategy that helped him earn billions.

Browder, who started out as a strong supporter of Putin, was out to make money. His attacks on companies like Gazprom, the giant state-controlled natural gas company, over asset stripping and other misdeeds, were aimed at maximizing share prices and profits. Browder did not become a leading advocate for human rights until years later, after he was expelled from the country, and his tax adviser Sergei Magnitsky died in a Russian jail after trying to expose a massive government tax fraud.

Navalny, on the other hand, had dabbled briefly in the stock market after getting a graduate degree in finance and lost most of his money in the early 2000s after the tech bubble burst. When he got back into stocks in 2007, it wasn't to make money but to pursue justice and expose corruption.

For Navalny, the initiative was his own personal approach to "impact investing"—taking up stakes that would give him the legal right to attend annual meetings, demand information from executives and corporate directors, and, when necessary, file lawsuits or criminal complaints.

By 2007, he had pulled together a stock portfolio that might have mortified any common-sense financial adviser—a curious collection of tiny holdings in some of Russia's biggest energy and financial companies, with little chance of delivering quick profits.

In addition to Surgutneftegas, they included other big Russian oil companies—Transneft, Rosneft, Lukoil, and Gazprom Neft—as well as two huge state-controlled banks, Sberbank and VTB; the power-generation giants, RusHydro and Inter RAO UES; as well as Gazprom, the state-controlled natural gas behemoth.

Navalny has often said that he simply doesn't like to get ripped off. But he also sensed that going after corporate corruption would inevitably reveal the malfeasance at the center of Russia's kleptocratic political system.

As it turned out, he was perfectly suited to be a crusader for shareholder rights. Trained as a lawyer, he was willing to comb through the fine print of quarterly earnings, annual reports, and other regulatory filings. But it was his instinct to stick up for the little guy and his utter disdain for graft that would prove most useful.

The auditorium for the Surgutneftegas annual meeting was filled with about 350 people, many of them Surgutneftegas retirees with nothing better to do than listen to the gray-haired corporate bigwigs recount the company's annual performance. Navalny was conspicuously out of place. Who was this tall, young stranger? Why was he there?

Vladimir Leonidovich Bogdanov, the company's general director, read through his report, droning on about revenues and expenses, and rattling off statistics: a 29 percent increase in capital investments for production; plans to commission fourteen small fields in Western Siberia. Total revenue for 2007 of $23.3 billion, with net profit of $3.46 billion.

Bogdanov had led Surgutneftegas since the mid-1980s, during Soviet times, and continued as its boss after the company was privatized in 1993. But unlike every previous shareholder meeting, where he delivered his report without question or debate, this time, a hand went up in the audience. "I have something to say," Navalny proclaimed.

The room froze.

Moving to the podium, Navalny launched into a speech. As always, he played to the audience by first expressing effusive thanks to the local workers. Then, he began a three-pronged attack. First, he criticized Surgutneftegas for paying out paltry dividends—only 31 percent of net profit, while comparable oil companies outside Russia typically paid 35 percent or more.

As part of this complaint, Navalny also voiced his suspicions that profits were being siphoned off by firms paid to transport and trade the company's oil, specifically Gunvor—a Swiss-registered firm then co-owned by Gennady Timchenko, believed to be a close associate of Putin. Navalny suggested that shareholders, including Russian taxpayers, were potentially being shortchanged.

His second line of criticism involved the secrecy surrounding the ownership of Surgutneftegas. "Surgutneftegas is one of the largest commodity companies in Russia, and it is owned by no one knows who," Navalny told the online Russian news site *Izbrannoe*. In reply, Bogdanov asserted, preposterously, that even he did not know who owned the company because he owned fewer than 2.5 percent of shares—not enough by law to demand disclosure.

Navalny's third issue was simply a demand for transparency. He pointed out that it was far too difficult to access company information, including its annual report, which could be obtained only by making a request in person. Navalny proposed a solution that was not particularly novel: publish all the corporate materials, including about the annual meeting online. "We insisted on publishing the company's financial statements on the internet," he said.

Navalny received a smattering of applause. His appearance at the shareholder meeting made news in *Vedomosti*, Russia's leading business daily. And in the end, while he did not get his answers, Navalny expressed satisfaction that he was permitted to say his piece. "We must pay tribute to Vladimir Bogdanov," Navalny told *Izbrannoe*. "He did not interfere."

* * *

That benign tolerance would not last.

While his attendance at the Surgutneftegas was his first public appearance as a shareholder advocate, Navalny had quietly mounted another campaign focused on an even bigger target: Gazprom, the crown jewel of Russia's state-controlled energy companies.

That case, which became public in late December 2008, marked the first time that Navalny's personal safety would be called into doubt. From then on, it was always a question of when—not if—the hit men would come after him.

The threat came in conjunction with Navalny's first notable "victory" as an anti-corruption crusader, in which he succeeded in being named as "victim" in a criminal case against Gazprom, the state-owned natural gas company. The case was a classic example of fraud that is rampant in the Russian gas sector, with money siphoned off by an unnecessary intermediary.

As would prove true with many of Navalny's future anti-corruption investigations, the Gazprom case did not originate with him but stretched back to 2005. Navalny stepped in and brought attention, publicity and, most important, tenacity, refusing to drop the matter even as the entire Russian system—the police, prosecutors, courts, and Gazprom itself—tried to make it all go away.

The fraud was so blatant that the Russian Interior Ministry felt compelled to investigate, beginning a yearslong tug-of-war as authorities repeatedly closed and reopened the inquiry. One of the biggest snags came when Gazprom itself refused to acknowledge suffering any damage and repeatedly declined to be named as a victim. That was where Navalny stepped in, putting himself forward in the summer of 2008 as a victimized shareholder, thereby salvaging the case—at least for a few months longer.

The complaint alleged that a Gazprom subsidiary called Mezhregiongaz had defrauded shareholders by purchasing gas from a supplier, Novatek. Rather than buying the gas directly, Mezhregiongaz used an unnecessary intermediary, Trastinvestgaz, which charged markups of up to 70 percent—bilking Gazprom investors of more than 1.5 billion rubles or $53 million.

But even as Navalny scored a small victory by being recognized as a victim and plaintiff in the criminal complaint, he was warned that he was putting himself in danger.

He described the case—and the accompanying threat—on his blog, under the headline "How They Saw at Gazprom." In Russian, the verb *to saw*—as in cutting wood or a tree branch—is slang for "to fleece" or "to steal" or "to embezzle," as in "how they saw up the budget."

Navalny's blog entry would become the first in a series of blockbuster attacks on mega-corruption schemes under similar headlines: "How They Saw at VTB." "How They Saw at Transneft." "How They Saw at Russian Railways."

Even back in 2008, Navalny had a knack for explaining complex transactions and financial frauds in simple, easy-to-follow language. The writing on his blog was cutting and sarcastic, and often peppered with jokes or witty observations. Sometimes he would inject acerbic or inappropriate remarks, even threats, but ~~stricken through~~ in the text, signaling self-awareness that he had perhaps gone too far.

Navalny opened his Gazprom post with a quick explanation about the basic monopoly of the gas market in Russia. Any business needing gas, he explained, had to buy from Mezhregiongaz, a division of Gazprom. "You can't buy from anyone else. Because the pipe belongs to Gazprom," he wrote. "And without a pipe, gas makes no sense. Without a pipe, you can only use gas to make a beautiful, fiery torch over endless snowy fields."

Navalny then went on to explain the egregious, if ingenious, fraud, in which the intermediary, Trastinvestgaz, suddenly stepped in to buy gas, which Gazprom itself had declined to purchase, from a relatively small producer called Novatek.

Two days later, Trastinvestgaz sold the very same gas, moving through the very same pipe, to Gazprom for nearly double the price. When Gazprom officials were pressed to explain why they hadn't bought the gas at the outset for the lower price, they initially insisted Gazprom didn't have the cash to complete the transaction. But, according to Navalny, Trastinvestgaz had bought the gas using a loan from . . . Gazprom.

"In such a simple way," Navalny wrote, "the effective managers from Gazprom, by moving pieces of paper around the table, earned 1.5 billion rubles [about $53 million]. Just in this episode. It is clear that this is only the tiny tip of the big iceberg."

While Navalny reveled in being named a victim in the case, he also described a sinister warning that accompanied his little victory.

"The investigator in the case, a very cheerful lieutenant colonel, said to me at our first meeting: 'Alexey Anatolyevich, I will now issue a decision recognizing you as a victim,' " Navalny wrote. " 'But I consider it my duty to warn you—a man in Novatek's leadership, who was aware of the scheme and signed everything, tragically died under strange circumstances after the investigation began. Looks like he crashed on a snowmobile.' "

Navalny's LiveJournal blog post that day—December 28, 2008—offered an early example of his dark humor about the risks to his own life in taking on Russian corruption and powerful corporate interests, as well as Russia's most powerful, and dirty, politicians.

"Just in case," Navalny wrote. "I officially declare: I do not ride snowmobiles. I do not plan to go skiing this year or next. I am not fond of rock climbing and hang gliding. I drive a car carefully. I do not wash windows, especially when they're open. I don't like to eat puffer fish or anything like that for breakfast. I don't run across the road at red lights. I swim very well. I don't make a habit of walking where bricks, slates or pianos fall from above, etc.

"This is not to say that I am very afraid of 'countermeasures'—just in case," he wrote.

* * *

The battle with Gazprom would drag on for years.

Meanwhile, Navalny was developing a knack for using his small stock holdings to stir up big trouble. Among those holdings were two shares of Transneft, the giant state-controlled oil pipeline company. And on August

6, 2008, Navalny launched another crusade on his LiveJournal blog: an effort to uncover how Transneft suddenly had become one of Russia's biggest charitable donors—giving away nearly 7.2 billion rubles, or roughly $300,000 million in 2007—and to figure out where the money had gone.

Navalny learned of the situation from an article in *Vedomosti* on March 24, 2008, about Transneft's third-quarter results, which showed the stunning giveaway. The article described how Transneft in 2007 had smashed all records for charitable contributions in Russian history, and given away far more money than it paid in dividends to shareholders—the main shareholder, of course, being the Russian government.

The huge amount of money being siphoned out of the company would have been enough to trigger Navalny. But the company's explanation was the sort of preposterous nonsense that makes him spitting mad. "Excess oil is found annually in the Transneft system due to inaccuracies in measuring instruments, oil evaporation," *Vedomosti* reported being told by Transneft managers. "How to spend the money from the sale of surplus oil is decided by the board of directors of the company." In recent years, the company told the newspaper, "all the proceeds from the sale of unaccounted for oil" were donated to charity.

Mikhail Barkov, a Transneft vice president, said the money went to support orphanages, cancer hospitals, sports organizations, and religious groups. Interestingly, Barkov seemed to go out of his way to note that Semyon Vainshtok, who had recently stepped down as Transneft's president, "had nothing to do with it" because the company had not sold any excess oil until after Vainshtok left the company in October 2007.

"The largest philanthropist in Russia is Transneft," Navalny proclaimed in mock amazement. "Last year the company spent 7,193,000,000 rubles on charity," he wrote. Apparently concerned that the magnitude wasn't coming across, he added: "In words: *seven billion one hundred ninety-three million rubles*.

"This is a very generous donation, because in the same year, Transneft spent only six billion rubles on the repair and maintenance of all oil pipelines," Navalny wrote. "That is, charity is more important for Transneft than oil pipelines, despite the fact that dealing with oil pipelines is Transneft's main and only task."

Navalny noted that Russia's blogger community should take special interest, given the rising popularity of online crowdfunding. Every day, it seemed, someone was posting another heart-tugging story worthy of donations. Navalny's question was simple: "For what laudable purposes is Transneft giving out such colossal sums?"

"I asked many people connected with charity about Transneft," Navalny wrote. He switched to all caps for emphasis: "BUT I HAVE NEVER MET A PERSON WHO WOULD KNOW THE FATE OF EVEN A SMALL PART OF TRANSNEFT'S CHARITY MONEY."

To Transneft, Navalny put the question very politely: "Please tell us which organizations were the recipients of the company's charitable assistance?" At first, he said, he got vague but polite replies about how the company provides "open and transparent charitable assistance to many organizations. Then," Navalny wrote, "they began to snap, like 'It's none of your business who we help.' Now that I have filed a lawsuit, Transneft claims this is confidential information.

"Can a state-owned company give $300 million confidentially to charity? It seems to me—no," Navalny wrote, answering his own question. "To Transneft, the government of the Russian Federation, the Ministry of Energy and everyone else that I applied to, it seems yes."

Navalny reflexively divides human beings into good and bad. Often his instincts are right. Sometimes he misfires. But he typically reserves special venom for people he perceives as bad who were put in positions that demanded they do the right thing. Identifying specific individual villains in the vast cesspool of Russian kleptocracy has always been one of Navalny's extraordinary talents. In the case of Transneft, at least initially, Navalny decided that the primary villain would be Oleg Vyacheslavovich Vyugin, who had been elected to serve as an independent member of Transneft's board of directors.

Navalny opened his public campaign against Vyugin in a blogpost on September 8, 2008, under the headline: "Next Generation Manager."

He began by linking to Vyugin's official biography as head of the Federal Service for Financial Markets of the Russian Federation. Vyugin's résumé was impressive: undergraduate and graduate degrees in the physical and mathematical sciences; teaching and research positions focused on consumer demand, trade, and economic forecasting; and then a series of important positions in government and in the private sector, beginning with his appointment in 1993 as head of the Macroeconomic Policy Department at Russia's Finance Ministry. From 2002 to 2004, he was first deputy chairman of the Russian Central Bank. "Ufff," Navalny wrote on his LiveJournal blog. "I'm tired just listing the merits."

Navalny noted that Vyugin, at that point, was chairman of the board of directors of MDM Bank—"but not only," he noted. "Because Oleg Vyugin is a very respected person, he is called an independent director in various places. Because it is a great honor to have Oleg Vyugin as an independent director. It has a very positive effect on our, and the foreign, business community.

"They know Oleg Vyugin very well as a man who stands up for transparency and efficiency," Navalny wrote, his sarcasm dripping down the screen. "Oleg Vyugin on the board of directors is like a signal: 'Everything is OK with us. Everything is transparent and efficient, because Oleg Vyugin himself vouched for us. His reputation is at stake, and he values it.' " Now, Navalny reiterated, Vyugin was on Transneft's board.

"And so," Navalny wrote, "O. V. Vyugin will receive (or has already received) an official letter. In which there will be no anthrax powder, but there will be a request from one of the shareholders of OAO AK Transneft to provide assistance in obtaining at least some information about the 12 billion rubles that were withdrawn from Transneft over the past two years as charity expenses."

Navalny's arch reference to anthrax offered a bit of insight into a man growing into his role as a major public figure. The bioweapon was back in the news that summer in a big way in the United States and international media, after the FBI named a suspect in a string of anthrax attacks that had terrified the U.S. in 2001 following the 9/11 terror attacks. The suspect, Bruce E. Ivins, was a longtime researcher on biological weapons who worked at an army laboratory. He had become interested in anthrax after a 1979 outbreak in Sverdlovsk, the Russian city now known as Yekaterinburg. At least sixty-four people had been killed by anthrax after an accidental release at a Soviet military facility.

Navalny is a news junkie. In those days, when not railing against corruption, he often used his blog to comment on current events and pop culture—mainly in Russia, but also from the United States and around the world. The anthrax joke was also the kind of stray, biting remark that in the future would make Navalny vulnerable to lawsuits and prosecutions. Was he joking, or had he threated Vyugin's life? As Navalny kicked up dust, and ticked off ever more powerful people, his opponents would file lawsuits or pursue criminal charges against him for far less.

Navalny's lawsuit was specifically aimed at Vyugin, demanding that he meet his obligations as an independent member of the board of directors. In November 2008, Navalny issued a "statement" following a hearing in the case in Moscow. He noted that Vyugin did not attend but had sent three lawyers, who argued that as an independent director he had the right to ignore the requests of minority shareholders.

"The position of Oleg Vyugin is bewildering," Navalny wrote in his statement. "This is a famous person with a good reputation. He was elected an independent director of the company and, obviously, should advocate for transparency in the work of the company and the fight against theft with it." He added: "I approached him expecting support for my legitimate claims. However, Vyugin prefers to sacrifice his reputation in order to cover up the dubious dealings going on in Transneft."

Navalny was pouring it on—counting, it seemed, on Vyugin actually being on his side. "We have serious grounds to believe that, under the guise of charitable activities, theft on an especially large scale has occurred and continues to occur," he wrote. "It is a pity that Vyugin ended up on the other side of the barricades. It remains to be hoped that he is not personally involved in these frauds."

Navalny ended with another sharp dose of personal invective. "I will add that not so long ago, Oleg Vyugin was awarded the Golden Diploma for his personal contribution to increasing the transparency of the domestic stock market.

"How this diploma is linked to Vyugin's support for the secret charity of Transneft is unclear," Navalny jabbed. "But I decided for myself that from now on all letters to Vyugin (and obviously there will be) will be addressed to: Oleg Vyacheslavovich Vyugin, an independent member of the Board of Directors of AK Transneft OJSC, winner of the award 'for personal contribution to increasing the transparency of the stock market' holder of the Golden Diploma."

About three dozen comments were posted in response, and Navalny relished the engagement. One reader posted, "Is there a chance after Vyugin to go higher? I wish for all the good people from Transneft to become not only owners of golden diplomas, but also golden cages as permanent residence."

Navalny replied: "Vyugin is just that—a side question. The real villain is Vainshtok and Co. Gradually, we will get to the bottom of them."

A month later, Navalny appealed again to Vyugin, noting comments that Vyugin had made after the assassination of Andrei Kozlov, the deputy chairman of the Central Bank of Russia, who had been targeted for cracking down on large-scale money laundering. Vyugin, speaking to journalists in Singapore at a meeting of G-7 finance ministers in 2006, had said that Italy's fight against the mafia and corruption had started "when people appeared who said to themselves: 'I am threatened, my work is dangerous, but I will do what my conscience tells me.' "

Navalny wrote: "I completely agree with you and believe now is the time to do what your conscience says."

"Now" was overly ambitious and optimistic. Transneft refused to divulge any information. But Navalny was making an impact. Journalists and other activists were also following his lead. In May 2009, *Vedomosti* reported that in the disclosure documents of a bond prospectus, a Transneft subsidiary had revealed making large charitable donations to two organizations, the "Assistance Fund" and "Kremlin-9." The amount of money involved was nowhere near the total that Transneft had said it donated to charity, but finally there was some indication of where such huge sums had gone. Kremlin-9 was particularly interesting, given that it was established as a charity to help employees and former employees of the Russian security services—in other words, to help people like Putin.

Not quite a year later, on September 3, 2009, Vyugin published an op-ed in *Vedomosti* calling for an overhaul of Russia's economy following the 2008 financial crisis. Navalny at first didn't read it, but then spotted praise for the article by Konstantin Sonin, a brilliant, Western-minded Russian economist. When he read the op-ed, Navalny was blown away and infuriated.

In the article, Vyugin had called for major reforms, including greater efficiency in public administration, and new mechanisms for publicly evaluating the quality and effectiveness of state institutions. He had also stressed the importance of the media's role in informing the public and facilitating accountability.

Lashing out on his blog under a headline of "excellent hypocrisy," Navalny praised the article, saying, "After reading, it even makes you want...to slam your palm on the table and exclaim, 'Why are we sitting here? It's clear what to do!' The wise Oleg Vyugin says a lot of right things."

But then Navalny called Vyugin a hypocrite and a liar, adding, "Transneft is essentially now an organized criminal group." About a month later, Vyugin wrote Navalny a letter saying that he was formally urging Transneft's chairman, Russian energy minister Sergei Shmatko, to publish full information about Transneft's claimed 15 billion rubles in charitable donations from 2005 to 2008.

Navalny declared a truce and proclaimed victory. "Well done. What can I say?" he wrote on his blog. "The man had the courage to be consistent and admit that he was wrong." But he also knew that Vyugin's change of position would not do anything to change Transneft's behavior. "I am quite sure the board of directors will reject the proposal," Navalny wrote. "But at least the question will be officially announced."

He also vowed to keep going after Transneft, warning: "Soon on our screens there will be a lot of interesting things about them." As it turned out, the estimated $500 million siphoned off through charity was just scratching the surface when it came to alleged fraud and embezzlement at Transneft.

* * *

While battling with Transneft, Navalny was simultaneously locked in arbitration with Rosneft, the state-owned oil company, demanding that it disclose basic corporate information as required under Russia's law "On Joint Stock Companies." Such information is typically published and sent to shareholders as a matter of routine in countries with normally functioning securities markets and regulatory and judicial systems. Not in Russia.

As Navalny mounted these shareholder-rights crusades, he discovered that his anti-corruption campaigns provided a strong organizational framework for his broader political activity, and helped generate publicity and name recognition.

On November 30, 2009, Navalny published his most explosive investigation to date, alleging a massive fraud at VTB Bank, which was 85 percent owned by the Russian government. The head of VTB's supervisory board was Finance Minister Alexey Kudrin, and in May 2007 Putin personally had urged Russian citizens to buy shares in VTB in a limited initial public offering.

In his post, headlined "How They Saw at VTB," Navalny described a scheme in which VTB managers invested in oil rigs, that would in turn be leased to drilling companies—specifically thirty rigs made by a Chinese manufacturer, Sichuan Honghua Petroleum Equipment, which amounted to 4,500 train cars of equipment.

The rigs would have cost $10 million apiece from the manufacturer. But VTB bought them through an intermediary company in Cyprus, which charged $15 million, inflating the overall price by $156 million—which, of course, was siphoned off. But there was a second layer to the scam. Rather than leasing the rigs directly to energy companies, VTB then created a shell company called Well Drilling Corporation, according to Navalny's investigation, which acted as another intermediary. The rigs were leased to Well Drilling for 200,000 rubles per day, and then to the final customer for double that. Over the lease term of eight years, Navalny calculated, $400 million would be stolen.

Except the scheme didn't quite come together. Only some of the rigs were leased. The rest were stashed in the remote northern region of Yamal, where Navalny traveled to see the hunks of metal laid out in snowy fields—"fifteen hectares," Navalny wrote, "littered with pieces of iron."

Now, he wanted his readers to understand the impact. With Putin encouraging them, 150,000 investors bought shares in VTB. "Do you still think that VTB shares fell from 13.6 kopecks per share (the price of the "people's IPO") to the current 6 kopecks due to one international financial crisis?" Navalny asked. "Or are the reasons for the fall also in . . . uh . . . specific management methods?"

He urged his followers to join the campaign. "Can we do something to help? Of course, you can and, moreover, we are in dire need of help," he wrote. "There are about 150,000 minority shareholders of VTB. These people were cruelly screwed over and robbed. I am now forming a pool of shareholders who are ready to enter into this business. Continue the investigation. Claim damages. Initiate a criminal case. ~~Torture and hang~~ etc." He added, "Remember the more publicity, the greater the chance of success."

Navalny was making a mark, infuriating his targets in government and business circles, and impressing journalists and citizens fed up with decades of boundless Russian corruption and malfeasance.

Vedomosti named Navalny, at age thirty-three, as its "private individual of the year" for 2009, as part of an annual rankings list. Calling him "minority shareholder of the largest companies in Russia," the newspaper said: "A lone hero, prudent businessman, or manager of the 'Bring State Companies to Clean Water' project? We do not know this about Navalny, a minority shareholder in leading companies. It doesn't matter. Navalny was not afraid to declare war on 'effective managers,' as he calls them, of state-owned companies. While professional investors quietly solve their problems, a simple person, invested with neither status nor power, is trying to fight the system."

The newspaper noted that Navalny might pivot back into politics, but more important, it said, he was setting an example: The little guy could fight back and make a difference. "One in the field is not a warrior," *Vedomosti* said. "Navalny encourages other shareholders to participate in their projects. This could be a springboard for his return to politics. But now something else is more important—by personal example he proves to citizens [they have] the ability to protect their rights."

In March 2010, Navalny teamed up with *Forbes* Russia to request routine company documents and information from ten of Russia's biggest companies to test the quality of corporate governance. The result was a hodgepodge of responses.

Gazprom provided the documents quickly, along with an invoice for the 643-ruble, or roughly $21, cost of photocopies. Other companies, like RusHydro and Inter RAO, provided partial documents, saying some material was confidential. VTB provided complete information but charged about $422 for 2,373 sheets of paper. Sberbank, Russia's largest savings and loan, responded after a long delay, but sent the documents for free.

Transneft, Gazprom Neft, and Rosneft did not provide information. Navalny in the article appealed to the Federal Financial Markets Service and to the prosecutor's office. The overall conclusion: "A total mess in the country with corporate government standards."

Navalny persisted with his own court cases and notched some small victories.

In May 2010, a court ruled that the police had not properly investigated Navalny's complaint against Transneft, and ordered them to do so.

Rosneft's lawyers, meanwhile, had gone to great lengths to justify not giving Navalny the information. One argument was that he simply did not own enough shares. As a result of a company court filing that September, Navalny said that he was glad to know that he owned 0.00000326 percent of Rosneft.

Navalny, who was on a fellowship at Yale University at the time, responded on his blog by feigning an American accent. "In America," he wrote, "in such cases, they say 'Oh my goodness.' What they say in Russian in such cases, you will now understand for yourself."

According to Rosneft's lawyers, Navalny wrote in disbelief, "Shareholders are big, small and insignificant. And their rights are respectively large, small or insignificant. But the most trash is that Rosneft decided to prove in court that A. A. Navalny is not an ordinary shareholder."

Indeed, in its court filing the company argued: "It is also an obvious fact that A. A. Navalny is not an ordinary shareholder . . . and his goals are inextricably linked with his socio-political activities."

Navalny, in his post, tried to tweak Peter O'Brien, a Rosneft vice president, writing in Russian transliteration: "Petrucho, what's up? I notice you enjoy being a bad Russian guy. Just remember you have the Bribery Act in your home country." O'Brien is actually American, so the Foreign Corrupt Practices Act would be the relevant statute, not Britain's Bribery Act, but Navalny's point was clear.

The arbitration court ultimately agreed with Navalny on his right, as a shareholder, to the disclosure of company information. In August 2010, the court ordered Rosneft to provide him with the minutes from meetings of the board of directors.

* * *

Initially, Navalny had used the LiveJournal blogging platform as a place to post transcripts of his radio appearances. But as he grew more politically active, the internet would prove to be his only way to get around the government's ironclad control of all television media. Kremlin propaganda was so widespread across the many different channels that Navalny derisively referred to Russian television as the "zombie box"—sort of like "idiot box" in English, but more insulting.

Navalny wasn't the only outraged Russian leveraging the blogosphere to engage in more open political discourse and to play online vigilante. But he was arguably the most effective—and the most popular.

On October 7, 2010, Yevgeniy Lerner, cofounder of a web design firm called Artus, published an outraged post on LiveJournal describing how Russia's Ministry of Health had put out a public tender calling for the design of a social networking site to connect medical providers and patients. The first issue: an absurd cost of 55 million rubles, or about $1.8 million. The second: it had to be completed within sixteen days.

"What a cool and most importantly new idea!" Lerner wrote, with scathing sarcasm. "In short, such an internet resource will dramatically improve the quality of medical literacy and services provided in our country. Glory to our own Ministry of Health and Social Development, the most caring ministry in the world. Hooray! Is there someone, besides the employees of the Ministry of Health and those who are going to do this, who believe that they will create something useful and worth that kind of money?"

Lerner tipped off Navalny, who posted about the tender two days later, calling on readers with web development expertise to weigh in, even though Lerner, in fact, was in the business and one of Moscow's top experts.

"Uh mmmm . . . I don't understand the cost of sites etc. at all," Navalny wrote. "But I have a little experience when other people made websites for me. Based on this experience, I personally can say that never, neve-eve-ever, can you make a complex site (especially a social network) in 16 days. But, judging by the price, the site should be VERY fancy."

Navalny, wasting no time, flat-out accused the ministry of fraud. "My first impression: The vendor is known. The site is ready. The money is sawed. And of course, I really want to take a stick with a sharp nail at the end and start poking it at the Ministry of Health." He urged his followers to file complaints with Russia's Federal Anti-monopoly Service.

Two days later, the tender was cancelled. Posting under the headline "Hehehehehehehe," Navalny crowed about his quick success.

Navalny's followers identified other tenders for similar health ministry IT projects at inflated prices. The official in charge of them, Oleg Simakov, head of the health ministry's digital information department—nicknamed "Eyebrows" by Navalny because of his unibrow—was forced to resign.

"Congratulations and thank you to everyone who participated in the sharp-stick poking," Navalny wrote gloatingly after the original tender was annulled. "And it only took two posts. One. Two."

Well, technically three, counting the original post by Lerner, who discovered the whole scheme. But after giving Lerner a brief, initial acknowledgment of the tip, Navalny wasn't about to let someone get in the way of his growing legend as Russia's main anti-corruption cowboy of the interwebs.

* * *

Indeed, Navalny's stature and name recognition were soaring. He was attracting new attention and new sources. And in November 2010, he published his biggest investigation yet.

This was the revelation Navalny had hinted at while pushing on the charity issue. Headlined "How They Saw in Transneft," Navalny's post alleged that Transneft executives, led by Vainshtok, had stolen at least $4 billion during construction of the 2,600-mile-long Eastern Siberia Pacific Ocean (ESPO) oil pipeline. Some Russian media reports later put the figure at $2 billion. In any case, it was a staggering sum.

The allegations, which Vainshtok and Transneft vehemently denied, dwarfed all of Navalny's previous disclosures and were based on documents leaked to him that were prepared as part of an audit, which had been ordered by Russia's federal Accounts Chamber. The audit of the pipeline project, and Transneft's responses to it, were immediately declared classified.

Navalny opened his report by noting the personal significance of the investigation. "This is a very important post for me," he wrote. "I have been working on this case with my colleagues for many months. I will be very grateful to everyone who reads and helps."

"But before you start reading, take a look in your wallet," he continued. "You may not have noticed, but about 1,100 rubles"—about $35—"was missing. Not much, for each of us, but this amount was stolen from every adult resident of Russia. In total, according to our estimates, at least $4 billion was stolen during this story."

Navalny's personal pitch reflected his growing realization that many ordinary Russians were as outraged and offended by corruption as he was, and that he had an opportunity to enlist them to fight against it. Along with his blog post, Navalny released a nearly five-minute-long YouTube video, testing out a format which would later become the main media platform for investigations by his Anti-corruption Foundation.

The video, with an opening credit declaring "Alexey Navalny presents," included some strange sound effects but mainly featured Navalny, in a blue button-down with a microphone attached to his lavender tie, delivering an engaging summary of the investigation's findings.

The ESPO scheme was just a bigger, sprawling version of frauds that Navalny previously investigated. Construction of the giant pipeline was outsourced mainly to offshore companies, which had no capacity to do the work but were merely shells used to hire subcontractors, inflating the project's cost for no obvious reason other than theft.

At the time, Navalny and his team could not fully get to the bottom of it all. He speculated that the whole situation was exposed only because the Kremlin had grown unhappy that more money from the ESPO project wasn't being funneled to the top of Russia's power vertical, and Putin had moved to replace Vainshtok with Nikolai Tokarev, who had served with Putin in the KGB in Dresden. It was Tokarev who had ordered a review of the ESPO project, and the compilation of documents that later ended up in Navalny's hands.

Ironically, when Tokarev took over the job in October 2007, *Kommersant* had reported that "he was the only one of the four presidents of Transneft whose appearance in the company was not accompanied by a scandal. His predecessor, Semyon Vainshtok, calmly completed the deadline in his contract."

Vainshtok and his associates denied any wrongdoing related to ESPO or the exorbitant charitable donations, and no charges were brought. Putin himself, at one point, commented on the case and indicated the allegations were unfounded. In a sign of his good standing with the Kremlin, Vainshtok was briefly put in charge of the government's overall construction efforts related to the 2014 Winter Olympics in Sochi. But after less than a year in the job, Vainshtok left Russia to live in London and later Israel, where he obtained citizenship.

He used his huge wealth for all sorts of investments, including the purchase of 35 percent of the Lipstick Building on the East Side of midtown Manhattan. More than a decade after Navalny's investigation, the Pandora Papers, a giant trove of leaked documents related to offshore wealth, confirmed that Vainshtok was one of three owners of Vniist, a Cypriot company, that won numerous contracts related to ESPO, including for design and survey work. Hundreds of millions of dollars were funneled through Vniist to family trusts in New Zealand created by Vainshtok and his partners, according to news outlets that reported on the Pandora Papers.

* * *

Until the fall of 2010, Navalny had been working with a small team from his own little law office in Moscow. But the Eyebrows escapade at the Health Ministry had given him an idea.

In early December 2010, Navalny announced the launch of a new antigraft website called RosPil—again playing on the word "saw." Its logo was a double-headed eagle, Russia's national insignia, with each of the birds wielding a handsaw.

The idea was to enlist the internet masses to scour for outrageous public procurement contracts, taking advantage of new public transparency requirements implemented by President Dmitry Medvedev, and to then blow them up by filing complaints that the government would be obligated, by law, to answer.

It worked. Millions of dollars in contracts were annulled as a result of RosPil's attention. And more important, Navalny was collecting record levels of donations for his work. In the week after his first request for donations to RosPil, some $120,000 came in. The framework for his future organization was quickly coming together.

Navalny expanded his team by hiring four lawyers, including Lyubov

Sobol, who would become one of his top lieutenants and closest confidants. And he would create several other initiatives aimed at crowdsourcing pressure campaigns to improve government administration in Russia, including RosYam, which focused on repairing potholes. In September 2011, Navalny brought all of these projects under the umbrella of the Anti-corruption Foundation,

In his own way, Navalny was creating outlets for a slice of Russian society fed up with corruption and the country's slow pace of development—including its stubborn adherence to strange bureaucratic rituals putting process over outcomes. And they succeeded.

Harvard Business School, among others, used RosPil as a case study in fighting public corruption. That said, Navalny's larger goal was not to cancel a raft of public tenders or fill a bunch of potholes, but to foster political change, and he was not yet making a major impact in shifting Russia's political landscape.

In 2011, Navalny told Miriam Elder of the *Guardian* that he believed there would need to be new leadership in Russia for anything to change. "Change cannot come about under this leadership. These people will never deny themselves billions of dollars. Sooner or later, something will change and these documents we gather will be used so they will all be put in jail."

Nonetheless, Navalny had no intention of giving up.

"To outsiders our efforts might appear futile, even impossible," he wrote in an article for Harvard University's *Nieman Reports* journal, which he coauthored with Maxim Trudolyubov, the editorial page editor of *Vedomosti*.

"Corruption, some say, is an internal issue and it is inevitable in countries that are moving from state-run to market-driven systems," they wrote. "But corruption is not just a pile of rocks placed in our way while we head down the road toward something different. It involves crimes that thwart the progress of entire societies; in Russia the consequences of widespread corrupt practices are disastrous."

They continued: "Corruption is not just theft. It leads to moral and physical suffering and the destruction of people. Thousands in Russia are serving prison terms on charges cooked up by those who took their businesses away or needed to get rid of witnesses."

Navalny, in any case, had found his central, defining political mission and ideology. The success of RosPil had proven the power of the fight against corruption to motivate thousands of Russians, not only to break out of the pervasive national apathy and actively join the fight, but to donate money to the cause.

The Anti-corruption Foundation, established in September 2011, was not only the organizational umbrella for Navalny's various projects but also what Andrew Roth of the *Guardian* called "a guerrilla newsroom, an opposition research center and a campaign strategy headquarters." In short, it was Navalny Inc.

The Foundation also provided Navalny with a stable source of financing. At the outset, a dozen founding donors agreed to commit roughly $10,000 a month. They included Boris Zimin, who had been living outside of Russia since 2004, and Vladimir Ashurkov, a former banker and top executive at the Alfa Group Consortium, the sprawling holding company founded by the oligarch Mikhail Fridman.

Navalny's slick videos, infused with his deadpan humor and arch sarcasm, generated millions of views, and helped him to build a network of supporters across Russia and to win sustained international attention.

After more than a decade of searching, Navalny had found a defining message that could unite many disparate opposition forces. And yet, in a country built largely on endemic corruption, it was by nature an anti-establishment message with little chance of winning popular support among the country's elite.

Navalny was not naïve about this, or about the excruciating difficulty of his crusade.

"It is foolish to expect that people who have at hand 2 million police officers, half a million FSB officers, administrative resources from executive authorities throughout the country, television, and billions of dollars will simply give up," he said in an interview with the *Moskovsky Komsomolets* newspaper. "The government is doomed. It devours itself and the country, but these people will resist for a long time. The coming to power of a man with views like mine means that they will lose their billions and their freedom. The country still receives huge incomes from commodity exports—and they do not want to give this money to anyone. These are concrete figures with many zeros in accounts in Swiss banks, which are guarded by the police, the press, Channel One."

But he was also blunt about the political motivations of his anti-corruption work. He was not some goody-two-shoes whistleblower, but a politician.

"In our country, politicians are treated badly, and many, knowing this, mimic, calling themselves 'civil activists,'" he told *Moskovsky Komsomolets*. "But I don't want to deceive anyone. My main activity is the fight against corruption. Corruption is the main political problem in our country. The corruption 'vertical' has become a system of control. So, my work is absolutely political. I don't write manifestos, but every line of my legal inquiries is full of politics."

—7—

BLOGGER, STREET FIGHTER, POLITICIAN

"Our police wagon is Number 2012. Attention! DO NOT SET IT ON FIRE. Just puncture the tires."

—*Alexey Navalny, Moscow, March 5, 2012*

However long overdue, Navalny's break with the Yabloko party in December 2010 brought freedom and uncertainty. "My life as a nonsystemic oppositionist began," he said.

The State Duma elections, which took place days before Navalny's expulsion from the party, were a disaster for the opposition. According to the official results, which were almost certainly falsified, United Russia won 65 percent. Putin had cemented his control. The Communist Party, the far-right Liberal Democratic Party of Russia, and A Just Russia, a centrist party with no clear ideology, were designated as the "systemic opposition" and permitted to clear the 5 percent threshold and enter parliament.

Yabloko, with a reported result of 1.6 percent, was completely iced out, losing its four seats in the parliament. The Union of Right Forces similarly lost its three seats.

Navalny voiced contentment that he had boycotted. "I feel great satisfaction from the fact that I did not go to the polls yesterday," he wrote on LiveJournal. "Let them go to hell with this clowning. The dumb idea to come and spoil the ballots also failed: 1.1% nationwide. It is clear that almost all are spoiled by accident."

Sergei Mitrokhin, then the deputy head of Yabloko, complained that the vote was rigged, and Yabloko had actually won 8 percent. Navalny posted Mitrokhin's gripes without adding further comment, but his silence was heavy with sarcastic derision. Mitrokhin complained of "colossal stuffing of ballots," carousel voting—in which groups of people are transported to vote multiple times at different polling stations—and other predictable dirty tricks. "There is nothing to celebrate here. It was a gigantic disgrace to the whole world," Mitrokhin wrote. "In order to maintain his influence, Putin once again humiliated the national dignity of the citizens of Russia."

There were other signs that Putin and his security services were tightening their grip. For instance, Natalia Morar, a co-founder of DA!, was suddenly expelled from Russia.

Morar, a citizen of Moldova, had written an article in *New Times* magazine describing a vast money-laundering scheme that the Kremlin used to finance—and control—all political parties in the country. She was just twenty-four and had only recently graduated from university. But her investigative digging had angered, among others, Alexander Bortnikov, a close Putin ally who was then deputy head of the FSB.

That December, Morar had gone on a reporting trip to Israel. When she landed back at Domodedovo Airport in Moscow, she was detained and deported on orders of the FSB. Moldovan citizens did not need visas to enter Russia and all of Morar's papers were in order.

Navalny heard about the situation while she was still in detention at the airport. "They found the most dangerous migrant," he posted angrily. "Cattle, freaks and scum."

In some ways, Morar was lucky. A little bit more than a year earlier, Anna Politikovskaya, a journalist with *Novaya Gazeta* who had reported aggressively on abuses in Chechnya, was shot to death in the elevator of her Moscow apartment building. Two years before that, Politikovskaya had survived an apparent poisoning attack, in which she fell ill on a flight between Moscow and the southern Russian city of Rostov-on-Don.

At that point, Navalny had no clue that, within a decade, the fates of Morar and Politikovskaya—exile or death—would become very real options in his own life.

Instead, Navalny, working with his collaborators in NAROD, organized an election postmortem roundtable event called: "The Death of the Russian Opposition and the Possibility of Its Revival. New Oppositional Discourse."

Among the topics to be discussed were "the systemic opposition as part of the political machine of the Kremlin" and the "possible creation of a qualitatively new opposition ready and capable of a real struggle for power." Navalny's announcement of the event included a note that it would be followed by a buffet. At least the opposition, or what was left of it, would not go hungry.

A report that Navalny published on behalf of NAROD summed up the conclusions of the roundtable and included a scathing indictment of the so-called systemic opposition.

"We can regard the actions of the systemic opposition in one and only way: a betrayal of the country and voters in the name of preserving its cozy commercial place in the Kremlin political system," NAROD said in the statement posted by Navalny.

"The opposition parties had a chance to adequately meet the test of 2007: to announce a boycott of the elections in September this year and thereby delegitimize the entire Kremlin political structure," the statement said. "However, the systemic oppositionists deliberately did not use this chance. Now, they are reaping the rewards. Even their humiliating defeat, they are not able to accept with dignity."

NAROD urged a quick and total overhaul of the approach to politics. "Ahead is the presidential election," they wrote. "The opposition could seriously compete with the current government only in one case: if it put forward a single and only candidate from all anti-Kremlin forces: left, liberal, nationalist. But there is practically no hope for this."

That prediction was accurate. Despite years of calls for Russia's democratically minded political forces to unite, the disparate groups remained fractured and they could not muster an agreed-upon presidential candidate to challenge Prime Minister Dmitry Medvedev, Putin's designated successor, in the March 2 presidential election.

Still, after eight years with Putin in power, the tandem switch created a sense that things might be changing. Medvedev, who had met Putin when they worked for Anatoly Sobchak in St. Petersburg's city government, was an academic, a law professor, and an author of a civil law textbook. Unlike Putin, he was never part of the Russian security services, from whose ranks came many of Putin's closest allies and confidants.

Where Putin was widely known as a technophobe, Medvedev was a lover of gadgets. He was interested in the movement toward electronic government services, even assigning members of his team to study the progress being made in neighboring Georgia. And, of course, for whatever it was worth, he had publicly proclaimed a commitment to fighting corruption.

Ultimately, it would all prove to be a mirage, deceiving not only Russians but also Barack Obama and Hillary Clinton, who were seduced into attempting their ill-fated "reset" with Russia.

* * *

For Navalny, the key deceptive development was Medvedev's December 2008 nomination of Nikita Belykh, the former leader of the Union of Right Forces political party, to be governor of the Kirov region, a forested area located between Moscow and the Ural mountains.

Belykh was a year older than Navalny and one of the brightest young prospects in Russian opposition circles. The Union of Right Forces was founded by Anatoly Chubais and Yegor Gaidar—the main proponents of Russia's post-Soviet liberal economic reforms—and would always be tarnished by the negative fallout of privatization, which yielded Russia's oligarchic system. Vast, previously state-controlled wealth, much of it tied to Russia's seemingly boundless natural resources, had ended up in the hands of a select few, many of them robber barons.

Originally, Navalny cheered those so-called reforms. But he later concluded that Chubais was a hypocrite and the man primarily responsible for Russia's path toward authoritarianism and crony capitalism. After preaching the gospel of private ownership, Chubais went on to earn a fortune running two state-owned companies, the power monopoly called

Unified Energy System of Russia, or UES, and Rusnano, the government-financed nanotechnology firm.

"As an erstwhile devotee of Yeltsin and Chubais, I can say that Chubais arouses more negative emotions in me now than Putin does," Navalny told Voronkov. "It's to none other than Chubais, I believe, that we owe the existence of Putinism."

In 2015, Navalny got a chance to confront Chubais personally with his allegations of hypocrisy, appearing opposite him during a live, televised debate moderated by Ksenia Sobchak on TV-Rainn. Navalny opened by quoting "a wonderful, very smart person" who in 2006 said: " 'State capitalism is inefficient, almost always corrupt, and strategically not viable.' In 2006, that person was Anatoly Borisovich Chubais." Navalny said Chubais had betrayed his younger self and that Rusnano should not exist in its state-owned form.

Chubais replied by saying that while Navalny had a potentially bright future as a politician, he was viewing the world in overly black and white terms. "Alexey Anatolyevich," Chubais said, "please don't confuse the term 'state capitalism' with the term 'state company'—these are not quite the same thing, or rather not at all the same thing."

Navalny accused Rusnano of squandering public funds; Chubais insisted that the state could play a useful role as an incubator of innovation. The debate was anticlimactic, with no knockout blow from either side.

Future disagreements and disappointments aside, Navalny, in the late 2000s, had good reason to find common cause with the Union of Right Forces, known by its Russian acronym SPS.

Other founders of the party included avowed democratic politicians like Boris Nemtsov, the first post-Soviet governor of the Nizhny Novgorod region who later served as energy minister of Russia and as deputy prime minister in the late 1990s. He went on to become a deputy chairman of the State Duma, and the head of the SPS faction in the Duma, from 2000 to 2003.

Belykh had been a member of the legislative assembly in his native Perm region, which is adjacent to Kirov. He then served as a deputy governor of Perm before being catapulted into the SPS leadership in May 2005. In that role, he became allies with Maria Gaidar, who had joined the party following in the footsteps of her father.

Belykh had participated in the first DA! public debate. With Navalny moderating, Belykh had argued that "classical Italian fascism" was embodied by the forces in the Kremlin. The Russian authorities, he said, operated according to a well-known principle, being the loudest in the crowd to shout "Stop thief!" when in fact they themselves were the thieves. When one member of the audience asked the prominent journalist Oleg Kashin, a member of the jury, why he had voted for Belykh, Kashin replied: "Belykh looks like me, a fat, kind guy from the provinces. I like him."

Navalny also liked Belykh, and the feeling was mutual. When the final debate ended in a bloody brawl, Belykh went to the police station to give a witness statement on Navalny's behalf. And when Belykh was appointed governor of Kirov, he invited Navalny and Maria Gaidar to join his team.

Gaidar was reluctant. She was engaged to be married and had plans to spend time in the United States. Navalny, however, was enthusiastic. After nearly a decade of working on the political fringes—campaigning, advocating, and criticizing, but never making decisions—he saw Belykh's offer as a chance to make a difference from the inside.

"Nikita invited me and Alexey to come with him, to work with him," Gaidar recalled. "And Navalny accepted. I wasn't sure because I had my personal life plans. I was about to get married and to leave to go to the U.S. for a while to study. But then, I remember, Navalny told me, 'No, you have to go. You have to use this opportunity. You have to do something. You know, it's a great opportunity.'

"I remember that he visited Kirov region even before, ahead of me, like one week or two, and he said, 'It's cool. We're going to do great things here. You should come. You should work here.' "

In Kirov, their paths diverged. Gaidar focused on social services, particularly health care and welfare programs, and she became a deputy governor. Navalny worked on economic affairs and, because he was still contemplating his own political ambitions, preferred to remain an outside adviser to Belykh. He did not accept an official government position.

"Navalny was from the beginning focused on corruption and business transparency," Gaidar said. "I think that even Belykh offered him a position, but Navalny wanted to continue his political work and do it just part-time, not take any position, still be an adviser."

* * *

Navalny started out with a quick success, spotting a scheme to dilute the value of a region-owned distillery with a new public stock offering. He managed to stop it and trumpeted his initial victory.

The main industry in Kirov, however, is not booze, but forestry and timber, and Navalny quickly learned that it was rife with corruption. Following a common pattern in post-Soviet Russia, the costs of doing business were largely centralized and borne by the government, while the profits were decentralized and gobbled up by private entities.

The government-owned timber company, Kirovles, was losing money, in part because the thirty-six timber mills it controlled were selling directly to customers and pocketing the cash. In Russia, timber is the common man's extraction industry. Most regular people can't just dig an oil well or build a gas pipeline. But they can cut down trees.

In Kirov, Navalny tried to clean things up and impose reforms, but mainly he just made enemies. "Navalny got engaged in that, and I think that was his biggest mistake ever," Gaidar said. "Because it's a very decentralized corruption. It's not a corruption that you can fix with just abolishing one law or just taking out some unneeded procedure at the top level.

"All the Kirov region really lives on that," she said. "Everybody gets some money out of it. Police at the local level. Some customs officers. Somebody working on the railroad. Somebody from measurements... Usually it's some bureaucrat's corruption, or some oligarch's corruption. Then, it was people's corruption. It's not that there was a great corruption that goes to Swiss banks or to offshores."

People representing these entrenched interests complained repeatedly about Navalny to Belykh, and tried every possible strategy to preserve the old corrupt system that Navalny was working to destroy, including by filing legal cases against him. Years later, one of those cases would come back to haunt him, revived by the Kremlin to convict him of serious crimes and bar him from running for public office.

But at the time, Navalny was just stuck in a thankless and fruitless crusade against endemic corruption. "He ended up having all the region fighting against him," Gaidar said, while Belykh had grown exhausted with all the complaints he was getting about Navalny.

"Their relationship started to deteriorate, and actually he stopped listening to Navalny at some point," she said. "Belykh didn't listen to Navalny, didn't want to help him anymore. Even though they agreed together on the plan . . . Navalny was very angry and very disappointed. He was feeling that he was wasting his time."

Navalny began a series of intermittent blog posts under the heading "100 Facts About Kirov Region" in which he complained about his frustrations there, and poked fun at the bureaucracy he encountered. This included local officials insisting that they could not install Wi-Fi in the main regional administration building, and unsuccessful attempts by maintenance staff to use glue or a heavy weight to hold down loose tiles on the building's front steps. The posts, unsurprisingly, did not win him local friends.

Navalny appeared to take particular pleasure, so to speak, in relaying an item from the local newspaper *Vyatsky Observer* headlined: "FSB Loves from Behind." A Federal Security Service officer in the Kirov region had been involved in four car accidents within two years, the most recent being the "rear-ending: of a vehicle." Navalny quoted the newspaper, which reported that the FSB officer had "recklessly violated the integrity of an Opel hatchback."

Meanwhile, Yulia Navalnaya, who had moved to Kirov with a seven-year-old and a new baby, was miserable. A cosmopolitan Muscovite, she was living away from family and friends, in a place where hunting was the main recreational activity, and local residents were deeply suspicious of outsiders.

The Navalnys' daughter, Dasha, was bullied in school. At one point a teacher cut her out of a school performance, demanding that she give her costume to another child. "The teacher just comes in and says, 'You don't fit here, give your costume to another girl,' " Gaidar recalled. Yulia, indignant, refused. She took a crying Dasha and the costume, and stormed out.

* * *

While things were going badly in Kirov, Navalny's reputation as an online anti-corruption crusader was soaring. Day after day, he waged combat against Gazprom, Transneft, VTB, and others on his blog, in the courts, and in newspaper and radio interviews.

In October, Navalny blogged about Sergei Magnitsky, a tax adviser to Bill Browder, once Russia's largest foreign investor. Magnitsky had been arrested and imprisoned after exposing a massive tax fraud by the Russian authorities.

Government officials had seized some of Browder's companies, then filed tax returns fraudulently claiming a refund of 5.4 billion rubles—roughly $230 million—which was promptly issued. The money quickly vanished.

Navalny expressed amazement at the scheme, but he also seized the moment to take a shot at Browder, who was once an ardent Putin supporter. "Browder himself is not at all perceived by me to be some bunny-boy. He's still an Uncle," Navalny said, using Russian slang for a wise guy in the mob sense. "A few years ago, he praised Putin enthusiastically and argued he was being picked on unfairly.

"Well," Navalny added with his mocking tone, now Browder lost $230 million "and changed his mind."

Magnitsky had been sent to jail after blowing the whistle on the officials who stole the $230 million. He was imprisoned, denied medical care, and then died in captivity.

Navalny set aside his annoyance at Browder's flip-flop and reacted to the news with horrified dismay. "They killed him," Navalny wrote on

LiveJournal on November 18. "The news of the death of Sergei Magnitsky in 'Matrosskaya Tishina' is monstrous.

"The damage done to the country by this assassination has yet to be assessed but I'm sure it will be very significant," Navalny wrote.

He was wrong. Nothing was done to Magnitsky's tormentors, and Browder undertook a yearslong crusade to win some semblance of justice by securing passage of "Magnitsky Act" laws targeting human rights abusers.

Navalny's blog for the balance of 2009 showed him still trying to weave his personal political views into a coherent ideology with popular appeal. He was still convinced that the right balance would be a mix of liberal economics, progressive social-welfare policy, and conservative positions on migration and gun rights.

Under the headline "God Made Man, but Samuel Colt Made Them Equal," Navalny again extolled his support for gun rights. He described the case of a Moscow businessman who was nearly murdered but fended off his attackers because he owned a private security company and, therefore, was licensed to carry a gun, a Makarov IZH-71 pistol.

"Arm yourself with whatever you can," Navalny wrote. "And demand the legalization of short-barreled firearms. If the most corrupt and unlawful people in the country (I mean the police) are armed, then why is it forbidden for normal citizens?" He included a link to his strange pro-gun YouTube video, which he made after the creation of NAROD.

Meanwhile, Navalny scored a huge win with his investigation "How They Saw at VTB," about the drilling rigs purchased at inflated prices.

After the investigation was published, Navalny employees of VTB and VTB-Leasing reached out to tell him that managers were in a panic, running around with copies of his blog post, as one put it, "like rodents in a burning grocery store." Days later, Kostin, the head of VTB, announced it had fired the head of VTB Leasing and was taking steps to avoid major losses.

But the company did not admit wrongdoing and said it would cooperate with authorities if anyone could provide evidence of misconduct. Navalny, of course, immediately began laying out that evidence.

Navalny's fights were gaining recognition, including internationally.

"Although I am not a rock star, I have realized the dream of any rock star," he wrote on his blog on December 6. "~~Got a Grammy.~~ Gave an interview to *Rolling Stone* magazine.

"But there is a problem," he added. "In the city of Kirov, where I now live most of the time, it is absolutely impossible to buy *Rolling Stone* magazine."

That December, Maria Gaidar's father, Yegor, the former prime minister and market reformer, died. Navalny lamented that he never had the chance to meet him, though they had long planned to arrange it.

"I was his fan in the romantic time of the formation of a market economy," Navalny wrote. "To the point of hoarseness, I cursed everyone who was against him. The romantic time has passed, and Gaidar remained one of the few who retained unconditional respect and reverence for himself. Didn't steal. Didn't become an oligarch. Didn't grab the oil fields. Although he had more opportunities than others."

"It was always disgusting to hear stories about Gaidar's incredible wealth, because I saw with my own eyes that the family lives modestly," Navalny continued. "Even in liberal political circles where, let's face it, specific people love to pour mud on each other, no one would ever dare to reproach Gaidar," he added. "We are all orphaned."

* * *

Despite his limited success in cleaning up the timber industry, Navalny was using his time in Kirov to make other progress. He completed the requirements for being admitted to the bar as a lawyer, and he studied English. But it was clear Navalny's days in Kirov were numbered.

Navalny had been making snarky remarks about Kirov virtually from the outset, and now he began to take jabs at his boss, Governor Nikita Belykh.

At one point Belykh announced that he had decided to forego his salary and would donate the money instead to build handicap access ramps in Kirov.

Navalny sarcastically joked that other officials would follow Belykh's lead and "the world's largest ramp for the disabled will be built in Kirov."

He conceded that his boss was not pleased. "Belykh did not appreciate the idea," Navalny wrote. "He said that they don't understand my jokes in Kirov. And the local deputies of the United Russia have already complained, like, 'Navalny in his LiveJournal denigrates the Kirov reality.' "

That year, for Christmas, Navalny and his wife traveled to the United States, visiting Los Angeles, San Francisco, and Las Vegas. In a sign of his emerging public personality, Navalny kept blogging while on vacation, maintaining the banter with his followers and allowing them to tag along virtually on his trip.

But Navalny was also discovering that his followers would hold him accountable—for his words and deeds.

At one point, he asked the Russian blogosphere for advice on buying an iPhone in the United States without a contract, which was not possible at the time. "To get a contract, you need an American ID," Navalny complained. "Give someone some useful advice: How to deceive the American system?"

One follower quickly fired back a comment: "Interesting . . . you yourself write how officials scam the Russians. At the same time, you ask for advice on how to deceive the Americans."

Navalny answered: "I'm not going to rob anyone. You can definitely buy it without a contract." Other followers suggested he was wasting his money.

Upon returning to Moscow, Navalny was infuriated by the delays and hassles at Moscow's Sheremetyevo airport, especially outside where most of the cars coming to the arrivals terminal were clogged into just one of three roadways. Navalny railed against what he presumed was a money-making scheme reserving a two-lane roadway, left mostly empty, for specially branded taxis.

"In general, the Sh-2 airport is an ideal illustration of the fact that despite the huge number of people in uniform in the country, there is no power at all. Not vertical, not horizontal, not anything else," Navalny wrote. Describing his airport experience, he added: "This is hardcore hell."

The post struck a chord, garnering 887 comments, and prompting

Navalny to later joke that some of his followers were now worried that he had given up the protection of minority shareholder rights and was instead going to dedicate himself to air passengers. That post also yielded what may have been Navalny's first presidential endorsement.

Rustem Adagamov, who had long ranked as the most popular LiveJournal blogger in Russia, posted a link to Navalny's diatribe against the airport. "P.S.," Adagamov wrote, "If someday normal, fair presidential elections took place in our country and Alexey began to apply for this place, I would vote for him with both hands. Seriously."

By late January, it was clear that Navalny was under siege in Kirov. The regional legislature's Ethics Committee held a hearing to scrutinize his objectionable blog posts.

"Here he swears, but here he defames, and here he laughs at the Kirovites and here the police are offended," Navalny mocked them, adding that in his view the local lawmakers were not just opposed to him but intent on obstructing any advancement whatsoever.

"Well, my appeal to the deputies of the Legislative Assembly of the Kirov region," he wrote. "Be afraid. I'm a popular blogger. They read me in the Kremlin. High-ranking ~~idle~~ officials. They will read this post and punish you. For disobedience and ~~Holocaust denial~~, disbelief in modernization: forced to live on one salary."

Maria Gaidar said Navalny began pushing to leave Kirov, though she was committed to completing some of her projects, which were achieving some success. She had managed, for instance, to win World Bank funding for a project that was helping to train local officials.

"He was disappointed," Gaidar said, recalling Navalny's reversal after he first urged her to work in Kirov. "He was saying, 'You have to leave.' He told me, 'You have to come' and then he told me, 'It's stupid there's no way to do anything, to achieve anything here. We should focus on politics.' "

With Gaidar's encouragement and recommendations from Albats, Sergei Guriev—then the rector of the New Economic School in Moscow—and others, Navalny applied for a place in Yale University's World Fellows Program. In late April, he was accepted. His experiment working in government proved a failure, but he had learned firsthand about the excruciating difficulties of public service, especially in trying to eradicate corruption.

* * *

Ahead of his departure for New Haven, Navalny promised his followers that he would continue, and even expand, his crusade against the corrupt "effective managers" of Russia's companies. He also told them that he looked forward to learning more about anti-corruption laws in the United States and European Union, opening up new legal strategies.

"We should be able to piss off EMs where the greedy crooks from the Prosecutor General's Office and the Russian courts won't protect them," he wrote. He also urged his followers to keep up their own efforts and he reassured them that he would not disappear. "After all, I spent a year stuck among the bears, snows, and manatees of the Kirov region," he wrote sarcastically. "The internet in New Haven is definitely better than the internet in Kirov."

"Now on to the Oscar speech," Navalny blogged. "That is, I have not received an Oscar yet, but I already have a lot of gratitude. Here are the people who made it happen. Thank you very much—in the order they appeared on screen."

The list included Maria Gaidar and Sergei Guriev; a professor at Yale, Aleh Tsyvinsky; Albats; Garry Kasparov; Maxim Trudolyubov, the editorial page editor at *Vedomosti*; and Alexey Sitnikov, his English teacher in Kirov.

* * *

As Navalny and his family planned for their adventure in America, Russia's hopeless democratic politicians gathered once again, on June 15, 2010, in Moscow. This time they met under the banner of Democratic Choice, an organization created earlier in the year to replace the Union of Right Forces, which succumbed to Kremlin co-option and collapsed.

On its website, Democratic Choice was described as "a political organization founded in 2010 by a group of Russian politicians who advocate

Russia's return to a democratic, European path of development, against anyone's monopoly on power, for open, fair and free elections, and freedom of the media. We are for Russia to finally become a normal, civilized European country."

The group was led by Vladimir Milov, a former deputy energy minister. Navalny was cited among the notable personalities supporting the initiative along with Yashin; Boris Nemtsov; another former deputy prime minister and former head of the Republican Party of Russia, Vladimir Ryzhkov; and the economists Evgeny Gontmakher and Irina Yasina.

In its founding manifesto and other public proclamations, Democratic Choice said that it was committed to participating in elections and would forgo boycotts, which Navalny, among others, had advocated in the past. Instead, the group said that it was committed to using elections as a way to reach out to voters even if the Kremlin made it virtually impossible for new parties and candidates to register or win a place on the ballot.

On that Tuesday in June, Democratic Choice met at the Ararat Hyatt Hotel, for an event titled: "Electoral Cycle 2011–2012: What Should the Democratic Opposition Do?"

Posting on his blog the following day, Navalny laid out his own answer to that question in a long treatise, explaining among other things why his past instinct to boycott elections was a mistake. But the most important part of the Ararat hotel meeting was not what happened, but *who* Navalny met—and he described the situation obliquely, perhaps not even realizing the significance of it himself.

Navalny had been struck by the account of an independent city council candidate in Yekaterinburg who, against all odds, had used online campaigning to win a seat. "The dudes from the regions spoke very interestingly," Navalny wrote, "about the specific practical experience of slapping United Russia in the elections."

The "dudes" were really just one dude: Leonid Volkov, a physics, math and computer programming whiz who in March 2009 had gotten himself elected to the city council in Yekaterinburg, after running a groundbreaking campaign largely online.

Volkov was born in 1980, part of that same post-Soviet generation of 1976–1982, and he quickly became Navalny's most important political ally, forging a partnership that would take them through Navalny's historic campaign for mayor of Moscow in 2013, and his renegade campaign for president in 2017-18 when he was barred from the ballot.

Their work together, developing political parties and a nationwide network of local offices, as well as a system called "Smart voting" designed to break United Russia's monopolistic grip on Russian politics, ultimately led to Navalny being poisoned and imprisoned, and to Volkov living in exile.

Navalny and Volkov were not just kindred spirits. They had an instant mind-meld, as if they shared some special sequencing of political DNA. Consider this post on LiveJournal and try to guess which of the two wrote it:

> According to my political views, I am a liberal, a democrat, and I consider the European path to be the right way to develop Russia. My dream is for our country to become a normal European country, while retaining its identity and culture. Therefore, I am disgusted by the policy pursued by our government in recent years: a policy aimed at re-creating totalitarian procedures, imperial thinking, economic and political isolation from the outside world, a policy of saber-rattling.
>
> The logical consequence of this policy was the restriction of freedom of the press and freedom of elections, the independence of the judiciary was completely violated, the executive and legislative powers merged in ecstasy, and the Constitution of the Russian Federation was violated.
>
> The immediate consequence of this was rampant corruption, simply put, all-consuming theft. That is why the global financial crisis hit Russia much harder than most developed countries. I believe that it is not too late to return Russia to the normal path of development of a democratic country: with free elections, free courts and the press; with a free market with the proper level of

> state regulation, but without state corporations; with fair competition and without raiding by law enforcement agencies; with a transparent and accountable government, with a low level of corruption, with a large and stable middle class, with a really working local government. It is necessary that people themselves decide how to live their lives.

Those lines were written by Volkov laying out his positions for voters in the municipal elections in Yekaterinburg. But Navalny could have delivered those same lines in any campaign speech of his own without changing a word.

Volkov was one of just two independent candidates to win seats on the thirty-five-member city council, which was otherwise dominated by members of United Russia.

Volkov shared Navalny's visceral hatred for the authorities in power. On Election Night, even as he was on the cusp of victory, Volkov lashed out. "The election campaign was very dirty," he wrote. Incumbent candidates used public resources for their own campaigns, he complained, and election rules demanding fair competition were just ignored.

Volkov took credit for a groundbreaking candidacy. "No one has ever done what I'm about to do," he wrote. "But after all nobody also conducted a municipal election campaign on the internet; no one has ever collected more than 100,000 rubles by voluntary donations via the internet; and my 82 meetings in courtyards... were also worth a lot."

But with the final tally still not in, Volkov wanted everyone to know that the fight wasn't fair. "Now, when nothing is clear, I repeat once again: even if I win, I will still know and remember that my victory could have been much bigger."

Volkov recalled how he was often invited to meetings in Moscow, like the Democratic Choice gathering, as a token representative of the regions. "Someone 'from the regions' was me," he said. "Because I was elected, so I was a member of the council, and I was, well, rich enough to come on my own. So they didn't have to cover my tickets."

"This conference, it was quite stupid," Volkov recalled in an interview in Vilnius, adding that in the crowd of tired elders of the Russian opposition, "Navalny was such a contrast. He was so different."

The old crowd of liberal lions, Volkov said, offered nothing beyond a tired strategy of expressing offense and outrage without any concrete action.

"The typical modus operandi for these famous and really renowned opposition politicians, like Kasyanov who was a former prime minister, and Kasparov who was Kasparov," Volkov explained, was this: "Putin does something bad, something we don't like, and we issue a statement—we condemn it and say we are gravely concerned. So, they didn't do anything."

Navalny by contrast was a doer. "Navalny was such a difference because he actually operated projects," Volkov said. "Like, OK, here's the issue. Let's tackle it. I liked his approach very much."

* * *

In his own treatise summing up the Democratic Choice conference on LiveJournal the following day, Navalny laid out what would become his and Volkov's main electoral strategy for the next decade: urging voters to back any party other than United Russia and any candidate other than those loyal to Putin. Navalny also advised his democratic compatriots to give up any hope of uniting—what he called "an all-galactic unification"—for the foreseeable future.

But his main point was an anything-but United Russia strategy. (He had not yet branded them as the Party of Crooks and Thieves). "We must urge everyone to go to the polls and vote for anyone, but against [United Russia]," he wrote. "Even if we ourselves do not have the opportunity to run."

"I don't give a damn if, as a result of my work, the mandate goes to Yavlinsky or Zhirinovsky," he added, referring to his old boss in Yabloko, and to the head of the far-right Liberal Democratic Party. "The main thing—to destroy the monopoly."

While Volkov could fairly claim to be the first to have run and won an internet election campaign in Russia, in the fall of 2010, Navalny scored his own precedent-setting triumph in online voting—but it was only a simulation.

While Navalny was on his fellowship at Yale, two Russian news outlets, *Kommersant* and *Gazeta.ru*, decided to hold a virtual election for mayor of Moscow, aiming to gauge who city residents would want to replace Yuri Luzhkov, who had been dismissed by the Kremlin.

Navalny won in a landslide, garnering 45.02 percent of the vote; second place went to "against everyone" at 13.64 percent. Nemtsov scored 11.99 percent.

Just 2.82 percent went to Sergei Sobyanin, a deputy prime minister and chief of staff of the Russian government, who would actually be appointed to the mayoral post by President Dmitry Medvedev two weeks later.

Just a few weeks later, in Washington DC, Navalny's victory would be cited in his introduction at a hearing of the U.S. Helsinki Commission focused on "advanced fraud schemes in the Russian market."

Noting Navalny's crushing victory in the virtual mayoral election, Kyle Parker, a policy adviser on the commission, said: "So Alexey, sort of, in a sense, represents a generation that has been locked out of politics and have taken to other means. And Alexey has made extensive use of new media and other modern technologies to advance his message."

Navalny offered a bare-bones introduction of himself and his work. "My law practice focuses on the shareholders' rights," he said. "We work within the corporate system by pressing management to maintain transparency, to respect the law and to abide international standards of accountability. We use both traditional media and grassroots methods, especially blogs, to rally public interest in corruption. My personal blog has about 50,000 readers daily and has proven very efficient and effective."

Navalny's hope was to explain to the American authorities how big-ticket corruption was ultimately connected to the highest echelons of Russian power, and to lay out how Washington could help, particularly by tightening enforcement on Russians who funnel the proceeds of their corrupt schemes abroad, purchasing real estate and other assets in the United States and Europe.

Navalny, wearing a dark suit and pink tie, described how a gas pipeline stretching across Europe had cost triple to build in Russia, compared to a similar section in Germany despite wages and materials being far more expensive in Germany. "A construction company was engaged to build the Russian part of the pipeline without even bidding," Navalny testified. "This company belongs to Vladimir Putin's former judo coach, Arkady Rotenberg. He and his brother were named the main construction contractors for Gazprom, the largest company in Russia."

Navalny recounted his efforts to expose the dealings between Russia's major oil companies and Gunvor, the secretive trading firm headquartered in Switzerland. "All companies refused to give any information about their cooperation with Gunvor, so I filed suit," he said. "Finally, the judge held all Gunvor's documents to be privileged and we can understand pretty well the real reason of this decision because the only one piece of information about Gunvor is well-known. That one of the owners of this middle-man company is Gennady Timchenko, old friend and colleague of Vladimir Putin."

Navalny accused Timchenko of making a fortune but gave no proof that he had done anything illegal. Timchenko successfully sued the opposition politicians Boris Nemtsov and Vladimir Milov for defamation after they published a report alleging that he owed all his business success to Putin.

"His position allows him to skim a small percentage off the top of each of millions of barrels sold and all legally—very good business," Navalny said of Timchenko. "And he's a billionaire as well. Actually, it's a very interesting Russian phenomenon why all friends of Vladimir Putin who want to be in business, they became billionaires so soon."

Navalny also tried to give Washington incentive to join his fight. "So why does it matter for you?" he asked. "Corruption in Russia affects share pricing for shareholders around the world, which hurts corporate portfolios and the retirement funds of the little American guy. It also made a hit to your tax base and your economy because U.S. funds have invested billions of dollars in Russian companies."

At that moment, in Washington, Barack Obama's much ballyhooed "reset" with Russia was underway. Navalny cautioned his American listeners not to be overly romantic. "I don't want to push this idea of bad president and good president," he said. "Actually, it's not true that we have a bad Mr. Putin and a good Mr. Medvedev."

Still, he acknowledged that Medvedev and some of his top advisers, notably Arkady Dvorkovich, seemed open to reforms, including greater transparency requirements. "They're open-minded and they understand that it's much more profitable to be more transparent. You can attract cheaper money and you can attract more investors and so on and so forth," he said.

Navalny had described his effort to expose the suspicious "charity" at Transneft, and now he explained how Medvedev had suggested privatizing the company and also had proposed removing government officials from corporate boards to be replaced with independent directors.

"Transneft was powerful enough to cancel this idea," Navalny said. "And a couple of weeks ago the government declared that they are not going to privatize this company." What Navalny did not point out was that the head of Transneft, Nikolai Tokarev, was a close friend of Putin's, a colleague from when they served together in the KGB in East Germany.

The hearing in many ways was emblematic of Navalny's overall time at Yale. He was learning a lot about the American system, and one of the things he learned was that the U.S. system did not have very much interest in learning from him. In fact, it did not have very much interest in Russia at all, a surprise given Russia's obsession over its rivalry with the United States.

For whatever it was worth, though, Navalny left his listeners in Washington with a key point about himself, and about his country.

"I'm not a dissident," he said. "I'm an activist. I consider investment in Russia to have very high potential. I hope Americans will continue to invest in Russia, but we need a little more political leverage to protect those investors."

* * *

Throughout his time in New Haven, Navalny continued to push his anti-corruption work and he had come up with an answer to a question that had nagged him for years: how to harness the many offers of assistance from readers of his blog.

By creating the RosPil website, he would crowdsource the scrutiny of government procurement contracts and identify those that seemed corrupt. Anyone could spot a potentially fraudulent tender and then submit it to Navalny's team, which would carry out verifications and pursue the cases most worthy of attention.

Upon Navalny's return to Moscow, his name recognition was soaring, and it was then supercharged when he uttered the famous "Party of Crooks and Thieves" line on the radio. Journalists were calling nonstop. When he returned to Finam FM to debate the Duma member Yevgeny Fyodorov, two magazine writers, Julia Ioffe of the *New Yorker* and Yulia Gutova of *Russian Reporter*, were in the studio gathering color for long profiles of him.

In March 2011, Navalny went on the attack against proposed changes to Russia's government transparency laws, which had allowed RosPil to identify vast amounts of graft. Navalny noted that the new law had been drafted at the Higher School of Economics, where the rector, Yaroslav Kuzminov, was married to Elvira Nabiullina, then Russia's minister of economic development.

Kuzminov, offended by the allegation of collusion, challenged Navalny to a public debate. It was held at the school on the evening of March 18, and livestreamed on the internet. The hall was packed, and it remained full for much of the four-hour event, even as Navalny and Kuzminov sparred over the minutiae of procurement law.

Konstantin Sonin, a prominent economist and newspaper columnist, called the debate "a landmark event."

"Navalny could very much emerge as the political leader of a new generation of Russians," Sonin wrote in the *Moscow Times*. "They have been waiting for a leader with Navalny's qualities for more than a decade." He added, "The Navalny-Kuzminov debate was the first meaningful discussion by prominent individuals to be aired in many years."

The larger problem, Sonin lamented, was that active Russian citizens following the debate would have no way to act on what they had concluded. "Ideally, Russians would now be able to choose between the important positions taken by Kuzminov and Navalny as voters in democratic countries everywhere do—through free elections," Sonin wrote.

But Russia was not a democratic country, a point that would be driven home mercilessly on September 24, 2011, when Medvedev and Putin, speaking at a convention of the United Russia party, announced that the tandem would switch places again: Putin would return to the presidency.

The announcement infuriated many Russians, including Navalny and Volkov. That day, Volkov was attending a conference at the Institute for Contemporary Development, a think tank in Moscow that was close to Medvedev. A year earlier, the institute's top policy analysts had published a report, "Russia in the 21st Century: Vision for the Future," that favorably envisioned Russia joining NATO and the European Union. Now, as they watched the United Russia conference on television, Volkov could see many of them were crushed.

"All people on Twitter started to calculate like, how old am I going to be in 2024," Volkov said, "because everyone realized it was decided Putin will stay until at least 2024."

Anger over the tandem switch would simmer for months before finally boiling over after reports of widespread fraud in the December 4 State Duma elections. Cheating in Russian elections was nothing new, but for the first time, ubiquitous cell phone cameras yielded instant video evidence of ballot stuffing, carousel voting, and other irregularities. It wasn't enough that Putin had made clear that voters' opinions were worthless, and they would have no real say in the presidential election. Now, they could see firsthand that the parliamentary vote was also rigged.

Solidarity, another coalition of democratic political forces, had obtained a permit for a public rally to be held the day after the elections on Chistye Prudy, one of Moscow's charming public squares.

Navalny, on his blog, implored people to attend no matter their political leanings.

"There will be a rally in protest against election fraud," he wrote. "It is a must to come to it. The meeting is permitted. Its formal organizer is Solidarity, but that doesn't matter now. Whether you like it or not, you have to come. This applies to everyone. Nationalists, liberals, leftists, greens, vegetarians, Martians." The Party of Crooks and Thieves, he wrote, "stole everyone's votes."

Privately, however, Navalny had little hope for the event. "I went, although I thought that the rally would be a failure," he said days afterward, speaking to a journalist from prison.

Yashin had heard Navalny's pessimism firsthand. "I have a funny correspondence with Navalny an hour before the rally," he said. "I wrote him an SMS: An hour ago, the Communists gathered 100 people on Pushkin Square."

Navalny replied: "I'm afraid that not much more will come to us."

He was wrong.

Thousands turned out for what stunningly became one of the biggest protests Moscow had seen in many years. To get to the stage, Navalny actually had to fight his way through the crowd and scale over a police barrier. Once on the main platform, he delivered a fiery speech.

"Hi everybody," Navalny began. "While jumping over the fence to get to this rally, I forgot everything I wanted to say."

He asked for a show of hands from those who voted and thanked them for fulfilling their duty as citizens. "Thanks," he said, then his tone shifted.

"Thanks for telling these goats, we're here," he said. "For telling the bearded [Central Election Commission Chairman] Churov, we exist!

"We have our voice and we exist!" he shouted.

"Yes," the crowded shouted back.

"We exist!"

"Yes," the crowd shouted again.

"They hear this voice and they're scared," Navalny said.

He then turned his attention to the derision directed at them by the propagandists on Russian state television, the idiot box that Navalny feared was turning Russia into a zombie-nation. "They can laugh in their zombie box. They can call us microbloggers or internet hamsters. I am a net hamster! And I am going to cut the throats of these beasts! Together we'll do this. Because we exist!"

Navalny said he did not understand why he bothered to go to the polling station to vote, and that some jerk had asked if he voted for United Russia. "I said no," he shouted to the crowd. "Tell me: Did you vote for United Russia?"

"No," the crowd shouted back.

"What is this party called?"

"Crooks and Thieves," the crowd shouted.

"It's the party of crooks, thieves and murderers," Navalny thundered. "These people should be afraid of us. And they should understand that we hate them.

"We repeat it every time and maybe some think it's a joke. We don't forget and we don't forgive," he said, launching a new chant.

"We don't forget! We don't forgive! We don't forget! We don't forgive!"

"They are no one. With us are these astronauts in camouflage uniforms," Navalny said, referring to the helmeted riot police. "That means we are the power; they are no one. And we say: We are the power. After these elections, these Kremlin thieves have no right to tell anyone they are the rightful authority. They are no one.

"We don't need these crooks and thieves," he said. "We want another president. Not a crook."

Moving to wrap up, Navalny said he would try an experiment, but the crowd wasn't done and began shouting, "Putin's a thief! Putin's a thief! Putin's a thief."

But one more thing that's important to understand, Navalny said, picking up a line he had used at the nationalist Russian March. "All for one and one for all," Navalny shouted. "There's no other choice."

"All for one," he shouted.

"And one for all," the crowd shouted back.

"See, it works not only for the Russian March," he said, adding: "We're correct! We're here! We exist! All for one and one for all!"

It was the first of a series of electrifying performances by Navalny at the front of large crowds that assembled in Moscow for the so-called white-ribbon protests, which were held over the three months ahead of the March 4, 2012, presidential election.

It was also the night of his first arrest.

After the rally, many of the participants marched toward the FSB headquarters at Lubyanka. They had no permit to do so. Among others, Navalny and Yashin were detained and ferried to a distant police station far from the boisterous crowd. Video showed Navalny being hustled away to a police van, a helmeted officer on each arm.

Navalny was sentenced to fifteen days, beginning a pattern of arrests and short sentences over the ensuing months.

Four days after his arrest, Navalny spoke by phone from jail with *New Times* magazine and said the conditions were uncomfortable but not inhumane, though he said he had not yet been allowed to shower.

"This is clearly not a sanatorium and not a resort. It is rather unpleasant to be here, but it cannot be called some kind of 'torturous conditions,'" he said. "However, I believe that we are all being deprived of our liberty quite illegally."

Navalny said there was a clear need for continued protests but he urged that they be carried out peacefully, and said far more people were needed than the seven to ten thousand who appeared on December 5, 2011.

"On the one hand, it's a lot, and I'm glad that so many came," he told *New Times*. "On the other hand, it is not enough: After all, they stole the votes from millions quite brazenly and openly! There are many videos that talk about this, and as far as I understand, now no one doubts that there were falsifications... We need to continue actions, but we need to hold them only in a legal format. No need to set fire to cars and beat the police. But we must go out."

He also sought to deflect attention from himself. "I am very grateful to those people who go to pickets with slogans: 'Freedom for Navalny,'

'Freedom for Yashin,'" he said. "But these slogans must be changed. 'Freedom for all political prisoners!' There are about sixty-five people in this special detention center for political people. No need to single out one person. And this slogan should be used on a par with another: 'We demand fair elections, we demand a revision of the election results.'"

When the journalist asked Navalny if he would run for president, he refused to answer, saying it was a stupid question under the circumstances.

A few days later Putin hosted his annual "telethon." Typically held each December, the Russian leader spends hours fielding questions from constituents on live TV. And that year, he used the event to mock the protests, which he said were being fomented by the United States. He said that when he saw the protesters wearing white ribbons, he thought they had condoms pinned to their shirts and were speaking out against AIDS.

The derision from the once-and-soon-to-be-again-president only fueled the anger and future protests, which continued at times in a joyous, carnival atmosphere.

Navalny missed a follow-up demonstration on December 10 because he was still in jail. But he was again the most electric speaker at a huge rally on Sakharov Avenue on December 24, which drew a crowd of more than eighty thousand.

"Who is the power here?" he shouted.

"We are!" the crowd roared back.

"They stole our votes," Navalny said. He added at another point: "I can see that there are enough people here right now to seize the Kremlin and the White House"—Russia's government headquarters building, where the prime minister's office is located. "We are a peaceful force and will not do it yet. But if these crooks and thieves try to go on cheating us, if they continue telling lies and stealing from us, we will take back what is ours."

To keep things organized, the opposition formed a Coordinating Council. Navalny was elected to it, of course. But his public stature clearly had shifted in a way unlike others. Calls grew for Navalny to seek public office, and in Russia only one office really matters: the presidency.

"Navalny went to jail as a blogger, and came out as a presidential candidate, unexpectedly for himself," the writer Viktor Shenderovich said on Ekho Moskvy radio that January.

"Obviously he changed his status while sitting in prison, and it is clear that he himself is not ready for this. Just like we ourselves are not ready," Shenderovich added. "We are trying to comprehend what is happening on the fly, and it is clear that our analyses of a month ago have nothing to do with reality."

The protests were the largest public outpouring that Russia had seen in decades. But they were confined mainly to Moscow, with only a smattering of small demonstrations elsewhere. In hindsight, it is also clear that conditions were simply not right for a full-scale uprising that could take down the government. Unlike in many countries that had just experienced the Arab Spring, quality of life was good in Russia, especially in big cities, and still improving.

Many of the Russian protesters were simply too comfortable—especially Moscow's young, middle-class professionals. Their participation in rallies would often fit in between other items on the urban social calendar, which included meals in Moscow's hip restaurants or grabbing drinks in the city's trendy bars.

Navalny himself, after participating in the December 24 rally, flew off for a Christmas vacation in Mexico.

"¡Feliz Navidad!" he posted on LiveJournal, wishing his followers Merry Christmas from the ancient Mayan city of Chichén Itzá. There, in the Mexican sun, he continued to work on RosPil projects and to give media interviews about the budding protest movement. In a blog post published on Orthodox Christmas, Navalny offered a detailed explanation of how RosPil was managing its thousands of online donations.

On March 4, 2012, Putin was overwhelmingly reelected to the presidency, a deflating moment for the opposition. Still, the next day, several thousand demonstrators, including Navalny, gathered at Pushkin Square in the center of Moscow. By evening, many of them had been arrested and the crowd was dispersed.

Navalny, flashing his signature humor, continued tweeting even after getting bundled into a police wagon. "Our police wagon is Number 2012," he posted. "Attention! DO NOT SET IT ON FIRE. Just puncture the tires."

* * *

With Putin restored to the Kremlin for at least a dozen more years, the opposition suddenly lacked a clear mission.

One lesson was that they had failed to mobilize Russians outside of the capital, so Navalny and others turned their focus to the regions, looking for ways to be relevant.

They found an initial cause to take up in Astrakhan, a regional capital in southern Russia located on the Volga River delta. An opposition mayoral candidate, Oleg V. Shein of the Just Russia party, was on a hunger strike to protest what he said were falsified tallies that robbed him of victory in the March 4 election. Appeals to election officials and to the courts yielded nothing.

By the time Navalny and other activists from Moscow, including Ilya Yashin and Ksenia Sobchak, arrived in Astrakhan on April 9, Shein and a small group of supporters had not eaten solid food for twenty-six days.

At a downtown plaza in Astrakhan, Navalny gathered with about two hundred supporters of Shein. "It's a crucial moment," Navalny said in an interview. "We need to inspire these people. You know these small little conflicts; we have a lot of them.

"The local authorities, they just don't care," Navalny continued. "When the federal media is promoting this information and it's promoted from the internet, it's a real problem. That's why it's so important to attract people from Moscow." But the paltry number of protesters who turned out that Tuesday—fewer than five hundred people in a city of five hundred thousand—did not bode well for the Russian opposition, in Astrakhan or anywhere.

The following month, in Moscow, protesters clashed violently with police at a demonstration on Bolotnaya Square on the day before Putin's inauguration. Navalny was among those arrested. Once again, he got a fifteen-day sentence, but others who were implicated in fighting with the police were charged with serious crimes.

Navalny had proven that he could electrify a crowd, and he had crossed over from his niche as an anti-corruption blogger into a new role as arguably the leading voice of the opposition. But the path forward was unclear.

There were rivalries and tensions in the motley array of opposition forces. Eduard Limonov, the writer, poet and founder of the left-wing National Bolshevik party, wrote a brutal assessment of Navalny as part of a series of political profiles published on the *Svobodnaya Pressa* news site. Limonov, who fled the Soviet Union in 1974 and returned to Russia in 1991, derided Navalny as an ineffective "front man" for a group of capitalists:

> An oversized guy, a big frame in blue jeans and a shirt without a tie, preferably small-check. When contemplating him, the thought arises of the American type of health, of oatmeal and milk... The Navalny phenomenon testifies that our intelligentsia has successfully adapted the American figurative range for themselves. Not a Stalinist in a clumsy suit, not a protest rocker in a leather jacket, not a fat deputy in a Brioni suit, not a Russian intellectual with a scraggly beard and glasses (half-Chekhov, half-Trotsky...), but really a citizen of the world, instead of a tie—a smile.
>
> A pinch of Assange, vaguely reminiscent of Ralph Nadar... the second, young edition of Boris Nemtsov—that's Navalny for you. In fact, that's all. Navalny has no other advantages. He is not witty or smart.
>
> Navalny is not the leader of a political party or even a prominent activist in any party. As a fighter against corruption, Navalny is ineffective. It is not his fault... he is probably a good corruption investigator, but the authorities do not want to prosecute the corrupt officials he discovered. [So] he is still ineffective.

Limonov, who died in 2020 at the age of seventy-seven, claimed that Navalny had visited him to talk about the elections to the opposition's

Coordinating Council. "He called himself a politician so often that I realized that he did not believe that he was a politician. But he was told that he was a politician," he wrote. "Navalny was created by the media."

Limonov's criticism also reflected annoyance, or envy, at how Navalny had become the centerpiece of protests. "The masses took to the streets not because they were fascinated by Lyosha Navalny," Limonov jabbed, "but because they were outraged by Vladimir Putin."

* * *

Emboldened by Putin's victory, and shaken by the volatility of the Moscow protests, the Kremlin started cracking down on dissent and on perceived foreign influence, which Putin insisted was responsible for the unrest rather than genuine public anger over outright fraud in the Duma elections, and his decision to return to the presidency for a third term.

In June, Putin signed a law raising the maximum fine for participating in an unsanctioned public rally to 300,000 rubles, or about $9,100, from 1,000 rubles, or roughly $30. Organizers of such protests could be hit with triple that: fines of 1 million rubles.

In July, the squeeze tightened again. Putin signed a law vastly expanding government control over internet content. Under the guise of combating child pornography, the law authorized the government to shut down sites it considered a threat.

Putin that month also signed amendments to existing laws that created new requirements for nongovernmental organizations and other nonprofit groups to register as "foreign agents" if they received any financing from abroad, even if the money was not used for political purposes. Once registered or designated as a foreign agent, a host of other daunting administrative obligations followed. The new rules threatened to destroy many civil society groups, including some that were not at all political but focused on issues like public health.

Late that December, Navalny took aim at one of the main champions of all this draconian legislation, a United Russia member of the Duma named Sergei Zheleznyak.

"I'm sure you hate this lying, hypocritical scoundrel as much as I do," Navalny wrote on his blog. But then, for effect, he argued with himself. "Stop. And why did I call Zheleznyak a 'deceitful, hypocritical scoundrel'? What right did I have? After all, a person has the right to a striped suit and his own point of view... He is a patriot. He is sincerely rooting for Russia. He prefers everything Russian... Agents of influence must be fought."

Navalny explained: Zheleznyak's children were attending expensive schools in Europe, including one daughter at the American School in Switzerland and one at university in Britain. At the same time, Navalny posted financial disclosure information showing Zheleznyak owned assets that seemed to far outstrip his income as a member of parliament, including expensive real estate and cars.

Navalny noted that at the same moment, United Russia—at Putin's behest—was moving to ban the adoption of Russian orphans by U.S. citizens, as retaliation for Congress approving Browder's Magnitsky Act. Putin was enraged by the law, which created mechanisms to levy sanctions against alleged human rights violators, including in Russia.

"These scoundrels still have enough conscience to shout that sick orphans cannot be adopted by foreigners," Navalny wrote. "[Zheleznyak] himself sent three children abroad, but on the other hand he will stand as a wall [against] some unfortunate three-year-old autistic person, lying in dirty diapers and having the prospects of only a nursing home until age 18, being taken abroad."

The battle escalated when Zheleznyak hit back at Navalny on Facebook, calling him a "scumbag" and saying it was out of bounds for Navalny to involve Zheleznyak's children in a political fight. Navalny was apoplectic.

"Nothing terrible will happen to your children, Monsieur Zheleznyak, fortunately," he fired back. "They are safe, abroad, studying in elite educational institutions. Their dad, of course, is a corrupt scoundrel, but there's nothing to be done about it."

But then he pointed out how many children had been harmed by Putin's crackdown on their parents, whose only crime was supporting the political opposition. This included his own eleven-year-old daughter,

Dasha, "whose children's belongings were seized during a search, and whose computer, phone and photographs have not yet been returned."

Navalny noted the government's efforts to sever the custody rights of Yevgeniya Chirikova, an environmental activist, and Maria Baronova, a member of the protest group Pussy Riot. Similar actions, he pointed out, were taken against those charged with crimes for fighting with police at the rally on Bolotnaya Square before Putin's inauguration, including Maxim Luzyanin, who had a fifteen-year-old son.

"He won't go to Switzerland," Navalny wrote in a scathing post. "His mother now spends money on lawyers."

"This bastard here on TV talked about patriotism, and flew to his family abroad for the weekend," Navalny wrote, noting that Zheleznyak's family was enjoying a pampered life while United Russia was banning adoptions and depriving orphans of families. "They are literally ready to eat children," he wrote, "just to have their own privileges and status, to be outside the law."

Many of Navalny's darkest warnings about Putin and Putin's enablers and supporters proved awfully accurate, though not necessarily in the ways he expected. Slightly more than a decade later, in 2023, the International Criminal Court issued an arrest warrant for Putin and Russia's children's rights commissioner, Maria Lvova-Belova, accusing them of war crimes by illegally transporting Ukrainian children to Russia.

But as the year drew to a close, Navalny faced several challenges. Among the opposition, there was still no unified political movement. The protests of 2012 had been squashed. Putin had been reelected for another six years and was certain to stay, as Volkov warned, until at least 2024, and Navalny had not yet managed to form a viable political party structure. Navalny, however, had emerged as the brightest light—or most "fashionable," to use Limonov's word—among the opposition leaders, putting a target on Navalny's back. He was no longer just an annoying blogger or occasionally cutting voice on the radio. He was now a threat to Putin's regime with clear, if not entirely formed, political ambitions—a threat that would potentially need to be silenced, or eliminated.

—8—

PROSECUTION, PERSECUTION, PRISON

"I am not afraid and, once again, I call on everyone else in the room not to be afraid either, because there is nothing to be afraid of here."

—Alexey Navalny, Prison Colony No. 2, February 15, 2022

Navalny was in a large room in Prison Colony No. 2, which had been transformed into a makeshift courtroom, to face the latest criminal charges against him. It was February 15, 2022, and Navalny had been in jail for more than a year since his return from Germany.

This time he was facing an allegation of fraud, that he had misappropriated donations to the Anti-corruption Foundation and used them for personal expenses. Navalny brushed aside the accusations as absurd, noting that his organization maintained meticulous accounting and could prove how each kopeck was spent.

He also had zero expectation that the legal proceedings would correspond to reality.

"I understand," he said. "This is not my first trial. I am not a naïve person. The verdict will be guilty. It will be a rather long term . . . since I insulted this dark lord of yours, Putin. I not only survived, but I returned. So he said, 'He kind of thinks that he is so cool, let him sit in prison and stay there for life.' And there will be this case, and the second case, and the third. And you will endlessly increase the term for me.

"Well then what can I do," Navalny asked. "My activities, the activities of my colleagues, are more important than just the specific fate of a person. And I think the worst thing I can do, the real crime I can commit, is to be scared of you—you and those behind you. I tell you again: I am not afraid, and once again I call on everyone else in the room not to be afraid either, because there is nothing to be afraid of here."

Indeed, at that point, Navalny had been under prosecution—or persecution—in the Russian judicial system, one way or another, for fifteen years.

The first effort to bring a criminal case against Navalny appears to have been after the bloody brawl that erupted at the thirteenth DA! debate in the fall of 2007. Navalny was brought to the police station, and it was quickly clear that he, rather than the hooligans who instigated the fight, was under scrutiny of the police.

Despite video evidence and numerous witness statements by Belykh, Yashin, and others, it took six months before the case was finally closed without charges. Navalny described the situation in a December 2007 email to Frank Conatser, a grant officer for the National Endowment for Democracy, which had helped finance the debate series.

"You may have heard that our project has faced more than just provocations from the Kremlin youth organizations," Navalny wrote. "Now these are provocations with the use of violence." He included links to photographs of the episode. "In addition, after the last debate, they are trying to fabricate a criminal case against me personally. We've hired lawyers and hopefully they'll settle this case."

Russia's corrupt and politicized judicial system is regularly used to carry out vendettas and settle scores, even more often in business than in politics. And the next investigation of Navalny grew out of his effort to clean up the timber industry in Kirov.

In February 2010, the FSB had arrested another adviser to Governor Belykh in Kirov, Andrey Votinov, and accused him of extracting a bribe of 2 million rubles from Vyacheslav Opalev, the head of Kirovles, the regional-owned timber company. In return, according to the FSB, Votinov let Opalev keep his job despite substantial evidence that he was incompetent or corrupt or both. Opalev was also arrested.

At the time, Navalny and his main colleague in Kirov, Pyotr Ofitserov, had been working to get Opalev fired as part of what they hoped would be a broad shake-up of Kirovles. Instead, Navalny and Ofitserov got shaken up—prosecuted on fabricated charges of embezzlement.

As a result of mismanagement, corruption, and the 2008 financial crisis, Kirovles led by Opalev had accumulated massive losses, totaling some 240 million rubles, or $7.5 million. Navalny and Ofitserov initially faced criminal charges over losses totaling just $42,000, or 1.5 million rubles.

The case was as absurd as it was byzantine. And yet, Navalny acknowledged there was reason to be concerned. Votinov was actually the second Belykh adviser to be arrested in what appeared to be retribution against the new governor and his team. Another adviser, Roman Shipov, had been arrested in the summer of 2009 and charged with fraud. So when rumors began swirling that Navalny would be the third, he did not wait around to find out. Navalny and his family returned to Moscow.

Sure enough, within weeks news reports appeared in Kremlin-connected media outlets saying that Navalny was under investigation. "Adviser to the governor of the Kirov region Alexey Navalny, better known as a fighter for the rights of private shareholders, may be brought to trial for fraud," the government-controlled newspaper *Rossiyskaya Gazeta* reported. "Law enforcement agencies of the Volga Federal District, with the support of the Federal Security Service, are conducting checks on the involvement of the well-known blogger in gray schemes in the forest complex of the Vyatka region," the newspaper said.

Navalny was at Yale when news of the case broke. At the time, he described the situation in Kirov as a simple matter of revenge—perhaps organized by Transneft or VTB as retribution for his investigations into their corporate malfeasance. He also suspected that it was payback from the disgruntled Kirovles director, Opalev, who, as a cooperating witness against Navalny, was providing the trumped-up evidence that the authorities needed.

Kirovles, Navalny noted on his blog, had an effective monopoly on the forest business in the region yet had lost tons of money. "Despite such a privileged position, the office was (and still is) in a very deplorable situation: huge debts, salary delays, etc.," he wrote. "The director of the enterprise was a hellish swindler by the name of Opalev. He organized some completely unthinkable schemes for the sale of forests, through 36 different branches, and no one really understood where, what and for how much. I began to squash this crook on the subject of centralization and transparency of sales... I got him fired and a decision was made to conduct a full audit."

Navalny said he planned to post all the information about the Kirovles case online "both for those who want to understand in more detail and for those who are interested in the mechanics of the fabrication of a criminal case."

But he also said that the case was so weak that he doubted the authorities actually intended to bring it forward. Instead, he said, it was designed to scare him into staying in the United States.

"As I understand it, the main idea is that I should not return to the Russian Federation, frightened by a fabricated case," Navalny wrote. He added: "My dear crooks! It was obvious that you would depict something like that and I was ready for it.

"I'm not scared and I'm coming back."

A pattern was beginning to emerge.

* * *

Some commentators noted that as an unofficial adviser to Belykh in Kirov, Navalny did not even have authority to make or enforce any governmental decisions, so he could not possibly be held responsible for anything that occurred with the timber company.

As Navalny predicted, the Kirovles case was flimsy and investigators in the Kirov region could not make it stick. They decided to drop it. But suddenly, officials in Moscow intervened; the headquarters of the Investigative Committee declared the case reopened. But now it would be sent, instead, to investigators in the Volga Federal District to reexamine, suggesting that the local authorities in Kirov had failed in their assigned task to make a case.

"The investigation of the century continues," Navalny proclaimed on his blog.

He noted with some amazement how the decision was announced on television by Vladimir Markin, the chief spokesman for the Investigative Committee. "Funny, right?" he wrote. "All the cases that I investigate for hundreds of millions and billions tend to go downhill and are never commented on TV. The case against me for 1 million rubles is rapidly traveling up and is receiving active comments from the leadership."

Officials in the Volga Federal District also did not see any merit to the case. But in May, the Investigative Committee headquarters in Moscow announced that a case was opened and Navalny would be prosecuted.

"Navalny convinced Opalev to sign a deliberately unprofitable contract... for the sale of timber products," Markin said, announcing the case. "In fact, I can say that Navalny, in his actions, applied the tactics and techniques that raiders use when seizing enterprises."

Navalny marveled at the audacity. "In order to mold a real criminal case out of a complete fiction, it was necessary to raise it to the highest level—the Investigative Committee of the Russian Federation," he blogged. "At the level of Kirov, they issued a refusal to initiate a case, at the level of the Volga Federal District, too. In total, as I understand it, there are already five 'refusals' in the case."

The charge against Navalny actually did not even amount to theft. He was accused of causing damage "absent signs of theft" that resulted in a significant loss. And yet, it carried the possibility of a five-year prison sentence.

The harassment, however, was just getting started. And the Investigative Committee made little effort to disguise its plans. Markin, the spokesman, said that Navalny had put a bullseye on his own back.

"If a person tries with all his strength to attract attention, or if I can put it, teases authorities—'Look at me, I'm so good compared to everyone else'—well, then interest in his past grows and the process of exposing him naturally speeds up," Markin said.

On the evening of Friday, May 13, 2011, three police officers knocked on Navalny's apartment door and demanded to see him. He wasn't home. His wife reached him by phone and Navalny referred the cops to his lawyer, thinking the visit was connected to Kirovles. In fact, a whole new investigation was underway: Navalny had been accused of desecrating the Russian Federation's official emblem of a two-headed eagle, which he had used in the logo of RosPil, his antigraft initiative.

Playing on the Russian slang for "embezzle," which is "to saw," each of the eagles in the RosPil logo held an old-fashioned hand saw, and one of United Russia's Duma members had taken offense. Navalny's real "crime," of course, was criticizing the man's extravagant official travel.

"Remember the puffy-loafer from the party of Crooks and Thieves, deputy Pavel Zyryanov?" Navalny asked his LiveJournal followers. "The one whose deputy activity consists of business trips to Cuba, Germany and Taiwan?"

"Well, at the request of this senseless creature, the Prosecutor General's office is conducting a powerful check to see if the RosPil logo is a desecration of the state emblem of the Russian Federation," Navalny wrote.

Another, more sinister, development also emerged that spring.

Navalny had been running RosPil on record-setting private donations, which he summarized in intermittent blog posts laying out the operation's finances in detail. Most donations were made online, through Yandex Wallet, typically by bank transfer. The Yandex system was supposed to be confidential.

But suddenly that May, donors to RosPil got strange phone calls demanding to know why they donated to Navalny's organization.

"About four weeks ago I received the first letter from the series 'Morons, who did you tell my number to!!?' " Navalny wrote on LiveJournal.

He described donors' nearly identical complaints: A woman, claiming to call from a nonexistent media outlet, demanded information about why they had given money to Navalny and asked who had given them the money to donate. It was clear to the donors that the caller also had information about other financial transactions.

Navalny explained that despite craving more information about his donors, he typically could see only a Yandex Wallet user's account number. Surnames would be visible only if the donor specifically added a note. Navalny stressed that he had anticipated such meddling when he first opened the account. "I asked the Yandex people a direct question: The Kremlin Thieves will definitely not like the project . . . to whom and on what basis can transaction data be provided."

The answer, Navalny said, was only "at the formal written request of the special services."

"On this I calmed down," he wrote. "Paper is paper. You can't hide it later. It will be clear who is interested and you can ask the question: For what purpose are you interested? For the request, some grounds are needed. There should be something formal where it says:

> Navalny is financed by the CIA
> The CIA is financed by Navalny
> Navalny is financed by Bin Laden
> Bin Laden is financed by Navalny
> RosPil is a terrorist network
> Navalny eats children
> Everyone who transfers money to RosPil eats children
> RosPil was created to ban Medvedev from dancing and take away his iPad.

"Imagine my surprise," Navalny continued. "When Yandex replied: The information regarding your account was transferred to the FSB of the Russian Federation at their official request."

Navalny expressed anger and disbelief. "After all, I've been trying to get the attention of these guys for so long," he wrote. "For the last three years I have been regularly writing various complaints and statements to this department. And never. Not once did these powerful fighters for banknotes consider my writing worthy of their attention."

"But," he added, "the parasites see a threat just in the fact that people themselves unite to fight corruption, and even finance such a fight themselves."

Navalny urged "the blogger Medvedev, whom some also call President Medvedev" to intervene and demand that the FSB adhere to the law. Of course, nothing came of it.

* * *

Navalny, looking back, has said it was clear the Kremlin shifted tactics after Putin's return to the presidency, ramping up its harassment and persecution of opposition figures. "Putin realized that it's not affordable for his system to give people more democracy," Navalny told the U.S. news program *60 Minutes*. "He completely changed his strategy, and started to arrest people, started to fabricate criminal cases."

Navalny's tactics also began to evolve, as he increasingly positioned himself as *the* leader of the Russian opposition.

A three-part "dialogue" with the writer Boris Akunin on LiveJournal, initiated by Akunin, reflected a rising demand among supporters for Navalny to clarify his positions.

In essence, it was a call for him to grow up as a politician, to show that he was capable of taking charge. The need for such leadership grew even more urgent as the protests of the first half of 2012 petered out, and the opposition entered a bleak period.

As Putin cracked down, Navalny's clash with the authorities grew more personal, and more visceral. With the Investigative Committee leading the push on Kirovles, Navalny hit back hard at its head, Alexander Bastrykin, a friend and university classmate of Putin's who reported directly to the president.

In early July, Navalny published a post called "Bastrykin with a Gun in the Forest," accusing the Investigative Committee chief of ordering subordinates to fabricate the Kirovles case against Navalny. The headline had a double meaning understood by most Russian readers: The month before, Bastrykin had been publicly accused of escorting a deputy editor of the *Novaya Gazeta* newspaper, Sergei Sokolov, into the woods outside

Moscow, threatening to kill him, and gloating that he would then be in charge of the investigation.

Several of *Novaya Gazeta*'s journalists were murdered over the years, and the newspaper's chief editor, Dmitry Muratov, who years later would win the Nobel Peace Prize, issued a public appeal to Bastrykin, recounting the episode and demanding security guarantees for Sokolov. Bastrykin apologized for the forest incident and kept his job.

Navalny, in his blog post, also referenced past examples of erratic behavior by Bastrykin, including an incident in 2004 in St. Petersburg, in which he pulled a gun and threatened a man walking a dog.

In late July, Navalny hit Bastrykin again, this time under the headline "About Real Foreign Agents," in which he recounted allegations that Bastrykin owned substantial real estate in the Czech Republic that he had failed to disclose, as required by Russian law, and that he had failed to pay certain taxes.

"Let's talk about foreign agents," Navalny wrote. "Not those nonexistent ones that United Russia is trying to expose, but the real ones: high-ranking, cynical, deceitful. Those who prefer to earn (steal) in the civil service of Russia, but associate their cozy future with living outside of it."

Navalny acknowledged the futility of his attacks on one of Russia's most powerful law enforcement officials with personal ties to Putin, someone who could threaten to murder a journalist and face no consequences.

"Of course, we understand that the more crooked, thieving and criminal an official is, the more stable his position in Putin's system of power is," Navalny wrote. "I personally understand that the more I piss on this or that swindler, the dearer he is to Putin."

Still, Navalny said he was formally appealing to Putin and to the Investigative Committee to open investigations into Bastrykin.

"It's funny, yes, but the crimes of the head of the Investigative Committee Bastrykin should be considered by the Investigative Committee," he wrote. In September, Navalny slapped Bastrykin again, calling him a "double foreign agent" and linking to a report in *Novaya Gazeta* that Bastrykin and his wife also owned real estate in Spain.

There were other signs that Navalny's battles with the government had escalated to a new level.

On August 6, 2012, on a bit of a lark, an employee of the Anticorruption Foundation returning from summer holidays decided to sweep the office for bugs, only to discover a listening device and video camera stashed in the walls.

Navalny described the situation in a blog post titled, "Just Because You Are Paranoid Doesn't Mean You Aren't Being Followed." He included a video of roughly a dozen police officers in the office after he reported finding the bugs. "Honestly, I thought they would hide them better," Navalny said.

On December 14, 2012, as the Kirovles case slowly churned forward, the Investigative Committee announced another major criminal case. This one, against Navalny and his younger brother, Oleg, accused them of a bizarre scheme to defraud the French cosmetics maker Yves Rocher by overcharging the company for shipping its products.

Oleg Navalny had worked for the Russian postal service and started a business providing commercial shipping for customers like Yves Rocher.

Navalny, who had been invited to serve on the board of directors of Aeroflot, Russia's main airline, was in an audit committee meeting when his phone started blowing up with news of the case. His parents and brother also called. The police were carrying out searches.

The day before the announcement of the Yves Rocher case, Bastrykin had a "working meeting" with Putin at the Kremlin. According to a partial transcript, published by the Kremlin, Putin asked about developments in key areas including organized crime, terrorism, and drug trafficking. Bastrykin claimed success on all fronts but emphasized a different area of focus: About 10 percent of cases were "corruption-related," he said.

"In the first nine months of this year alone, we initiated more than twenty thousand criminal cases of corruption, that is, every tenth case that was investigated is aimed at combating corruption," he said. "Of this number, about sixteen thousand are cases against officials at various levels: municipal, subject, federal, and cases against special subjects—these are deputies at various levels, officials, administrators and law enforcement officers."

The numbers, which were impossible to verify, seemed outlandishly high. Navalny, meanwhile, suspected that he was a topic during the meeting.

"Yesterday Bastrykin met with Putin, got the go-ahead to start a fake case," Navalny alleged to the journalist Oleg Kashin. "This is complete bullshit."

The opposition had been planning a march on December 15, and Navalny and his supporters immediately interpreted the Yves Rocher announcement as an intimidation tactic.

Navalny's mother, Lyudmila, was so angry she went on Ekho Moskvy radio.

"The statement of the Investigative Committee on the eve of the Freedom March says that they want to blackmail my son through his family so that he does not go to this march, so that Alexey stops his political activities altogether," she said. "But I want to say that they will not succeed, because the whole family supports Alexey. And we ourselves, and all our friends, of course, will definitely go. We cannot call anyone, but I just want to say that by our example everyone can understand how opposition figures are persecuted in the country.

"And the last thing I want to say," Lyudmila Navalnaya added. "I hope that during my lifetime I will hear that Mr. Bastrykin and all his classmates at St. Petersburg University, who are involved in the political persecution of Alexey, will wake up in the same morning and hear the same news about themselves."

The Investigative Committee accused the Navalny brothers of a massive theft, totaling some $1.8 million. "Oleg and Alexey Navalny fraudulently embezzled the funds of a trading company in the amount of more than 55 million rubles," the press release declared. "The Navalny brothers spent most of this amount on their own needs."

Navalny was even more furious than usual. He tweeted a photo of Oleg standing in his tiny kitchen holding his baby in his arms. "I stopped by my brother's to find out how things are going and see if he hides 55 million in his kitchen of 5 (five) square meters," Navalny tweeted.

On LiveJournal, Navalny admitted that there was something different about seeing his family in the crosshairs. "Well, I'm not going to lie: This is an unpleasant thing," he wrote. "It's one thing when Kremlin-crooks climb specifically at you. You are ready for this. The wife is ready. It's another thing when they have already gone to a wide circle of relatives."

The next day, Navalny went to the Freedom March. Demonstrators gathered on Lubyanka Square, outside the headquarters of the FSB, where many placed flowers on a monument to victims of oppression. Predictably, Navalny and the other organizers were arrested as police cleared away the protesters. They were released later that night.

But Bastrykin wasn't done.

Three days later, the Investigative Committee announced that it had launched another case against Navalny, this one involving the privatization of the Urzhum distillery in Kirov, which had been Navalny's initial focus. In fact, Navalny had stopped an effort to dilute the company's value. The privatization had gone forward two years after he left the region. On Twitter, Navalny expressed disbelief. "Hahaha. WUT?!" he posted.

Speaking to the Interfax news agency, which had reported the latest case, Navalny said that the Investigative Committee had a new strategy: "Not a day without a new case," and, he said, "Every new press release must mention me." He added, "We are going to pin every crime that happens in Russia on you. And if you are innocent and can prove it in one case, we'll pin 10 others on you, and you will not be able to do anything except come to the Investigative Committee."

Navalny's assessment was pretty much spot-on. Within a week after the distillery announcement, the Investigative Committee brought forward yet another potential criminal case—this one dating to 2007, when Navalny and Gaidar used a corporate entity Navalny created called Allekt to do campaign advertising and publicity work for Gaidar's party, the Union of Right Forces, which was led at the time by Belykh.

Approximately 100 million rubles, roughly $4 million, had moved through the Allekt, according to the Investigative Committee, but it insisted that there was no evidence that any advertising work had actually been done. Belykh insisted that everything was in order and the work was related to advertisements placed on outdoor billboards.

No one had ever complained—and by that point, even if money had disappeared, the Union of Right Forces no longer existed as a party. No matter. The Investigative Committee used the case as the basis to order searches of Navalny, Gaidar, and their associates. Among those to be targeted was a Navalny employee, Georgy Alburov, who was still in high school in his native city of Ufa in 2007 when the alleged crime occurred. Another was the head of Navalny's Anti-corruption Foundation, Vladimir Ashurkov, a financial whiz and former senior executive at Alfa Group Consortium, one of Russia's biggest private investment firms, owned by the oligarchs Mikhail Fridman and Petr Aven.

As flimsy as the Allekt case might have been, the allegation was not new. It first surfaced after a 2010 hack of Navalny's e-mail that exposed correspondence with Belykh, and they had denied any wrongdoing. Back then, Yevgenia Dillendorf, a spokeswoman for Yabloko, raised a different question—about the propriety of Navalny working for the Union of Right Forces, a rival party, when he was still in the leadership of Yabloko.

It was clear that the Investigative Committee was going to throw everything it could at Navalny. And not quite three months later, it attacked again, alleging that Navalny had falsified his credentials as a lawyer.

To be admitted to the bar in Russia requires documenting professional experience, which the Investigative Committee said Navalny had improperly claimed as head of legal services for Allekt. The Kirov bar association, where Navalny first applied, said that everything had been in order. Navalny later transferred to the Moscow bar association.

The Allekt case also led to a different strange case, in which the Investigative Committee accused Navalny of possessing a stolen painting that they had seized from his apartment during a search.

The drawing, called *Good-Bad Man*, was made by an artist, Sergei Sotov, in the city of Vladimir, and hung on an outdoor fence along with many other pictures. It was brought to Moscow as a gift for Navalny by Alburov.

The artist said he routinely left pictures outdoors to be taken or discarded. But the authorities insisted that it was stolen—an example of the extreme crackdown against Navalny and his associates. Navalny said he thought it was a joke and that Bastrykin merely wanted the poster for himself after seeing it on Navalny's Instagram.

* * *

This was Navalny's new reality. His existence going forward would be defined by police searches and court appearances, including repeated trips to Kirov, where the Kirovles case was being heard by a judge named Sergei Blinov, who was exactly Navalny's age.

Blinov was from a small town about forty miles outside of Kirov, where he had been a judge in the local district court. He was married with two children and loved to play hockey. According to *New Times* magazine, in the previous two and a half years he had issued 130 verdicts—all guilty. The parallels between Blinov and Navalny were equally striking and mystifying: two accomplished young lawyers from the same generation who as teenagers had watched the Soviet Union collapse. Somehow, one emerged as a major threat to Russia's authoritarian regime, fighting it at every chance; the other was its dutiful servant, delivering guilty verdicts as expected. Why, after all, would the authorities bring charges in the first place, if not to pronounce guilt?

Before the start of the trial, however, Navalny made a calculated bet to raise the stakes by publicly declaring that he intended one day to run for president of the Russian Federation.

"I want to become president," Navalny said in an interview on TV Rain on April 4, 2013. "I want to change life in the country. I want to change the system of government in the country." He said that given Russia's vast wealth of oil and gas reserves, its 140 million citizens should live at least as well as people in neighboring Estonia.

Simply by voicing his presidential aspirations aloud, Navalny had reset the terms of the case in Kirov. Putin's henchmen in the law enforcement bodies were no longer prosecuting an annoying blogger who had insulted United Russia. They were now persecuting Putin's declared rival.

Shortly before the opening of the Kirovles trial in April 2013, Mark Galeotti, an expert on Russian history and security issues, explained why the Kremlin regarded Navalny as such a threat.

"He has brought the issue of the corruption elite into the center of Russian politics, and has done more than anyone else to connect that with the United Russia bloc, that bastion of the cynical, the careerist and the corrupt," Galeotti wrote on his own blog. "At present, there is no one else who can assume his mantle, no one else who has a chance—no more than a chance—of being able to turn the middle-class metropolitan opposition into a credible political force. Which is, of course, why the Kremlin wants him out of the way, whether in prison or, much more likely, smeared and given a suspended sentence which will preclude him from standing for political office."

That April, following one court hearing in the case, Navalny submitted a petition to Judge Blinov asking for the travel restrictions that he had been placed under to be lifted during the May holidays—when Russians who aren't attending shareholder meetings in Siberia typically go on vacation.

Navalny and Blinov, after all, were part of the generation of Russians that had grown up with the ability to travel freely and see the world. "I would like to go to Egypt," Navalny told the judge. "But if I can't go abroad, at least somewhere to the south, for example, to the Astrakhan region. Yes, [or] at least to some Nizhneivkinsky sanatorium." He was referring to a spa located in the Kirov region.

At that, Blinov cracked a rare smile and declared: "The court does not issue vouchers to the sanitorium." But he granted Navalny's request.

Meanwhile, other machinations were developing in the Kremlin.

The appointed mayor of Moscow, Sergei Sobyanin (whom Navalny trounced in the virtual vote in 2009), announced that he was resigning to force early elections.

Legislation adopted the previous year had revived the possibility of a direct mayoral election, which had not been held in Moscow since 2003, and Sobyanin's masters in the Kremlin had decided the moment was right to carry out a bit of political kabuki theater.

While the government had managed to squash the protests, many Russians were genuinely offended by the tandem switch and left feeling that their votes were meaningless. The Kremlin seemed to sense a need to restore a veneer of democracy. And what better way than to allow Navalny to campaign for the country's second most important public office?

On June 4, the same day that Sobyanin announced his resignation to trigger early elections, Vyacheslav Volodin, the first deputy head of Putin's presidential administration and overseer of the domestic politics portfolio, gathered a group of political scientists and laid out his vision for orchestrating real, participatory elections in Moscow.

The absurdity and inherent contradiction of *staging* a genuine election did not seem to register. Or, as often happens with absurdities in Russia, everyone just nodded and went along as if it was the most normal thing in the world.

Volodin told his assembly of experts that Russian politics needed "to become more transparent and competitive, candidates from the government need to participate in debates, and opposition members should be allowed to participate," according to the *Gazeta.ru* news site. When asked specifically about Navalny, Volodin said: "His participation in the Moscow mayoral elections would benefit the political system."

Konstantin Kostin, the head of the Civil Society Development Fund, told *Gazeta.ru* that Volodin expressed a desire to create a political system that was "not manually managed" but that also "maintains stability and predictability"—again with no nod to the contradiction.

Volodin stressed that Navalny's legal fate was in the hand of the courts. That offered a convenient way for the Kremlin to hedge its bets and keep up the appearance of a separation of powers between the president's office and the judiciary where clearly none existed. If Navalny's campaign somehow did well, he could always be imprisoned.

Putin and his team, however, were clearly calculating that the slew of news about criminal charges had weakened Navalny's public standing and eroded trust in his anti-corruption investigations. This was reflected in opinion polls, including by the Levada Center, which conducted its surveys without the government putting a thumb on the scale.

By allowing Navalny to run for mayor—and lose—the Kremlin could create a mirage that the Russian election system was free, fair, and open for competition, and also that Navalny was an unworthy candidate who could not even persuade his core base of supporters—urban elites in the capital—to entrust him with a position of authority.

One of Navalny's weaknesses is his inability to walk away from a confrontation, even when it is clear that he is being provoked, or that he will be forced to fight on someone else's terms, or on unfriendly turf. Even when, with a bit of perspective, it is clear that victory, at best, would prove hollow and likely carry a cost.

When challenged to a public debate, Navalny could never refuse.

The Finam FM radio host Yury Pronko had used this weakness to draw Navalny back in the studio for a clash with the United Russia deputy Yevgeny Fyodorov. And it was this instinct, born from his days growing up as a military brat, as a fighter among fighters, that propelled Navalny out onto the street to brawl with the hooligans after the DA! debate.

So, when invited—challenged, really—by Putin's top political technologist to run against Sobyanin, Navalny could not resist. This was not a virtual poll conducted by newspaper editors but an election campaign, with his name on an actual ballot, for mayor of Moscow, a world capital of more than 11 million people. Navalny took the bait.

In many ways, the crafty operators in the Kremlin had left him with no choice. If Navalny had refused to jump into the ring, it would confirm that he was not a serious politician but just an attention-seeking harpy, as Putin and his proxies alleged. But it was clear from the outset that the situation was entirely "manually managed"—to use Volodin's phrase—and Navalny's defeat was preordained.

Navalny, for instance, could not even get on the ballot without accepting the help of United Russia to obtain the minimum number of required signatures from municipal lawmakers to qualify as a candidate. Then, he would be running in a snap election, a situation that always favors the incumbent. The vote would be held on September 8, with many of the city's residents caught up in the frenzy that follows the postsummer return to work and school routines.

The Kremlin, of course, also made sure that Navalny got minimal to no exposure on the federal television channels, other than the continuing negative coverage of his legal prosecutions. Kirovles, in particular, was an insurance policy. The outcome of the trial could—and would—be manipulated to achieve the Kremlin's goals.

Navalny, however, would not shy away from the fight, no matter how unbalanced. With the deck clearly stacked against him, he began building a campaign operation with his friend Leonid Volkov as its manager and chief strategist. He also needed the backing of a party, which he got from RPR-PARNAS, the Republican Party of Russia—People's Freedom Party coalition, of which Boris Nemtsov was then a leader.

In a fifteen-page campaign "program," Navalny laid out the basis of his candidacy: a need to end corruption and raise the standard of living in the capital. "Moscow has sufficient resources to become a comfortable city that does not lag behind other European capitals in terms of quality of life," Navalny declared, "a city in which free citizens have a sense of their dignity and can directly influence the policy of city authorities."

Noting that Moscow's budget was comparable to New York City's, Navalny asked: "Why despite these huge resources, have the Moscow authorities still not been able to cope with traffic jams, crime, arbitrary police, poor quality of medical care, education, and poor urban spaces? The answer is very simple: theft and inefficient spending of the city's funds."

"Moscow," Navalny's program continued, "needs full transparency of all decisions, accountability of the authorities to citizens and a victory over corruption. It is thanks to this that it will be possible to free up huge resources that will help solve the key problems of our city." Noting that many candidates would make identical promises, Navalny added: "Choose the one who will not deceive the voters."

The campaign program boasted that "Navalny has unique long-term experience successfully combating theft and inefficient spending of budget money. Only the RosPil project prevented the inefficient spending of more than 50 billion rubles of budget funds"—roughly $1.65 billion.

Plus, it said: "Navalny knows Moscow's problems firsthand. He lives in an ordinary apartment in Maryino, is stuck in traffic with us, his children going to ordinary schools and kindergartens; the whole family uses an ordinary district medical clinic." The program noted his role creating and directing the Committee to Protect Muscovites combating illegal construction. "Navalny conducts all his activities public and transparently, reporting on his every project, every step he takes." It added, "Navalny owes nothing to the federal government. He is not bound hand and foot by a system of undercover arrangements with the current bureaucratic clans."

The campaign platform was consistent with Navalny's positions over many years, and among his priorities it included "reducing illegal migration, which has negative impact on the labor market, leading to an increase in crime and social tension." The trope of the criminal immigrant was as low as it was predictable and false.

On this basis alone, there could be little doubt that Navalny was a genuine politician. But Navalny had learned from past criticism and was also working to adopt mainstream positions that would prove durable. As a result, his platform on migration also included efforts to protect migrants from exploitation in the labor market.

Still, it was clear that he had fallen into the Kremlin's trap. He told voters that they should choose the candidate who would not deceive them, and yet the cloud of criminal cases around him raised all sorts of doubts. He insisted that Moscow was in a miserable situation but in fact, residents of the Russian capital were genuinely living better than at any other point in their lives.

The problems Navalny cited were quite real, but in relation to how Russians had suffered over the decades, they were miniscule. The shelves of the "hyper" supermarkets like Aushan and Perekrestok were overflowing with goods from all over the world. Sobyanin had launched a beautification initiative that was transforming the city's parks into magical oases. The city's arts, entertainment, and restaurant scenes were thriving.

In early July 2013, Navalny delivered an impassioned closing statement in the Kirovles trial, urging the court first of all to spare his codefendant, Pyotr Ofitserov, a father of five, who was entangled in the whole mess only because of his ties to Navalny.

"Our remarkable trial resembling a TV series—and sometimes it looks like a TV series resembling a trial—is coming to an end," Navalny said. "All of us including myself know perfectly well that the main purpose of this trial was similar to a TV series: to make it so that the federal channels could mention my name in the news in the context that this is the man who stole all timber in the Kirov region, that this is that crook. As if this can change all that I write about the swindlers who really steal billions from all of us and who seized the power in our country."

This was the first of the "last word" statements that Navalny would make in a series of criminal trials in the ensuing years, and a pattern was being set at the outset. Navalny used the speech to slam the crooks and thieves who were plundering Russia's wealth and, in Navalny's view, driving the country into despair and geopolitical disrepute. He disregarded and disrespected this judge and all the future judges as pathetic bit players in a larger political drama—a saga in which Navalny and his nemesis, Putin, fundamentally refused to hear each other. Neither man was going to stop or go away.

"If somebody thinks that having heard the threat of the six-year imprisonment I would run away abroad or hide somewhere, they are mistaken," Navalny said in the drab courtroom in Kirov. "I cannot run away from myself. I have nothing else but this and I don't want to do anything else but to help my country, to work for my compatriots."

Navalny also denounced the indifference that was pervasive among his fellow citizens. He had long maintained—and would for years to come—that Putin enjoyed a core of genuine support, having effectively used soaring oil and gas prices to raise standards of living. Putin's officials took vast bribes, and Putin himself had bribed the country. By all evidence, he had bought their complacency at a discount, with millions still living in poverty without indoor plumbing, or a normal, well-paved national highway system.

"I think that no one of us has the right to neutrality," Navalny said. "No one has the right to evade the work aimed at making our world better. We do not have this right. Because every time someone thinks, 'Why don't I step aside and wait?' he only helps this disgusting feudal regime which, like a spider, is sitting in the Kremlin. He helps these 100 families, which are sucking from all of Russia. He helps them to put the Russian people on the path of degradation and drinking to death, and to take away all of the national wealth."

Navalny warned that he and his supporters would not be deterred—either by the Kirovles case or by the stiff charges brought against those arrested at the protest on the day before Putin's 2012 inauguration. "If anyone thinks that myself or my colleagues will cease our activity because of this trial or the Bolotnaya trials or the many other trials going on all around the country," he said, "they are gravely mistaken."

Two weeks later, on July 17, Navalny's mayoral candidacy was officially registered, after he accepted forty-two signatures of municipal deputies gathered by United Russia. The next day, Navalny, his wife, a phalanx of prominent supporters, and a flock of Moscow-based journalists were back in Kirov to hear the verdict in the Kirovles trial.

During the hearing, Navalny projected his usual aloofness and disdain for the proceedings. He spent much of the three-hour proceeding posting messages and photographs on Twitter, ignoring an order from Blinov to shut off all cell phones.

As expected, Navalny and Ofitserov were found guilty. The shock was Blinov's sentence: five years for Navalny in a penal colony and four years for Ofitserov. The sentences were shorter than the eight-year maximum, and less than the six years that the prosecutor requested, but still strikingly harsh.

For more than thirteen years of Putin's rule, the Russian authorities had generally refrained from using blunt force to sideline political challengers. Instead, they were banned from government-controlled television, co-opted with jobs or government financing, discredited by the release of embarrassing material, or hounded by repeat arrests and short administrative sentences of perhaps fifteen days at a time.

In the drab courthouse, journalists gasped. Ofitserov's wife burst into tears. So did Navalny's press secretary, Anna Veduta. Yulia Navalnaya, stone-faced, kept her composure. Navalny posted one last message for his followers: "O.K. Don't miss me. And most importantly—do not be lazy." Navalny hugged his wife. Then, he and Ofitserov were led away in handcuffs.

Outside the court building, fittingly located on the same street as a puppet theater, Navalnaya said that her husband would not be intimidated. "Alexey was as ready for this as one can be," she said. "If anyone believes that Alexey's investigations will cease, that is not the case. The Anti-corruption Foundation will continue working as before."

—9—

MAYORAL CANDIDATE, STATESMAN

"Is Crimea a bologna sandwich or something, to be passed back and forth? I don't think so."

—*Alexey Navalny, Ekho Moskvy Radio, October 15, 2014*

Upon news of the verdict and prison sentence, thousands of demonstrators in Moscow took to the streets, clogging Manezh Square near the Kremlin in a spontaneous display of fury.

There was also widespread international condemnation.

The White House spokesman, Jay Carney, said the "United States is deeply disappointed and concerned." He added: "Navalny's harsh prison sentence is the latest example of a disturbing trend of government actions aimed at suppressing dissent and civil society in Russia."

But the Kremlin's script was still unfolding. In Kirov, the public prosecutor called on Blinov to release Navalny the following day and allow him to remain free pending his appeal—a move that would keep Navalny out of prison for more than a month, temporarily neutralizing anger over the verdict, and allowing him to play his part in the mayoral election scheduled for September 8.

The next day Navalny was set free, his release requested by the very same prosecutor who had asked that he be locked up immediately upon his conviction.

Opposition politicians insisted that the protesters in Moscow the night before, shouting "Freedom!" and "Navalny!" had forced the Kremlin to back down. But others speculated that Navalny was just a pawn in a larger game that was still going precisely according to plan.

The authorities and Navalny said that his campaign for mayor would proceed. Sobyanin, in a television interview, urged that Navalny be allowed to stay in the race. "I think it would be wrong to remove any of the candidates," Sobyanin said. "We have spent a lot of effort so that Muscovites had the right to a choice, the maximal choice, and to register, among others, Navalny's candidacy. So, I consider it necessary to do everything so that all registered candidates continue to participate."

Navalny's supporters were jubilant, but the celebration was premature. He had been convicted of a serious crime, which meant that even if he won the election, he would be barred from serving in public office unless he also won his appeal. There seemed little chance of that.

Blinov, the trial judge, had proclaimed the contradictory testimony of the main witness, Opalev, the disgruntled former director of Kirovles, to be convincing and persuasive, and he had barred the defense from calling most of its witnesses.

At the court hearing where he was set free, Navalny was offered the chance to make a statement. He accepted, only to mock the process and urge the three judges to check if something was wrong with the prosecutor.

"I request that you verify the identity of Prosecutor Sergei Bogdanov," Navalny said. "It's possible that it is not Prosecutor Bogdanov, but his double. Because it was namely Prosecutor Bogdanov who demanded that I be arrested in the courtroom."

One of Navalny's lawyers, Vadim Kobzev, called his client's release "clearly a political decision." Among Moscow political commentators, debate raged over whether the whiplash developments reflected Kremlin incompetence or exquisitely planned strategy.

Outside the courthouse, Navalny acknowledged that the situation was bizarre. "We understand perfectly that what just happened is a completely unique phenomenon in Russian jurisprudence," he said. "Nothing like this has happened to anyone else."

And he conceded that his capriciously granted freedom could be snatched away at any moment. "Even if we have just a couple more months to fight," he said, "we will fight."

* * *

Navalny spent the rest of the summer on the campaign trail. In one campaign newsletter, a headline declared: "He Does Not Lie and He Does Not Steal." But many people, including some of Navalny's opponents, complained that the mayoral race was fixed and that Navalny was just a tool of the Kremlin.

"Deception!" the candidate of the Just Russia party, Nikolay Levichev, declared in a campaign flyer. "Instead of discussion of the different candidates' programs they serve up this fixed match between Sobyanin and Navalny."

Even as Navalny campaigned in an electoral process devised by the Kremlin, Russian law enforcement agencies kept hounding him. Following a complaint by Levichev, Moscow police raided the apartment of a Navalny supporter and seized campaign materials, allegedly printed in violation of electoral rules. Meanwhile, prosecutors said they were investigating Navalny's campaign for taking illegal donations from foreigners.

On its website, the Navalny campaign offered advice to its volunteers about how to deal with hecklers and provocateurs: "If a maniac with a chainsaw grabs the leaflets off you, it's better to hand them over. We can easily print more leaflets, but printing a new one of you will be more difficult."

Despite the suspicions of a fix, there was a sense of excitement on Election Night—a rarity in Russia. Navalny lost, as expected. But his campaign performed far better than predicted. He and his supporters were convinced that they had managed to deny Sobyanin the 50 percent majority needed to avoid a runoff. Navalny immediately disputed the results and demanded a recount.

The results were slow to come in, which only fueled Navalny's initial allegations of malfeasance. "We regard what is happening as falsifications," he said. "I once again call on both the Kremlin and the Moscow City Hall to abandon falsifications and go to the second round."

Several hours later, the election commission announced its final tally:

Sobyanin at 51.37 percent; and Navalny at 27.24 percent, with 100 percent of precincts reporting.

The next day, Navalny spoke to supporters in the courtyard outside his election headquarters and demanded a recount. "We do not recognize these elections," he said.

Navalny and Volkov said their exit polling data indicated that Sobyanin got 46 percent of the vote, and Navalny up to 35 percent. They also alleged that Sobyanin won significantly more support than average at polling stations without observers present, and an unusually high percentage among voters who requested to vote from home because they could not physically get to the local polling station. Under the law, local election stations were required to have portable ballot boxes that could be brought to voters who met the requirements for at-home voting.

"Sobyanin cannot consider himself the mayor of all Muscovites, he cannot consider himself a legally elected mayor if he does not agree to our demands and does not agree to a recount," Navalny said.

Tens of thousands of supporters attended a demonstration on Bolotnaya Square, which Navalny proclaimed a victory rally. "Every third voter voted for us—and this is a victory," Navalny said. Supporters chanted, "We are the power!" and "Second round!"

"We are not calling for unrest, we want a reasonable solution: a recount in problem areas," Volkov said. He insisted that Sobyanin had not crossed the 50 percent threshold required to avoid a runoff.

The election commission, however, refused to budge. There was little point in protesting. As September wore on, Navalny thanked his supporters, claimed victory, and moved on. By early the next month, he was back to defending himself in the litany of criminal cases—so many, in fact, that he faced an absurd scheduling conflict in which the Kirov court and a Moscow court each demanded his appearance on the same day, October 9.

Navalny's lawyers told the Kirov court that he could not make it; he was due at a previously scheduled hearing in Moscow. The Moscow court sent a fax, saying it had agreed to change the date of its hearing. Then, it sent another fax, rescinding the change.

Navalny, sarcastic as ever, posted: "Of course, I am pleased that I am such a sought-after criminal that there is direct competition in the courts. But I would like the shaman who gives instructions to the courts to make up his mind."

On October 16, Navalny finally returned to court in Kirov to hear the outcome of his appeal. Toward the beginning of the proceedings, a judge asked about the presence of journalists in the courtroom: "Do the parties have objections to the work of the press?"

Navalny quickly quipped: "In terms of objections, we would like Channel One, Channel Two, and NTV to cover the case more objectively."

Outside, on the street, Navalny's supporters protested on his behalf. In the courtroom, the trio of appellate judges rejected a request by Navalny's lawyers to call the witnesses that had been barred by Blinov during the original trial.

Navalny, given the chance to make a final statement, noted the Groundhog Day aspect of the entire exercise. "There is a sad joke on Twitter, that the decision of the Kirov Regional Court can be appealed in the proper manner only on Manezh Square," he said.

Navalny continued: "The 'last word' is considered a kind of dramatic moment in a person's life," he said. "But here in the city of Kirov, I am already saying a third 'last word.' There are already so many cases against me that I will have to say many more last words."

The judges ruled that they were converting the prison terms of Navalny and Ofitserov into suspended sentences. The decision set them free, but it also barred Navalny from holding public office, at least for the length of the suspended sentence.

"It's strange to call it 'victory,'" Navalny wrote later on LiveJournal. "We're just so used to the lack of justice that when an innocent person is put in jail, we feel sad. And when the authorities, frightened, give an innocent person five years probation, we rejoice and congratulate each other." Still, he acknowledged that he was happy not to be going to jail.

"So, I want to say thank you again: this is your merit, of course, and not mine," he wrote. He urged his supporters to keep pressing for the release of the defendants in the Bolotnaya case, who had been arrested during the protest ahead of Putin's inauguration.

"If it worked for me, it can work for them," he wrote. "So, we will find the right formats of work."

At the same time, Navalny acknowledged that Bastrykin and Putin had won this battle, if not the longer fight.

"The most important Kremlin goal that they set for themselves when starting these criminal cases—to ban me from participating in the elections—was achieved by them technically," he wrote. "I can't run. But participation in elections is not only 'being a candidate.' And I, and those who are around me, we are engaged in politics to make life better. For your future and the future of your children."

Navalny added a warning: "If someone there believes that I will now shy away from every rally and any activity in fear of an administrative offense that will turn a suspended sentence into a real one, then this is in vain."

* * *

In late November 2013, public anger in Ukraine at President Viktor Yanukovych boiled over, setting off the Maidan Revolution. The 2014 Winter Olympics—in Sochi, Russia—was also fast approaching. Whatever little tolerance Putin might have had for dissent soon evaporated.

Putin held back until the closing ceremony of the games. Then, he ordered the invasion of Crimea, the Ukrainian peninsula that holds near-mythic status in Russia as a favorite summer holiday destination.

Two days after Yanukovych fled Kyiv for Russia, abandoning his presidency, Navalny and hundreds of others demonstrated outside a courthouse in Moscow where defendants in the Bolotnaya case were being sentenced. Many of those at the court later joined other demonstrators in Manezh Square. Navalny was among those arrested, and he was accused of violating his suspended sentence in the Kirovles case. He was put under house arrest.

As a result, Navalny was confined to his apartment in Moscow; the revolution on Maidan in Kyiv reached a bloody climax; and then Putin's soldiers without insignia, the so-called "polite green men," seized control of the Crimean peninsula and Kremlin proxies carried out a referendum declaring independence from Ukraine.

Navalny was prohibited from using the internet. But he was following the news and, with his wife posting on LiveJournal on his behalf, Navalny voiced unequivocal solidarity with the protesters camped out in the Ukrainian capital, demanding Yanukovych's ouster.

On February 20, after shooting broke out on Maidan and scores of protesters were wounded, Navalny urged his followers not to pay attention to reports on Russian "zombie" television that they were "radicals with firearms." The demonstrators, he said, linking to a list of the dead, were "ordinary people, hard workers."

Navalny blasted Yanukovych for shooting people to protect his ill-gotten wealth and wrote that he "should immediately call early elections" and the Ukrainian parliament, he said, "should start constitutional reform."

The next day, Navalny expressed hope that one day Russians would rise up for democracy like the Ukrainians. "The mafia power of Yanukovych fell precisely because in Kiev there were a sufficient number of people who were ready to patiently stand on the street in the cold for as long as necessary," he wrote. "Without fear of arrests and detentions, they will not detain everyone. Whether such people will be found in Moscow is a question that only we ourselves can answer."

On Saturday, February 22, Yanukovych fled Ukraine, and Putin's soldiers quickly arrived in Crimea.

On March 2, 2014, after the Russian parliament authorized the use of military force in Ukraine, Vladimir Ashurkov posted a statement on behalf of the central council of Navalny's Party of Progress, calling on Putin to put a stop to any military activity:

> In the coming hours or days, our country may begin aggression against a neighboring state whose people are closest to the Russians from a historical and cultural point of view. Over the past two months, the Ukrainian people have come a long way in liberating

> themselves from the authoritarian, corrupt system of power that violates the constitutional rights of citizens, which was personified by President Yanukovych.
>
> Military aggression will lead to the violation of international treaties, the destruction of relations with Western countries, and to the international isolation of the country. The reputation of a reliable partner in foreign policy will take decades to restore. A significant deterioration in the economic situation in Russia will inevitably follow, and the introduction of economic sanctions against the aggressor country by the international community will become probable.

The statement noted that there was no evidence to support Putin's wild assertion that Russian-language speakers in Ukraine were under threat. "It's not too late to stop this adventure," the Party of Progress declared. Putin, of course, did not stop.

He annexed Crimea later that month and fomented a separatist war in the eastern Ukrainian regions of Donetsk and Luhansk. In Russia, nationalist fervor soared after the illegal annexation. Ilya Ponomarev, the only member of the State Duma to vote against annexation, ultimately had to flee the country. "Crimea is ours" became a national rallying cry, even for young Russian children.

Navalny, from house arrest, said he recognized he had a duty to issue an opinion, and to comply with terms of his house arrest, he said he would write it out on paper and have others post it to LiveJournal on his behalf.

Navalny issued an extremely long statement, explaining why Putin could not accept a successful democracy movement on Russia's doorstep. "In Ukraine, there was a popular uprising against the corrupt, thieves' government," he wrote. "The core of this uprising was Kyiv and the western regions of the country, but it was supported (tacitly) by most of the southeast"—Yanukovych's base.

"The people have the right to revolt in conditions when other political methods of struggle have been exhausted," Navalny continued. To illustrate his point about corruption, he described how Yanukovych's son, a dentist by professional training, had become a billionaire, and one of the wealthiest people in Ukraine, after his father came to power. "What better illustration of monstrous corruption?" Navalny asked.

Navalny also noted that Ukraine's ex–prime minister Mykola Azarov had railed against Europe but then went to live in Austria where his family had amassed huge wealth. "What could better illustrate the monstrous hypocrisy?" he asked. Azarov, like Yanukovych, later sought refuge in Russia.

Navalny asserted that Putin could not tolerate the images of ordinary Ukrainians walking through Yanukovych's abandoned and opulent residence, with its private zoo and a golden toilet—the type of extravagance that Navalny's investigators alleged had been installed for Putin in his own palaces.

"We all understand that Putin is going to be the president of Russia for life with the rights and lifestyle of an emperor sovereign," Navalny wrote. "An uprising against a fellow thief-emperor in a neighboring country is a threat, a challenge, and a terrible example.

"Therefore, Putin is simply personally taking revenge on the entire Ukrainian people and the entire country of Ukraine. This is not crazy revenge; he believes that it is very rational—to go to any lengths, to show that such revolutions end badly. Like, 'There will be a collapse of the country.' So he arranges the collapse of the country."

In his post, Navalny repeated his long-held belief that there was a fraternal bond among Russians, Belarusians, and Ukrainians—a view that he acknowledged was controversial and would lead to accusations of ethno-chauvinism.

"You can call me a Slavic chauvinist, but I believe that Russia's most important strategic advantage in this raging world is not oil, gas, or nuclear bombs, but friendly (and even fraternal, whatever) relations between Russians and Ukrainians and Belarusians," he wrote. He described spending a week in jail with a Belarusian, an Azerbaijani, and an Uzbek—all "good guys"—but Navalny said that with a Belarusian or Ukrainian, he felt instant "unity and common cultural codes."

"I don't know how to call it more precisely," Navalny wrote. "No one forms any fraternities and does not oppose other nationalities, it's just immediately clear: They are the same as me. I understand that this is a rather politically incorrect idea." He tried to explain, noting that he felt no common bond with someone from Uzbekistan, under age forty. "They don't know Russian. We read different books, we watched different films, we have different proverbs, we have different values and guidelines.

"I do not want to say that there is a contradiction, and the inhabitants of Central Asia are our enemies, but still, with Ukraine and Belarus, we are like brothers in different apartments, and not just neighbors," he wrote. "It is clear that there are nuances, different territories, and so on.

"Arriving in Kyiv, do you feel like you are in a foreign city? No. Me neither," Navalny wrote. "That's the point."

His larger point, however, was that violence between Russians and Ukrainians was unthinkable to him. "If Russians and Ukrainians are told to shoot at each other, then they should stand back-to-back at the border and shoot at those who give such orders," he wrote.

Navalny's views were complicated and, in some aspects, contradictory, and definitely controversial. He voiced deep unhappiness that Crimea had ever become part of Ukraine.

"Crimea was handed over by the illegal voluntaristic decision of the tyrant Khrushchev," he wrote.

But he also said that he did not support any effort to absorb Crimea into Russia—a point that many Ukrainians who now disdain Navalny often forget or choose to overlook. "International agreements and Russia's word must be worth something," Navalny wrote, citing the Budapest Memorandum of 1994, under which Russia committed to respect and protect the territorial integrity of Ukraine in exchange for Kyiv surrendering its nuclear arsenal. Also, he added: "Changing the borders of states in Europe using troops and force is unacceptable."

But Navalny's post, published four days before the staged independence referendum in Crimea, contained some grave underestimations of Putin—an early indication that he did not fully grasp how far his nemesis was willing to go.

Navalny predicted, wrongly, that Putin would balk at fully absorbing Crimea into Russia. "We will see the classic Putin story, 'two steps forward one step back'... That's what he always does."

Not this time. Putin moved to annex Crimea on March 18, and days later the Russian Parliament ratified the move.

Consequently, Russia came under a barrage of international sanctions. International flights to Crimea were cut off. Yet public opinion in Russia was overwhelmingly in favor of what Putin had done.

That March, Navalny was feeling the pressure of house arrest. Ahead of his son Zakhar's birthday, he submitted a petition asking for permission to take him to the movies to see the animated film *Rio 2*. "Zakhar is six years old today," Navalny wrote on LiveJournal. "He also demands that I take him to *Rio*, which, in modern times, is not a trivial task."

Navalny also had the Anti-corruption Foundation embark on a new project: sociological research and opinion polling. This included an effort to measure Russian public opinion about what was happening in Crimea, and the picture was complicated. More than 55 percent believed the rights of Russian speakers were being infringed upon in Crimea, a main Kremlin propaganda point. More than 85 percent said they wanted Crimea to become part of Russia. But nearly 75 percent also said they viewed war between Russia and Ukraine as "impossible."

In the following months, Navalny would continue to calibrate his public statements on the Crimea question, trying to balance his criticism of Putin's illegal annexation and Navalny's personal view, shared by a majority of Russians, that Crimea was rightfully Russian.

During a radio interview in October 2014, Navalny offered a blunt and realistic but controversial update to his position, which set off a storm among Ukrainians.

"Is Crimea ours?" the editor in chief of Ekho Moskvy, Alexey Venediktov, asked Navalny on-air.

"Crimea belongs to the people who live in Crimea," Navalny replied.

"You will not escape answering. Is Crimea ours? Is Crimea Russian?"

"Crimea, of course, now de facto belongs to Russia," Navalny said. "I believe that, despite the fact that Crimea was seized in blatant violation of all international norms, nevertheless, the reality is that Crimea is now part of the Russian Federation. And let's not fool ourselves. And I strongly advise Ukrainians not to deceive themselves either. It will remain part of Russia and will never become part of Ukraine in the foreseeable future."

Venediktov pressed the point, asking if Navalny would return Crimea to Ukraine should he ever become president of Russia.

"Is Crimea a bologna sandwich, or something, to be passed back and forth? I don't think so," Navalny said.

He was then pressed on whether Russians and Ukrainians were the same people. "My opinion, as a person who spent a lot of time in Ukraine, with relatives, etc.," he said. "I don't see any difference between Russians and Ukrainians at all." Navalny understood, though, that his position would not sit well with everyone: "I think that such a point of view will cause some kind of monstrous indignation in Ukraine," he said.

* * *

Two months later, Navalny was back in court, this time in Moscow, where he and his brother, Oleg, faced a decision in the bizarre Yves Rocher fraud and embezzlement case.

The verdict, of course, was guilty. But in a dastardly move, the judge suspended Alexey Navalny's sentence while condemning Oleg Navalny to a real sentence of three and a half years in a prison colony.

Navalny, enraged, practically choked on his words as he berated the young judge, Yelena Korobchenko. "Aren't you ashamed of what you are doing?" he cried out, tears in his eyes. "Why are you jailing him? What a dirty trick. I don't even understand. All of this is being done to punish me more?"

Oleg Navalny hugged his wife and kissed his mother, before being led away. Navalny had turned his back to the crowd, his arms folded and head slightly bowed. Yulia Navalnaya put an arm around her husband's neck and pressed her lips to his cheek. In more than a decade as an oppositionist, it was by far the most difficult moment Navalny had faced.

Outside the courthouse, his rage continued to burn. He called for a huge street demonstration. "This government does not deserve to exist," he told a crush of journalists and television cameras. "It should be destroyed. I am calling on everybody today to take to the streets until this government, which is simply tormenting innocent people, is removed."

Infuriated, Navalny left the courthouse and began walking through the streets toward Manezh Square, near the Kremlin, where the unauthorized rally was to take place, but he never made it. The police grabbed him outside the Ritz Carlton Hotel on Tverskaya Street, which he had just joked that his supporters should take by storm because it would be more comfortable than where he would probably spend the night.

The police, however, did not arrest him. They merely brought him home to his apartment and posted five officers outside his door to enforce his house arrest. Meanwhile, riot police dispersed the crowd in Manezh Square, which had dwindled to about 1,500.

In an interview with *Novaya Gazeta* before the verdict, Oleg Navalny, who was married with two young children, said he understood that the government might extract revenge on him for his brother's political activity. "We absolutely knew that sooner or later this all would touch us," Oleg Navalny said. "It is easy to influence a person through his family."

The jailing of his brother had a profound impact on Navalny, fueling his desire to see Putin's lackeys brought to justice. In his conversation with Michnik, the Polish historian, Navalny described his fury and hunger for accountability. "I can forgive my own persecutors," Navalny said, "but I've no moral right to forgive those who persecuted others. Lots of people are now behind bars as a result of their support for me, and I can't very well tell them, 'Sorry, but I've forgiven your persecutors.'"

—10—

PRISONER

"Our friendly concentration camp—that's what I call my new home."

—Alexey Navalny, Prison Colony No. 2, March 2021

Pobeda Airlines Flight 936 was descending toward Moscow's Vnukovo Airport, located on the southwest edge of the Russian capital.

The airport, built in the late 1930s by prisoners from Likovlag, a forced labor camp that was part of the brutal Soviet gulag system, has a special VIP hall, and is frequently used by President Vladimir Putin and other top officials. It is also favored by oligarchs and corporate titans with private jets.

Pobeda, whose name means "victory" in Russian, serves the opposite end of the air travel market—as the ultra-low-cost subsidiary of Aeroflot. But on this particular Sunday, January 17, 2021, Flight 936, a Boeing 737-8AL originating at Berlin's Brandenburg airport, effectively had been converted into a VIP charter of a different sort: carrying Navalny, his wife, Yulia, and dozens of Russian and international journalists who were alerted in advance so they could travel along to document Navalny's triumphant, brave, and arguably reckless return home.

Navalny, once again, was in his favorite spot: as the protagonist of yet another episode of high drama in his fight against the evil forces of Putin. Brought back, literally, from the dead after surviving the poisoning attack, here he was in Seat 13A, his wife next to him and his lawyer, Olga Mikhailova, across the aisle.

With Covid rules still in place, Navalny wore a black face mask; Yulia wore purple. Stewardesses crouched down to take selfies with him.

Reporters from news organizations around the world leaned over the seats, shouting questions at him, taking photos and videos with their cell phones, begging him for a word or two. Many posed variations of the same throwaway queries: How does it feel to be going home? Aren't you afraid?

The plane, flying east, descended steadily for an on-time arrival. But as its altitude crossed just below seven thousand feet, the aircraft suddenly banked southeast, away from the airport, and then hooked north, according to the Flightradar24 tracking site, which was live-tweeting Navalny's return.

As Navalny's plane made these strange turns, other nearby airliners, including flights from UTAir and Rossiya Airlines, were ordered to circle in a holding pattern.

The pilot of Flight 936 came on the PA system to announce that Vnukovo was closed for "technical reasons" because an "aircraft rolled out of the runway," according to a reporter for the Russian newspaper *Kommersant* who was on board. Passengers snickered. The pilot said there would be a roughly thirty-minute delay. Reassuringly, he added: "We have enough fuel to wait." One passenger grumbled that Navalny was "the technical problem."

On the ground, Pobeda Airlines issued an absurd statement saying a brush from a snowblower was stuck on the tarmac at the intersection of two runways. "Due to the closure of Vnukovo for technical reasons, three of our flights left for alternate airfields," the airline said.

Meanwhile, mayhem was unfolding inside the Vnukovo arrivals hall, where hundreds of Navalny supporters had answered his public entreaty to greet him in person. Helmeted riot police brandishing truncheons—some in all black, others in blue-gray camouflage—began clearing the building, dragging people out into the minus-six-degree cold, arresting them, and hustling them onto waiting police wagons.

Russian media had speculated about whether Putin's government would be brazen enough to detain Navalny instantly at the airport—a slightly curious question, given the Kremlin had been brazen enough to send a team of assassins to kill him with a chemical weapon.

Commentators wrestled with the question of whether Navalny should risk returning to Russia. Some concluded that if he failed to do so, his political career would be finished. He would be relegated to near irrelevance, as an exiled dissident, they said, like the former chess champion Garry Kasparov, or the ex-oligarch Mikhail Khodorkovsky, who served ten years in a Russian prison before being pardoned by Putin in 2013.

Others said that the government would be making a huge mistake by jailing Navalny, instantly transforming him into a Mandela-like figure—a prisoner of conscience who would haunt the Kremlin until his release. The smarter play, they suggested, would be to prolong the cat-and-mouse game that had been played for years, leaving him free but under constant threat of arrest, closely monitored but not martyred.

Now, with the plane circling above Moscow, some observers wondered if Navalny would be allowed to land at all and, if so, where. On Flightradar24, as many as 530,000 people were following along at one point, as Navalny's flight was rerouted to Sheremetyevo airport north of the city.

Earlier on the flight, Navalny, with his trademark carefree confidence, had insisted to reporters that he had no fear and did not expect to be detained. Now, he apologized to those around him for the inconvenience.

In fact, there was no doubt Navalny would be arrested. The only question was when.

Top Russian prison officials had openly declared their intention to charge him with parole violations, and to convert his suspended sentence in the Yves Rocher case to a real prison term. They had even scheduled a court hearing in anticipation of his return—effectively pleading publicly with Navalny not to come back. All this presented Navalny with what Putin himself later called a clear, "conscious" choice: exile or jail.

For Navalny, exile was never a consideration. Asked during his first interview after emerging from the coma about his plans, Navalny told Yury Dud: "Recover—I don't know to what percent, no one knows—and after, I'll return."

When Dud pressed him about what might make him choose not to return to Russia, Navalny's face darkened, and he stared back as if the question was an insult. "I exclude this possibility," he replied.

People close to him were not surprised.

"You have to keep in mind that when we talk about Navalny, we're talking about two people," Albats said. "Politician Navalny is not one person, it's two—Alexey and Yulia Navalny, that's number one. And if even Yulia failed to convince him not to go—and she tried—nobody can."

Once Navalnaya understood that there would be no stopping Navalny's return, she instead pleaded with him merely to wait until he was fully recovered.

"He was still in the hospital, they hadn't discharged him yet, but he already understood everything," Navalnaya explained to Dud in the interview. "I told him, 'I know you want to go back as soon as possible, but I am really asking you: Recover fully and then you go back because we—I don't know what's waiting for us in Russia, and if you go not fully treated, it's possible that we won't be able to save you a second time.' "

"I am not afraid to go back to Russia," Yulia insisted at another point. "We are absolutely going back to Russia."

That Navalnaya could seriously contemplate needing to save her husband from another assassination attempt underscored that he would never choose exile. But it also revealed that Navalny, his wife, and his inner circle had not accepted the new reality.

Navalny, in interviews, had described his inability to fully comprehend the extent to which his life was at imminent risk. At the same time, he noted that there was virtually no point in obsessing over precautions given the multitude of methods Putin's assassins could employ.

Masha Gessen, of the *New Yorker*, who has known Navalny for years, spoke to him shortly after he emerged from his coma and noted that interviewers had long asked Navalny why he hadn't been killed yet. "So, you have this understanding that you should have been killed by now, and you have people you know who nearly died from being poisoned," Gessen said. "And yet somehow your mind tells you, 'this won't happen to me, because'—why?"

"Because you think rationally," Navalny replied. "There are a million ways to isolate someone or kill them, but this is like some trashy thriller. I find myself living inside of a James Bond movie." He added, "It's like if someone asked me if I believe that I'm at risk for being beheaded with a lightsaber. I'd say no, even if I saw that someone I know is missing an arm and it looks to have been lasered off."

But on the cusp of their return to Russia, the Navalnys were in denial about a broader point: Putin was done fooling with him. The cat-and-mouse days of suspended sentences, probation, home arrests, and the like were finished. Putin wanted him out of the picture. And since he refused to die, and refused to stay outside of Russia, he would go to prison.

* * *

Navalny, arguably Putin's harshest critic, had once again underestimated the Russian dictator. Putin, as would become clear, was already preparing to go to war against Ukraine. And if he was willing to start a land war in Europe, to kill thousands of innocent Ukrainian civilians, why would he hesitate to eliminate one irksome Russian citizen?

"Who needs him anyway?" Putin famously declared. If the Russian security services wanted to kill Navalny, he said, they could have done so.

Navalny, however, was still driven by the outrage and indignation that had fueled his entire public life—even after weeks in a medical coma, even after realizing that the state-sponsored assassins had tried to kill him multiple times and, on purpose or by accident, had poisoned his wife. He was also still driven by his political ambitions.

"I have every right to go back," Navalny said on the flight from Berlin, where he and Yulia tried unsuccessfully amid the commotion to watch an episode of *Rick and Morty*. "I don't expect anything to happen. Nothing will occur."

Moments after landing at Sheremetyevo, Navalny was confronted at passport control by a phalanx of police officers. Even then, Navalny did not flinch.

"This is my home. I'm back. People keep asking me if I'm afraid. I am not afraid," he said. "Because I know that I'm right. I know that the criminal cases against me are fabricated."

He added: "I don't just have the truth on my side, I have the courts on my side. They are threatening to arrest me in connection with a case on which the European Court has ruled in my favor. So, I'm not afraid of anything, and you shouldn't be afraid of anything, either."

In some ways, Navalny had been preparing for years for this moment. For a political opposition figure in Russia, imprisonment is inevitable. And for Navalny, as always, there was simply no backing down from the fight.

Yet, on some level, he still seemed to believe that he would be the exception—that his millions of followers, his honesty, his humor, his core patriotic Russianness, would somehow save him from his inescapable fate. That Putin would not dare jail someone visited in his hospital room by German chancellor Angela Merkel. That he had carved out a protected space in Russian political life.

But he had not yet managed to change Russia.

If Navalny thought that remaining outside the country would spell instant irrelevance, pinning the dreaded label of "dissident" to his shirt instead of "opposition politician," which he preferred, he had miscalculated his own ability to control the situation.

Navalny had worried that he would be irrelevant living in Berlin or Warsaw or Vilnius. Instead, he would struggle to remain relevant while locked inside an eight-by-ten-foot isolation cell. There was also the challenge of staying alive in Russia's brutal prison system. His access to food and to medical care were now controlled by the same murderous regime that poisoned him.

Whatever he thought, whatever he envisioned, Navalny's return home completed his transformation from gadfly, anti-corruption crusader, activist, and aspiring politician to dissident—and political prisoner.

* * *

After the police led Navalny away in the airport, the director of Amnesty International's Moscow office, Natalia Zviagina, quickly issued a statement declaring him a "prisoner of conscience" and demanding his freedom as well as the release of the numerous supporters who were arrested as Navalny arrived back from Germany.

"Alexey Navalny has been deprived of his liberty for his peaceful political activism and exercising free speech," Zviagina's statement said. "Amnesty International considers him a prisoner of conscience and calls for his immediate and unconditional release."

She also demanded a full investigation of the poisoning attack and an end to the Kremlin's crusade against Navalny and his team. "The Russian authorities must end their campaign of intimidation and political persecution against their critics, including the staff members and supporters of Navalny's Anti-corruption Foundation," Zviagina said.

The judicial proceedings against Navalny were swift and characteristically absurd, beginning with the makeshift courtroom set up at a police station where he was being held in Khimki, near Sheremetyevo airport, the day after he was detained. A lawyer for the Anti-corruption Foundation, Vyacheslav Gimadi, had tried to see Navalny at the jail, but was told that he was sleeping. An update only came the following morning.

Apparently, the authorities did not want to create an opportunity for Navalny's supporters to gather outside a courthouse, so they assembled a courtroom in the police station.

"Madness," Volkov tweeted at 12:35 p.m. on Monday, January 18. "They are afraid to take Alexey to the court. They are bringing the court to Alexey."

Mikhailova, Navalny's lawyer, received a written notification one minute before the hearing was scheduled to begin. As always, the Navalny media machine was in high gear. Kira Yarmysh, the press secretary, posted a video to YouTube of Navalny, wearing a blue hoodie, inside the makeshift courtroom ridiculing the hastily improvised proceeding.

"It's impossible what's going on here," Navalny said, sitting in the "hearing room" and looking directly into the camera as he spoke. He accused the authorities of tearing up Russia's code of criminal procedure, adding: "It's just lawlessness to the highest degree."

The authorities gave conflicting explanations. At one point they said the hearing was held in the police station to allow media coverage because journalists would have been barred from a courthouse due to Covid restrictions. Later, they said the problem was that Navalny did not have a recent negative Covid test and could not be brought to the court.

Only the state-owned Russia-24 television channel, and Life News, the pro-Kremlin news portal, were given access to cover the hearing in person.

Legal experts later noted that the location of the hearing was not in itself any violation of judicial rules, but that other aspects of the process broke Russian law. Given that Navalny's case was based on an alleged parole violation, he should not have been put under immediate detention. The outcome, in any event, was that Navalny was ordered jailed for thirty days, with another hearing set for February 2.

World leaders began calling for Navalny to be set free. Outgoing U.S. secretary of state Mike Pompeo issued a statement demanding Navalny's "immediate and unconditional release." Jake Sullivan, days away from becoming the national security adviser for President Joe Biden, tweeted: "The Kremlin's attacks on Mr. Navalny are not just a violation of human rights, but an affront to the Russian people who want their voices heard."

On January 23, and again on January 31, tens of thousands of Russians demonstrated in cities across the country to protest Navalny's arrest. Thousands were arrested.

The Russian watchdog group OVD-Info estimated that on January 23 "in 125 cities, the police detained at least 4,033 people" and it said that "in many cities, the police use unreasonable and excessive violence while making arrests."

In all, more than one hundred thousand people protested Navalny's arrest. It was the largest outpouring in Russia in years but, on the whole, in a country of 130 million people, it was not much. The heavy-handed response demonstrated Putin's diminished tolerance. OVD-Info called it "the most large-scale and flagrant attack on the right to freedom of assembly in the entire modern history of Russia."

In 2013, after the verdict and sentencing in the Kirovles case, the Kremlin quickly approved Navalny's release pending his appeal in response to the protests in Manezh Square in Moscow. But the nationwide protests in 2021 had no noticeable impact. Though thousands were arrested in more than one hundred cities, Putin paid no mind.

Navalny was transferred to the Matrosskaya Tishina, or "Sailor's Silence," prison in Moscow—also known as Pretrial Detention Facility No. 1—beginning his awful odyssey in the penal system.

In another video, just before being led away, Navalny reiterated his version of F.D.R.'s famous line that "the only thing we have to fear is fear itself."

"Well, that's it, if you believe the court documents, I'm going to Matrosskaya Tishina," Navalny said. "And I want to tell everyone one thing: You don't need to be afraid of anything, you can only be afraid of your own fear. Bye."

Navalny arrived at the detention center at about 8 p.m. Alexey Melnikov, the secretary of the Moscow Public Monitoring Commission, which oversees prison conditions, visited Navalny there, and reported that his cell had a refrigerator, an electric kettle, a television, and hot water, and that he would need to spend two weeks in quarantine.

Fifteen days later, following the February 2 court hearing—where Navalny proclaimed Putin to be "Vladimir, the Poisoner of Underpants"—the judge, Natalya Repnikova, found Navalny guilty of the parole violations and converted his suspended sentence in the Yves Rocher case to a real term. With the sentence adjusted for time spent under house arrest, he faced just over two and a half years.

Navalny's lawyers appealed. But as he waited for the case to play out, the Kremlin tightened the screws a bit further. At the detention center, Navalny was labeled as a prisoner "prone to escape." Navalny mocked the absurd designation, noting the obvious point that he had insisted on returning to Russia from Germany, despite the obvious risk of arrest. However ridiculous, the designation would follow him through the prison system and justify harsher treatment.

On February 20, a court in Moscow scheduled a Navalny double billing; his appeal of the parole violation decision and the trial in another trumped-up case in which he was accused of slandering an elderly military veteran.

Navalny lost both, of course. In the slander case, he was fined 850,000 rubles, or about $11,000. Losing the appeal, however, meant that Russia's penitentiary service could now transfer Navalny to a prison colony, which would make his cell with the electric kettle and television seem like a luxury hotel room.

Navalny was transferred out of that Moscow detention center on February 25, the first of several moves that for days would leave his lawyers and family without any knowledge of his whereabouts. In what would become a pattern, one of Navalny's lawyers, Vadim Kobzev, tried to visit him at Matrosskaya Tishina only to be told that no such prisoner was there.

Russian media had already been reporting that Navalny would end up at IK-2, or Penal Colony No. 2 in the Vladimir Region, which was infamous for being one of the toughest camps in the Russian prison system. It was known for "breaking" prisoners through rigid enforcement of oppressive rules—no talking, hands always behind the back, and so on.

News accounts focused, in particular, on the high-security barracks, or Sector of Enhanced Control A, which when abbreviated in Russian spells out the word *suka*: "bitch."

The news site *Znak.com* interviewed Dmitry Demushkin, a right-wing nationalist political activist who had been imprisoned at IK-2 after being convicted of "inciting hatred" for posting a photograph of a nationalist march. Demushkin described losing nearly half his body weight—dropping to 130 pounds from 230—while in the high-security barracks, where he said guards would often awaken inmates once an hour at night on the pretense of making sure they had not escaped.

Once again, Navalny's team moved to strike at the Russian authorities as quickly as possible, releasing a twenty-minute video detailing how IK-2 operates, including beatings of prisoners instantly upon their arrival, and the denial of medical care.

The video included interviews with Demushkin, who described how inmates live in open barracks, are kept on their feet most of the day, and how he was harassed with incessant commands—repeatedly ordered to state his name, the crimes he was convicted of, and the start and end dates of his sentence.

Dmitry Nizovtsev, a Navalny associate from the Far East city of Khabarovsk who anchored the video, accused the Kremlin of trying to banish Navalny into silence.

"Now, according to Putin's plan, there should be silence," Nizovtsev said. "Two and a half years of long-awaited silence. It seems to Putin that his main dream is finally coming true—Navalny disappears. No one knows where he is and what he is, no one follows what Navalny does and says. But, of course, we will not please Vladimir Vladimirovich like that."

In the video, Nizovtsev cited a report that Navalny had been spared a customary beating upon his arrival at IK-2, which was consistent with the accounts of Demushkin and of Konstantin Kotov, another political activist who had been jailed at IK-2 for participating in small, peaceful, but nonauthorized pickets in Moscow. They said that prisoners jailed for political activism were typically spared beatings to avoid public scandal.

There was one small issue with the video: Navalny had not yet reached IK-2. Six days after his disappearance from Moscow, he surfaced at a different pretrial detention center in the town of Kolchugino, in Vladimir Region, about one hundred miles northeast of Moscow, where he was placed in a "quarantine cell" with two other prisoners.

Kobzev, his lawyer, said on Twitter that the defense team had been able to see him: "He is in complete isolation, he does not receive letters." He added, "There is nothing in the cell except a television. There is no refrigerator, not even a kettle." The lawyers explained that Navalny had been placed there temporarily because some paperwork in the slander case had not been completed.

Intent on showing that his spirits had not dampened, Navalny's team posted for him on Instagram describing how he was toasting crackers with his two cellmates—Dmitry, charged with theft; and Sergei, charged with fraud. "Everything is fine with me," Navalny wrote, while adding that he had not yet been able to access the prison library. "Believe it or not we toast crackers, and I never thought it could be so exciting.

"Hope you are doing well and don't get bored," Navalny wrote. With a wink emoji, he added: "Don't forget to eat healthy."

Navalny's team also sent an update on his whereabouts from his Twitter account, posting: "He is in a great mood and says hello to everyone."

Exaggerated or not, that great mood would not last long.

On March 12, Navalny disappeared again. His lawyers went looking for him in Kolchugino. They were stalled there until 2 p.m. and then told he had left—but given no information about his destination. From there, they went to Pokrov, about an hour's drive south, where officials at IK-2 said they had no information about him and that the prison was closing early that day, at 3:30 p.m.

On Navalny's Twitter account, his team posted: "Where Alexey is, is still unknown." However, Tass, the state-run news agency, reported that he had been transferred to IK-2. In fact, he had arrived there the day before, on March 11.

Three days later, it was confirmed in an Instagram post, showing Navalny, unsmiling, and with his hair newly shaved off. Again, he tried to start out light. "Three things never cease to amaze me," he wrote: "The starry sky above us, the categorical imperative within us, and the amazing feeling when you run your hand over your freshly shaved head.

"Hello everyone," he proclaimed, "from the Sector of Enhanced Control A."

As the inmates who served time in IK-2 had predicted, Navalny was not beaten. But as they had also predicted, he was the target of other types of brutality, including his fellow inmates being told not to talk to him or acknowledge his existence.

IK-2 made a quick impression on Navalny. "I have to admit that the Russian prison system managed to surprise me," he wrote in comments that his team posted on Instagram. "I did not imagine that it was possible to set up a real concentration camp 100 kilometers from Moscow.

"I have not yet seen any violence or even a hint of it, but from the tense posture of the convicts, standing at attention and afraid to turn their heads," he continued. "I easily believe the numerous stories that here, in IK-2 'Pokrov,' quite recently people were beaten half to death with wooden hammers. Now the methods have changed."

He described a prison community hauntingly in order—"regime, charter, daily routine—the literal execution of endless rules"—a suffocating, Orwellian discipline—"there are video cameras everywhere, they are watching everyone, and at the slightest violation, they make a report."

Navalny also described torture through sleep deprivation, though he tried to make light of it. "At night, every hour I wake from the fact that a man in a peacoat is standing next to my bed," he wrote, describing his treatment as a prisoner deemed at high risk of escape. "He records me on camera, and says, 'Two thirty a.m., Convict Navalny... In place.'

"Our friendly concentration camp," he wrote in the post. "That's what I call my new home."

But within days, there was no more joking. Navalny began complaining of severe back and leg pain, of torture by sleep deprivation, and of being denied access to medical care.

On Thursday, March 25, Navalny's team published two statements in which he appealed to leaders of the Federal Penitentiary Service and to Russia's general prosecutor for proper medical treatment.

Two days earlier, his supporters had launched a new website, free .navalny.com, and announced their plans to campaign for his freedom.

"Today we are launching our big political campaign," they wrote. "We demand the release of Alexey Navalny. We see that all Putin's hatred was personified in one person. Because of Navalny, Russia is ready to withdraw from the Council of Europe, terminate agreements, and leave international organizations." They added, "Navalny is the Putin regime's biggest problem. And if we really want to fight this regime effectively, then now there must be one demand: freedom for Alexey Navalny."

Navalny had been warned by Mikhail Khodorkovsky, the oligarch who spent ten years behind bars, about the danger of becoming seriously ill in a Russian prison colony. "You will die," Khodorkovsky had said. Navalny, of course, also knew how Magnitsky had died.

In his public letters, Navalny complained of acute back and leg pain, for which he said he was given only ibuprofen, and he demanded that he be treated by his own doctor. Navalny's lawyers echoed the demand, and Yulia Navalnaya appealed to Putin to release her husband. But there would be no second chance to go abroad for treatment.

"We will not respond to this appeal," Putin's spokesman Dmitry Peskov told journalists on his daily conference call. "Now that this citizen is a convict and a prisoner of a colony, the recipient for such appeals is the Federal Penitentiary Service."

Was Navalny really in poor health? Not even five months before his arrest at the airport, of course, he had been poisoned with a chemical weapon, spent weeks in a coma and months in recovery, learning to walk again, his hands shaking. He was also now living in an open barracks with other prisoners; tuberculosis was common in Russian prisons, and Covid was still rampant in Russia.

At the same time, Navalny and his team were clearly leveraging everything they could to break the prison regime that was designed to break him, and to try to guarantee his safety by convincing the world that his life was in constant peril.

Prison officials said that on March 24, the day before Navalny's health complaints were published, he had been taken for an MRI scan. Navalny acknowledged this, griping that he had no idea where they had taken him for the scan or what, if anything, it had shown.

The authorities later said the scans revealed two herniated disks and a bulging disk in his back, confirming that his back pain and the accompanying numbness he described in his legs were real.

In any case, Navalny's ability to generate international media attention meant his complaints could not be ignored. A regional official of the Federal Penitentiary Service issued a statement saying, "Convict A. Navalny is being provided with all the necessary medical assistance in accordance with his current medical recommendations."

The penitentiary service also denied that Navalny was being tortured with sleep deprivation, insisting that the hourly security checks did not interrupt convicts' rest.

Vladimir Grigoryan, deputy head of the Public Monitoring Commission in Vladimir, flat-out accused Navalny of lying.

"Navalny is faking," Grigoryan told TV Rain, the independent television station. "So don't worry about him." Another member of the commission, Yuri Belokrylin, told the channel, "I don't trust Navalny," and added, "I have a very negative attitude towards him."

Navalny punched back, issuing a statement through Kobzev, his lawyer, calling the commission in Vladimir "a bunch of crooks and liars who serve the administration of concentration camps, worsening the situation of prisoners."

On March 28, a group of doctors sent an open letter, ultimately signed by more than five hundred physicians, to the head of the Federal Penitentiary Service warning of "serious consequences including irreversible, complete or partial loss of lower limb functions" and demanding that officials "immediately provide medical assistance" for Navalny. They urged that he also be evaluated by doctors who treated him in Germany and wrote that denying Navalny adequate pain relief "can be considered . . . direct torture."

Three days later, on March 31, Navalny raised the stakes, declaring that he was beginning a hunger strike, and generating worldwide headlines.

"I have the right to call a doctor and get medicine," Navalny's team posted on Instagram on his behalf. "Neither one nor the other is given to me, stupidly. The pain in my back moved to my leg. Parts of the right, and now the left leg lost sensation. Jokes are jokes, but it's already annoying."

Navalny complained again of "torture" by sleep deprivation. "Well, what to do," he asked in the post. "I went on a hunger strike demanding that the law be fulfilled and that a visiting doctor be allowed to see me. So, I'm lying hungry, but so far with two legs."

Navalny's initial success in continuing his battle with Putin from prison became clear the next day, when Maria Butina, a Putin-aligned member of parliament and personality on the pro-Kremlin, propagandist RT television channel, showed up unexpectedly at the prison colony in Pokrov. She ambushed Navalny with cameras rolling, as he lay on his bed reading a book.

Butina, who once worked as an assistant to a Russian senator, Aleksandr Torshin, gained worldwide infamy after she was arrested and convicted in the United States of acting as an unregistered agent of the Russian government. An investigation by the Senate Intelligence Committee concluded that she had tried to set up secret back-channel communications between Moscow and Donald Trump's presidential campaign.

Butina had used a romantic relationship with a U.S. Republican political operative named Paul Erickson to build ties to the leadership of the National Rifle Association, looking to use it as a way to improve relations between Russia and the Republican Party. In Russia, she founded a gun-rights organization called Right to Bear Arms.

Butina also had a romantic relationship with Patrick Byrne, the Overstock.com CEO, conspiracy theorist, and Trump supporter. She was arrested in July 2018, pleaded guilty later that year, and served five months at a federal prison in Tallahassee. Then, she was deported to Russia, where she was greeted as a national hero and given plum jobs.

In addition to her election to the Duma and her job at RT, Butina was appointed as a member of the Public Commission, an agency that functions as a sort of ombudsman body, which gave her authority to visit prisons, including IK-2 in Vladimir.

That Thursday, she arrived at the prison wearing what appeared to be a designer plaid overcoat, along with plastic gloves. Initially, she wore a common light blue face mask, adhering to the prison's Covid rules, but shortly after confronting Navalny, she removed the mask as RT's cameras recorded their tense exchange.

In many ways, it was a remarkable showdown, which revealed how petty and nasty the feud between the Kremlin and Navalny had become. But it also demonstrated why, for many Russian viewers, the entire

Navalny, age 33, then known as an anti-corruption blogger and activist, in his office in Moscow, Russia, on December 17, 2009. *(Oxana Onipko/AFP via Getty Images)*

Navalny speaks to Russian political opposition activists gathered in Khimki Forest outside Moscow at Anti-Seliger, an event to counter the pro-Kremlin Seliger Youth Camp, on June 18, 2011. *(Andrey Smirnov/AFP via Getty Images)*

Navalny electrifies the crowd at a rally to protest fraud in the Russian parliamentary elections on December 5, 2011, the first in a series of demonstrations that gripped Moscow in 2011–12. *(Alexey Sazonov/AFP via Getty Images)*

Navalny is released from jail on December 21, 2011, having served 15 days after being detained at the December 5 rally. Behind him is opposition Duma member Ilya Ponomarev. Three days later, Navalny addressed an even larger crowd, estimated at 100,000 people. *(Evgeny Feldman)*

Navalny and TV presenter Ksenia Sobchak, at a sit-in on April 14, 2012, in the southern city of Astrakhan held in support of Oleg Shein, a local legislative candidate who said that falsified tallies denied him victory in elections held a month earlier. Protests in Moscow, however, did not gain traction outside the capital. *(Author photo)*

At a rally for Navalny's mayoral campaign on August 21, 2013, a supporter watches him autograph the cover of the December 2011 Russian issue of *Esquire,* in which he recalled spontaneously coming up with the phrase "Party of Crooks and Thieves" to describe United Russia, President Vladimir Putin's political party. *(Evgeny Feldman)*

Navalny addresses a throng of supporters on August 25, 2013, during his campaign for mayor of Moscow. Although he was an officially registered candidate, Navalny was nonetheless detained by police shortly after the rally. *(Evgeny Feldman)*

Navalny and his brother Oleg exchange glances after they were convicted of trumped-up fraud charges on December 30, 2014. Alexey was let go with a suspended sentence but Oleg was condemned to three and a half years in a prison colony. *(Author photo)*

Navalny and Adam Michnik, a Polish historian and public intellectual, at an event in Moscow on October 2, 2015, to mark the release of their book *Opposing Forces: Plotting the New Russia,* a compilation of conversations between the two men comparing the development of democracy and opposition politics in Poland and in Russia. *(Evgeny Feldman)*

Navalny, his wife, Yulia, and top political aide Leonid Volkov, at a march on February 27, 2016, to mark the second anniversary of the murder of opposition politician Boris Nemtsov, who was shot to death as he walked on a bridge near the Kremlin. *(Evgeny Feldman)*

Yulia helps her husband prepare for a news conference in Yekaterinburg, Russia, on February 25, 2017, where he announced the opening of the local headquarters for his 2018 presidential campaign. Leonid Volkov sits to the right. *(Evgeny Feldman)*

Navalny is forced into a police van after being detained at a rally in Moscow on March 26, 2017, part of a nationwide series of anti-government protests that followed Navalny's publication of a video investigating alleged corruption by Prime Minister Dmitry Medvedev. *(Evgeny Feldman)*

Navalny leaving First City Hospital in Moscow on April 27, 2017, after being attacked by an assailant who threw green antiseptic liquid at his face, damaging his right eye, which ultimately required surgery by specialists in Spain. *(Evgeny Feldman)*

Navalny, with Yulia, admonishes his son, Zakhar, not to show any fear to the police who detained them at a rally in Moscow on May 14, 2017, to protest government plans to tear down Soviet-era low-rise apartment buildings in the capital. *(Evgeny Feldman)*

Navalny debates former Federal Security Service officer Igor Girkin in Moscow on July 20, 2017. Girkin had participated in Russia's invasion and illegal annexation of Crimea, was accused of extrajudicial killings in Russian-controlled areas of eastern Ukraine, and in 2022 was convicted in the Netherlands of murder for the downing of Malaysia Airlines Flight 17. *(Evgeny Feldman)*

Navalny and his advisers, including director of the Anti-corruption Foundation Roman Rubanov (left) and press secretary Kira Yarmysh (center), on their way to Russia's Central Election Commission in Moscow, where he was barred from running for president against Putin in the 2018 election. *(Evgeny Feldman)*

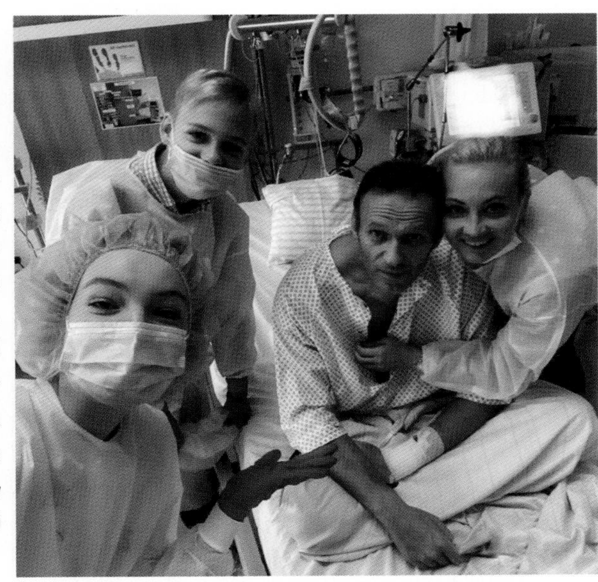

Navalny, with his wife, Yulia, daughter, Darya, and son, Zakhar, at Charité Hospital in Berlin, on September 15, 2020. He had spent days in a coma after being poisoned with a chemical weapon during an attempted assassination in Siberia on August 20, 2020. German Chancellor Angela Merkel personally announced that Navalny was attacked with Novichok, a prohibited military-grade nerve agent. *(Handout/Anadolu Agency via Getty Images)*

Police officers await Navalny at passport control in Moscow's Sheremetyevo Airport on January 17, 2021. He was arrested immediately upon his return to Russia from medical treatment in Germany. *(Kirill Kudryavtsev/AFP via Getty Images)*

Navalny flashes a victory sign from the defendant's dock, known as "the aquarium," at a hearing in Babushkinsky District Court in Moscow on February 20, 2021, where he appealed his detention on charges of violating parole during his treatment for poisoning in Germany. *(Evgeny Feldman)*

Yulia Navalnaya at the 95th Annual Academy Awards at the Dolby Theatre on March 12, 2023, in Hollywood, California, where *Navalny* won the award for best documentary feature. She is accompanied by her children, Darya and Zakhar, and the director, Daniel Roher (right). *(Kevin Winter/ Getty Images)*

Navalny speaks via video link at a court hearing on December 9, 2021, in Russia's Vladimir region, near the prison colony where he was being held, often in solitary confinement. On August 4, 2023, Navalny was sentenced to an additional 19 years for extremism. He has repeatedly accused prison officials of violating his rights and denying necessary medical treatment. *(Evgeny Feldman)*

situation felt scripted and theatrical. For some of those viewers, it undoubtedly succeeded in obscuring the fact that Navalny was a prisoner of conscience, unjustly deprived of his liberty because of his political views.

"Hello," Butina says, greeting Navalny formally. "I'm Maria. How do you feel?"

As she arrived, striding into the open barracks, Navalny was lying on a bottom bunk at the far end of the room, which RT on its website later characterized as a "place of honor" near the windows. He was apparently alone in the room, reading a book.

Butina approached the bed, but Navalny asked her to back away. "Let me try to get up," he said. "It's uncomfortable for me to talk to you lying down." As he walked toward the center of the room, Navalny gestured at damage to the floor, and Butina, glowering at him, immediately pounced.

"You, Alexey Anatolyevich, were not in an American prison," she snaps. "It's a perfect floor."

From there, a twenty-minute exchange of vitriol unfolded. Guards and other prison officials stood by as Butina scolded Navalny for refusing to fulfill work duties and accused him of forcing other prisoners to do his share, while Navalny derided Butina as a liar and Kremlin shill who was trying to put on a show.

The episode, which RT cut into several edited videos to avoid showing Navalny's face, got widespread attention on Russian state-controlled television, and it was ugly.

Butina clearly was on the attack, her jaw clenched, eyes narrowed in sarcastic fury. She gestured aggressively at the eggshell-blue walls and the surrounding room with mostly empty metal bunk beds, with her hands still in the plastic gloves as she accused Navalny of exaggerating about poor conditions and dismissed his allegations of torture.

She compared the colony to a summer camp for Pioneers, the Russian equivalent of the Boy or Girl Scouts. "Is this a torture correctional facility? Are you out of your mind? Have you traveled around the Russian regions," she said. "This is better than in a hotel in the village of Kosikha in the Altai Territory. I grew up there."

Navalny pointed out that he had been to Butina's native Altai Territory. He was splashed in the face with green dye in Barnaul, its capital, in 2017.

Butina claimed that she was visiting the prison colony in her official capacity as a member of the Public Commission, and later said that she was outraged by Navalny's description of the commission in Vladimir as useless. "I was obliged to stand up for my colleagues," she said in an interview with the news site *Gazeta.ru*.

Her assertion of professional solidarity seemed more than a stretch. Butina's ability to assert, on firsthand authority, that inmates in the United States suffered worse conditions—"I was in prison," she carped at Navalny—made the clash a classic set piece of Kremlin propaganda and whataboutism.

Her report for RT included interviews with other prisoners who said that Navalny refused to participate in the work regimen, or to clean the barracks. And she also interviewed the cashier of the prison shop who said that Navalny had come in once and bought chocolate and canned fish. That Navalny was able to stand up, walk around, and speak to her, was enough to cast doubt on his claims of being in precarious health.

Sergey Markov, the television commentator and former Putin adviser, posting on Facebook, wrote: "In general, it is clear that the story about Navalny, who is almost tortured and who does not receive medical assistance, apparently is a big lie."

In some of her own commentary afterward, Butina accused Navalny of being a "faker" and insisted that he showed no sign of being tortured with sleep deprivation. "Be a man," she said, addressing Navalny. "Serve your sentence."

But Butina also faced a torrent of criticism over her claim that the prison colony offered better conditions than hotels in Altai Territory. Some noted scathingly that there was not even a hotel in the village of Kosikha that she had referenced. Others said that her comment amounted to a less than ringing endorsement of the tourism industry, or of living conditions in the region where she grew up and that she was supposed to represent in parliament.

"So, what could be better than the confession of a propagandist that in Russia people live worse than in prison," the journalist, Anastasia Kirilenko, wrote.

Navalny's team, posting on his behalf in self-defense, said that instead of sending his requested doctor, prison officials had sent a "wretched propagandist" and that he had lost nearly eighteen pounds since arriving in prison, even before starting his hunger strike, dropping to about 183 pounds from 205. The post said Navalny had called Butina "a parasite and servant of thieves."

Lyubov Sobol, one of Navalny's top lieutenants, said that if Butina liked the prison colony so much, she should stay there. Yevgenia Albats was harsher, tweeting that Butina should "be pitied" for how she had been used and abandoned by the Russian government while in the United States but also noting how "she returned and once again collects for a life in prostitution."

Maria Pevchikh, furious, unleashed a thirty-tweet thread, describing Butina as an "extremely mediocre and untalented" person.

Pevchikh posted images of certificates showing Butina had participated in a knitting class and a life-skills course while in prison in the United States. She also posted a letter written by an Orthodox priest on Butina's behalf, assuring a federal judge that all she wanted was to return to her family in Russia "and start a Christian family."

She noted the priest's reference to visiting Butina numerous times while she was in prison to hear her confessions. "I remind you," she tweeted, "that not even a doctor is allowed to see Navalny, who is barely walking and starving."

"I could write as many more tweets about the adventures of the fools Butina and Torshin in the USA, but laughing at their absurdity distracts from the main thing," Pevchikh wrote, summing up. "Butina is an unprincipled corrupt creature who was sent to IK-2 to make fun of Navalny."

"Bedding," she added, using Russian slang for a trashy whore.

Days after Butina's visit, Navalny was sent to the prison infirmary—not for his back pain or the loss of sensation in his legs—but with a cough and high fever. Tests for tuberculosis and Covid came back negative, and he returned to his barracks after three days.

The Navalny team continued to drive the narrative. Within two weeks, there were headlines around the world saying that Navalny, still on a hunger strike, was near death. "Navalny's Health in Prison Is Dire, His Doctors Say," the *New York Times* proclaimed.

One of those doctors, Yaroslav Ashikhmin, had issued a statement saying Navalny could die "at any moment." Ashikhmin cited blood tests showing abnormally high levels of potassium and warned that Navalny could suffer cardiac or kidney failure.

Yulia Navalnaya told journalists that her husband had lost another fifteen pounds. Another doctor, Alexander Polupan, posted Navalny's blood test results on Facebook, and wrote: "This absolutely indicates hospitalization. If treatment doesn't start, he'll will die in the next few days."

The penitentiary service announced that Navalny would be transferred to a hospital in a nearby prison, and that he had agreed to "vitamin therapy." But Anastasia Vasilyeva, the head of the Doctors' Alliance trade union and one of Nvalny's personal physicians, said it was unsuitable. "This is absolutely not a hospital where they can diagnose and treat his problems," she wrote.

Navalny's supporters called for nationwide protests two days later, timed to coincide with a major speech by Putin to the Federal Assembly, Russia's upper chamber of parliament.

After the initial protests following Navalny's detention in January, his team had promised to hold another day of mass demonstrations to demand his freedom once five hundred thousand people registered to attend. Now, still forty thousand short of that goal, they said that Navalny's health had forced them to move faster. The timing, to coincide with Putin's speech, however, was not accidental.

In fact, Navalny's team had reason to believe that if they waited much longer, they would miss their last opportunity to organize street protests.

On April 19, Russian prosecutors went to court and initiated a legal process to declare the Anti-corruption Foundation an extremist organization, equating it with Al Qaeda, and potentially putting all its employees and associates at risk of arrest and prosecution. Borrowing the subtitle of Navalny's LiveJournal blog, the demonstrations were billed as "the last battle between good and neutrality."

On the morning of April 21, the authorities moved preemptively and arrested two of Navalny's top lieutenants, lawyer Lyubov Sobol and press secretary Kira Yarmysh. Wishful news accounts tried to portray the protests as impactful, noting that demonstrations got underway in the Russian Far East, even before Putin started his speech.

Turnout, however, was lackluster. In Moscow, an estimated ten thousand people gathered near Manezh Square and on streets near the Kremlin. Extensive police barricades, however, prevented demonstrators from coalescing, and there were relatively few arrests. Across the country, fewer than two thousand people were detained at protests. All in all, the opposition seemed deflated and defeated, with its leader jailed and reportedly on the brink of death, and his organization facing potential extinction.

A decision had to be made. Navalny's choice was literally to live to fight another day.

In a series of highly choreographed statements, five of Navalny's personal physicians issued a public plea urging him to end his hunger strike, which was now into its fourth week. In their statements, the doctors claimed partial victory—"thanks to the huge support of world and public opinion"—and announced that Navalny had been taken to a civilian hospital in Vladimir, where he was evaluated. They said he had undergone a procedure called electroneuromyography, which checks for potential nerve damage, and also had consultations with a neurosurgeon, a nephrologist, and a neurologist.

"All medical reports and examination results were submitted to us today for our opinion through lawyers and relatives," the doctors said. Warning that Navalny was at risk of dying, they added, "We understand that if the hunger strike continues even for a minimal time, unfortunately, we will soon have no one to treat."

Navalny, playing his part, issued a statement, carried forward by his lawyers and posted on social media, saying that he had agreed to follow his doctors' advice, based on their political diagnosis of victory.

"Doctors whom I fully trust made a statement that we have achieved enough for me to stop my fast," Navalny said in his statement, which was posted on Instagram.

And, just to add a dash of heroism to his self-preserving decision, Navalny described being moved to tears when his lawyers informed him that some supporters had gone on hunger strikes in solidarity. "Friends, my heart is full of love and gratitude for you, but I don't want anyone physically suffering because of me," Navalny said.

Volkov also declared victory, claiming the protests had secured Navalny's treatment.

"What can be achieved by rallies?" Navalny's top adviser tweeted. "As soon as the rally was announced, Alexey was taken for a multidisciplinary examination to a civilian hospital in Vladimir, and a large number of tests were carried out. As soon as the rally took place. As soon as the rally took place—today, all of a sudden, we were given all the survey materials."

When exactly Navalny went to the civilian hospital in Vladimir, or if he ever did, is unclear. The Federal Penitentiary Service—which on April 19 had announced his transfer to a prison hospital in a different camp, IK-3—did not issue any statement about taking him to a civilian hospital. And it's not clear when Navalny's lawyers or his wife would have been able to obtain medical records.

Within a week, Navalny appeared in a Moscow courtroom via video link for hearings related to his appeal of the slander case. He wore his blue prison garb and appeared gaunt, with his head shaved.

In his closing statement, Navalny was emotional but rambling. He railed against Putin, calling him a "naked, thieving king" who "doesn't give a damn about the country." He alleged that Russia's oil and gas wealth had been stolen from its people.

Navalny also blasted the effort to label the Anti-corruption Foundation as extremist, noting that he had investigated Moscow's chief prosecutor and linked him to luxury properties abroad. "This prosecutor is a civil servant here, stealing millions and investing abroad," Navalny said. "In a secret process, he is trying to recognize as extremists and 'foreign agents' me and people like me—patriots of the country who are trying to protect the country from you traitors."

The judge, Nataliya Kurysheva, tried to cut him off, but Navalny, characteristically, barreled over her. "You know everything I say is true," he snapped. "And I am very, very kind to you, given the fact that I consider you all traitors and the occupying power."

Wrapping up, he added, "Your government is quite successful, because for twenty years you managed to rob our people living in this country, deprive them of their future and take out their wealth. But it will end sooner or later." Judge Kurysheva, of course, denied his appeal.

It was a day of multiple defeats, as Volkov announced that there was no choice but to shut Navalny's network of regional offices. Six months later, Russia banned the "Smart voting" web site and Apple and Google removed the app from their download stores.

* * *

With his appeals denied, and the Kremlin refusing to flinch, Navalny's saga was entering a new and difficult phase, one that would test his ability to remain relevant, and the ability of his team to sustain public attention on his situation, while also operating almost entirely from exile.

But it was also a phase that would give Navalny time to reflect on his own political views and goals, on the future of Russia, and on the world. To open this chapter, Navalny returned to his core roots, as an anti-corruption crusader.

In August 2021, just before the first anniversary of his poisoning attack, Navalny published an op-ed in the *Guardian*, *Frankfurter Allgemeine Zeitung*, and *Le Monde*, calling on world leaders to address the scourge of corruption.

Navalny opened the piece with his trademark irony, crediting corruption with helping him survive the assassination attempt. "When a country's senior management is preoccupied with protection rackets and extortion from businesses, the quality of covert operations inevitably suffers," Navalny wrote. "A group of FSB agents applied the nerve agent to my underwear just as shoddily as they incompetently dogged my footsteps for three and a half years."

But Navalny then turned to a serious treatment of the role of public corruption in some of modern history's worst geopolitical debacles, making credible arguments that the failure of the U.S.-led coalition in Afghanistan was rooted in public corruption, and that Ukraine's Maidan Revolution—and Putin's backlash against it—had its origins in the corrupt regime of former president Viktor Yanukovych.

Navalny proposed five steps for addressing major state-sanctioned corruption.

He called for establishing a special formal designation of "countries that encourage corruption"—so that measures could be taken against a group of states, not just individual governments. Second would be "enforced transparency" so that any and all business dealings with countries deemed corrupt would have to be open to public scrutiny.

> You work for a state-owned company in a country at high risk of corruption and want to buy a villa on the French Riviera? Fine, go ahead, but you should know that all the information about the deal will be publicly available. You want to have dealings with an official in Minsk or the aunt of a Russian governor? No problem, but you will have to publish the entire paper trail of the transaction, and will no longer be able to conceal the bribe you pay through that "regional representative" or "local partner."

Third, Navalny said that superwealthy individuals who have benefited from corruption, notably Russian oligarchs connected to Putin, must be put under sanction. Fourth, he called for aggressive prosecution under existing laws such as the Federal Corrupt Practices Act in the U.S. and the Bribery Act in the UK. And fifth, he demanded creation of an international body or commission to crack down on former public officials enriching themselves.

"Legalized bribery is flourishing," Navalny wrote, "often in the form of board memberships at state-owned companies."

Stepping up his use of international media, Navalny agreed to a written question-and-answer interview with Andrew E. Kramer of the *New York Times*, sending out fifty-four pages of handwritten responses to the journalist's questions.

In the exchange, Navalny described the difficulties of his life in the penal colony, including being forced to watch state-controlled Russian television for many hours each day.

Navalny expressed confidence that Putin and his system could be defeated if only free and fair elections were permitted.

"I answer firmly and without a drop of doubt: Yes. If we could participate in elections, even without money or information resources, we would defeat Putin's party, United Russia," he wrote. "Our program is better, and we have a vision for the future of Russia while Putin does not."

Navalny insisted that Russia's core nature was democratic, a view not commonly shared by many Russians who readily acknowledge a historic, national preference for strongman rulers.

"Putin is not eternal, physically or politically," Navalny wrote to Kramer. "What is important is this: The Putin regime is an historical accident, not an inevitability. It was the choice of the corrupt Yeltsin family. Sooner or later, this mistake will be fixed and Russia will move on to a democratic, European path of development. Simply because that is what the people want."

Navalny, of course, used part of the exchange to bash Putin. "We clearly have to deal with a person who has lost his mind, Putin. A pathological liar with megalomania and persecutory delusion," he wrote.

Navalny also repeated his long-standing complaint that Western sanctions often harm too many regular Russian citizens, and are overly focused on midlevel government officials while allowing the wealthiest Putin-connected oligarchs to splash money around the West with impunity.

"For now, all sanctions were tailored to avoid almost all significant participants in Putin's gangster gang," he wrote "Do you want evidence? Name one real evildoer who suffered. The airplanes, the yachts, the billions in Western banks—everything is in its place."

But even as Navalny appeared to be adjusting to his imprisonment, the Kremlin stepped up its pressure campaign, arresting more of his associates, and initiating new legal cases against Navalny.

Navalny responded with trademark sarcasm.

"That moment when you ask the visiting lawyers: 'Well, how are things outside?'" he posted on Instagram in late September 2021. "And they: 'Yes, nothing; everything is the same.' And then after a pause: 'Ah, here. A new case has been opened against you! Creation of an extremist community! That's up to 10 years!'"

In all, Navalny noted then, he had four new cases pending, with potential sentences totaling twenty-three years. "They can, of course, come up with something else, but all the same, the maximum term for the totality of sentences is no more than 30 years," he wrote, adding a winking emoji. "So don't worry, I'll be released no later than the spring of 2051."

Some of Navalny's supporters hoped that he would be rewarded for his bravery in returning to Russia with the Nobel Peace Prize. Instead, the committee gave the honor to Dmitry Muratov, the longtime editor of *Novaya Gazeta*, an independent Russian newspaper, and Maria Ressa, a journalist from the Philippines. Since *Novaya Gazeta*'s founding in 1993, six of the newspaper's journalists have been murdered because of their work.

Some of Navalny's allies were furious, believing Muratov had made too many accommodations to survive in the Putinist system. Navalny, however, congratulated him and seized the opportunity to speak out about the importance of a free press.

On Oct. 20, the European Parliament announced that Navalny had won the Sakharov Prize for Freedom of Thought.

Though the award pegged Navalny as a dissident, he nonetheless expressed gratitude.

Addressing the Parliament and its members, he wrote: "I want to say (and I will take the courage to say this not only on my own behalf but also on behalf of many others): many thanks for creating this prize in general and for naming it after my great compatriot.

"I dedicate my prize to all kinds of anti-corruption fighters around the world," Navalny wrote, "from journalists to lawyers, from officials (there are some, yes) and deputies to those who take to the streets to support this fight. I wish them perseverance and courage even in the scariest of moments."

* * *

As 2021 drew to a close, the world was fixated on Russia's menacing military buildup on the Ukrainian border.

Navalny, who was learning about these events primarily by being forced to watch Russian state-controlled television, noticed the rising drumbeat of hostility toward NATO and the West.

"The TV set in our barrack hysterically fights NATO all day long," Navalny's team tweeted on his behalf. "On every channel, they talk about NATO threats. Putin himself laments that NATO is at our doorstep and we have nowhere to retreat."

On many levels, the developments seemed absolutely mad—but for Navalny they were also maddening. He had warned about the West's coddling of Putin and Putin's oligarch cronies for years. The response, as his daughter had told the European Parliament the previous week, amounted to a bunch of platitudes and repeated pleas for pragmatism.

Navalny's frustrations were clearly building, and his tweet thread wove the news developments into a scathing indictment not just of Putin, but of the Putin-connected, often UK-based oligarch Roman Abramovich, and of the European Union and the United States for hypocritically maintaining business ties and other dealings with Russia's elite.

Abramovich, who owned the storied British soccer team, Chelsea FC, was reputed to be one of "Putin's wallets"—known for opening his own checkbook to cover the costs of pet projects of the Russian leader. For years, Abramovich denied these allegations and even sued journalists who wrote about his ties to the Kremlin. But in 2023, Greg Miller of the *Washington Post* reported how a foundation connected to the oligarch paid for one of Putin's seemingly most endearing purchases—an apartment in Tel Aviv given as a gift to Putin's high school German teacher, who was living in Israel on a modest pension.

Navalny never had any doubts about the role of Abramovich and other oligarchs. In his thread, he described how Abramovich had managed to secure Portuguese citizenship and had also bought himself a new Boeing 787 airplane for $350 million—a nice sale for the American airplane manufacturer.

Abramovich managed to get citizenship—and an EU passport—through a program for people who claim Sephardic Jewish ancestry, but Navalny ignored this. He presumed instead that Abramovich had bribed his way to a new nationality, though the situation was not nearly so simple, and investigations so far have found no evidence of bribery.

"He finally managed to find a country where you can give some bribes and make some semi-official and official payments to end up in the E.U. and NATO—on the other side of Putin's front line, so to speak," Navalny wrote. He described how Abramovich made billions off the privatization of Russian enterprises and from buy-back deals.

"Well, there you go," he wrote. "'Putin's wallet' flies on an expensive plane to a NATO country. How brave of him. And everyone is happy. Putin and Abramovich steal from the budget and invest money in the West. The West scares itself with Putin's attack on Ukraine but gives citizenship to his trusted oligarch. Portuguese officials carry suitcases with money. The U.S. economy received $350 million. TV presenters praise Putin for his fight against NATO while foaming at the mouth. A perfect cycle of hypocrisy and corruption."

Investigations are still ongoing into how Abramovich became a Portuguese citizen, but the rabbis in Portugal and Russia who supported his application have denied any wrongdoing. And Portuguese officials have complained that Navalny's characterization of their country as corrupt was inaccurate and unfair. Abramovich, meanwhile, had also become a citizen of Israel, proving that Portugal was not the only U.S. ally willing to roll out a welcome mat for the Putin-connected business titan and his fortune.

Navalny's larger point, that Western nations remained all too happy to grant citizenship or sell airplanes to a Putin ally, was still valid. But he had reached beyond the facts. His lack of access to independent information was starting to take a toll.

Within two months, Putin proved to be more evil than even Navalny had ever warned, rolling tanks into Ukraine and unleashing a full-scale land war in Europe in the twenty-first century.

Navalny's I-told-you-so's piled up in abundance. The Russian military proved to be far weaker than anyone expected—hollowed out by years of corruption that left troops ill-equipped. The Kremlin launched an even more draconian crackdown on free speech, arresting not only political opposition figures but also ordinary citizens merely for speaking out in favor of peace. And Prigozhin, the billionaire who Navalny's team had targeted for allegedly poisoning school lunches, took on a central role in the war, deploying his Wagner mercenary group to fight in Ukraine.

While Navalny sat in prison, Prigozhin, who had served nearly a decade in jail for robbery and other crimes, began visiting prison colonies to recruit convicts to fight in Ukraine in exchange for being granted a pardon by Putin.

With the world's attention diverted, and a country of 40 million people under attack, Navalny found it harder to generate interest in his own predicament.

In March 2022, he was convicted in another case—this time trumped-up fraud charges—and sentenced to an additional nine years in prison. The judge ordered that sentence to be served in a maximum-security prison, and in June 2022, Navalny was transferred to IK-6, a penal colony in the town of Melekhovo, still in Vladimir Region, but two hours farther east.

In IK-6, his lawyers allege, he has been repeatedly placed in a punishment cell. Though prison regulations limit such brutal solitary confinement to fifteen days at a time, Navalny's team has said that prison officials pile on allegations of misconduct, so that as soon as he is released from the punishment cell, another reason can be cited to send him back.

Russia's full-scale invasion of Ukraine presented Navalny and his team with an extraordinary opportunity to leverage global sentiment against Putin. Suddenly, much of the world was coming around to a position that Navalny had articulated for years. As U.S. president Joe Biden put it, during a speech in Warsaw on March 26, 2022: "For God's sake, this man cannot remain in power."

But the invasion also vastly increased the challenge that Navalny's family and his team face in trying to sustain public awareness about his continuing incarceration, and about the abuses that he is suffering in prison. The Putin regime's repression of political opponents, even the alleged poisoning attempts, now paled in comparison to the war crimes that Russian soldiers were accused of in Bucha and elsewhere in Ukraine.

In a bid to position Navalny as a prominent critic of the invasion, he and his team turned to the question, suddenly of intense interest in capitals worldwide, of what a postwar Russia might look like.

From a legal and political standpoint, this was far more difficult, and potentially perilous, than it might seem.

Tough new laws prohibited any criticism of the Russian military or the war, so any antiwar statement by Navalny would risk new criminal prosecutions that could add years to his sentence.

Politically, war inevitably spurs national unity and a public demand for loyal support, if not for the goals of the conflict then at least for the soldiers who were sent to fight. Despite signs of public discomfort over Putin's September 2022 military mobilization campaign—which prompted hundreds of thousands of fighting-age men to flee the country—in public opinion polls, a majority of Russians still profess to support the war.

By speaking out against the war, which the Kremlin calls "a special military operation," Navalny risks seeming unpatriotic, and putting himself at political odds with the Russian public that he still hopes might vote for him some day.

On top of this, Navalny's compatriots in the Russian political opposition are either in prison like he is, or no longer in Russia. And the people most likely to support his political outlook have fled the country in large numbers, perhaps never to return.

Despite these risks and obstacles, Navalny and his team had no choice but to try to capture some of the global public attention focused on Russia and the war.

So, in a 2,135-word essay published in the *Washington Post*, Navalny set out to answer a question: "What does a desirable and realistic end to the criminal war unleashed by Vladimir Putin against Ukraine look like?"

In the article, Navalny argued that Western powers should strive not only for Ukraine to emerge victorious in defending its sovereign territory, but they should also commit to making sure that Navalny and the Russian opposition emerge victorious in their war against Putin.

"The issue of postwar Russia should become the central issue—and not just one element among others—of those who are striving for peace," Navalny wrote. "No long-term goals can be achieved without a plan to ensure that the source of the problems stops creating them. Russia must cease to be an instigator of aggression and instability. That is possible, and that is what should be seen as a strategic victory in this war."

The central point of his essay, if there was a central point, seemed to be that to achieve regional peace and stability, Russia must become a parliamentary republic with constitutional changes to limit the authority of the overly strong presidency.

That central point, however, was at times difficult to discern. The article rambled from one theme to another, trying unsuccessfully in the end to avoid numerous pitfalls. A pro-Russian argument would fall on deaf ears in the West; an anti-Russian argument would alienate his countrymen at home. Navalny seemed to be trying to make French president Emmanuel Macron's point that Russia should be defeated but not humiliated.

Navalny, in the op-ed, tried to reassure readers of his core belief that most Russian people are good, while also criticizing the West for misreading and mishandling the situation in Ukraine and, at the same time, pummeling Putin and "all Russians with imperial views."

He also issued a stern warning that simply defeating Russia militarily will not bring about the needed political change or the desired lasting stability:

> It is easy to predict that even in the case of a painful military defeat, Putin will still declare that he lost not to Ukraine but to the "collective West and NATO," whose aggression was unleashed to destroy Russia.
>
> And then, resorting to his usual postmodern repertoire of national symbols—from icons to red flags, from Dostoevsky to ballet—he will vow to create an army so strong and weapons of such unprecedented power that the West will rue the day it defied us, and the honor of our great ancestors will be avenged.
>
> And then we will see a fresh cycle of hybrid warfare and provocations, eventually escalating into new wars.

In the op-ed, Navalny insisted that many Russians were concerned about the terrible violence being inflected on Ukrainians.

> Yes, propaganda and brainwashing have an effect. Yet we can say with certainty that the majority of residents of major cities such as Moscow and St. Petersburg, as well as young voters, are critical of the war and imperial hysteria. The horror of the suffering of Ukrainians and the brutal killing of innocents resonate in the souls of these voters.

But this was no "Letter from Birmingham Jail" trying to rally the Russian people to take morally just action. It was a polemic against Putin. And it was a plea for the West to help Russia rewind the clock to the days shortly after the collapse of the Soviet Union, and let the country choose a different form of government without a strong executive presidency.

"Russia needs a parliamentary republic," Navalny wrote. "That is the only way to stop the endless cycle of imperial authoritarianism."

He then went on to make arguments that seemed to support his thesis but were historically inaccurate, claiming that Russia's neighbors that chose the parliamentary republic model (the Baltic states, according to Navalny) were thriving while those that chose a presidential-parliamentary model (Ukraine, Moldova, and Georgia) "have faced persistent instability and made little progress."

"Those that chose strong presidential power (Russia, Belarus and the Central Asian republics)," he wrote, "have succumbed to rigid authoritarianism, most of them permanently engaged in military conflicts with their neighbors, daydreaming about their own little empires."

In fact, these countries took a variety of paths. Lithuania has a semi-presidential system, not quite the same as its neighbors Latvia and Estonia. Moldova, meanwhile, has a parliamentary system that gives little real authority to its president.

A bigger flaw in Navalny's argument was his presumption that the West could exert much influence over Russia's future political choices. And his assertion that "parliamentary democracy is also a rational and desirable choice for many of the political factions around Putin" seemed far more aspirational than grounded in any reality.

Parliamentary democracy, Navalny wrote, "gives them an opportunity to maintain influence and fight for power while insuring that they are not destroyed by a more aggressive group." In fact, with Western sanctions biting, many members of the Russian elite seem fairly eager for Russia to return to being a relatively stable oligarchic kleptocracy—accused of public corruption and a rigged judicial system at home, but not atrocities abroad.

Despite these flaws, Navalny's op-ed included some important insights about Russia's war in Ukraine for Western readers trying to make sense of how it all came about:

> First, jealousy of Ukraine and its possible successes is an innate feature of post-Soviet power in Russia; it was also characteristic of

the first Russian president, Boris Yeltsin. But since the beginning of Putin's rule, and especially after the Orange Revolution that began in 2004, hatred of Ukraine's European choice, and the desire to turn it into a failed state, have become a lasting obsession not only for Putin but also for all politicians of his generation.

By unlucky timing that neither his lawyers nor *Washington Post* opinion editors could have predicted, Navalny's column was published on September 30, 2022—the day that Putin delivered a speech declaring his intention to annex four Ukrainian regions—Donetsk, Luhansk, Kherson, and Zaporizhzhia.

Navalny's op-ed got little traction and generated little public discussion. With Putin brazenly planning to redraw the boundaries of Europe, there was little bandwidth to consider the future of Russia.

On January 17, 2023—the second anniversary of his imprisonment—Navalny's supporters announced a new campaign to free him. But there was no reason to hope or believe it would succeed.

Navalny's daughter, Dasha, appeared in a video, urging his release, but now casting him as a victim of his antiwar statements rather than his decades of anti-Putin statements.

"Of course, the real reason my dad is in a punishment cell are his antiwar statements. And now they're tormenting him and depriving him of any connection with the outside world in order to silence him," Navalnaya said. "But my father is not afraid and will not stop fighting. My dad is an innocent man and deserves to be free."

Navalny also sent a message noting the anniversary.

"It has been exactly two years since I returned to Russia," he wrote. "I have spent these two years in prison. When you write a post like this, you have to ask yourself: How many more of such anniversary posts will you have to write?

"Life and the events around us prompt the answer: However many it may take," he wrote. "Our miserable, exhausted Motherland needs to be saved. It has been pillaged, wounded, dragged into an aggressive war, and turned into a prison run by the most unscrupulous and deceitful scoundrels."

Saving the Motherland, however, would have to wait. For the moment, Navalny's main task was to survive—at least until the end of the war—and to hope Putin wouldn't win.

—11—

LAST WORD

"This is the main thing in politics—people who just stand together somewhere."

—Alexey Navalny, Barnaul, March 20, 2017

Alexey Navalny and Leonid Volkov, his friend and chief campaign strategist, were walking along Molodezhnaya Street in the Siberian city of Barnaul. Piles of dirty snow lined the street. It was March 20, 2017, and they were in town to open a local headquarters in preparation for Navalny's plan to challenge Putin in the 2018 Russian presidential race.

Navalny, in a blue parka with a scarf tied tightly around his neck, stopped to shake hands with an older woman wearing a yellow beret and a man in a cap with a long white beard. Despite the subfreezing temperature, Navalny did not wear a hat. Suddenly, as Navalny turned away from the couple, a man in a black jacket threw bright green liquid into Navalny's face, bolted down the street, and jumped into a waiting Nissan Qashqai.

Other Russian political opposition figures had also faced these so-called *zelyonka*, or "brilliant green dye," attacks. The liquid, a common antiseptic, stains the skin and can take a week or more to remove. The assailant escaped, and Volkov later reported that the getaway car had been traced to the parking lot of the regional administration building.

Navalny quickly posted a video joking about his new likeness to Shrek, or the Hulk, or the main character in the movie *The Mask*.

"Maybe in the Kremlin they think I won't make video addresses with a green face," he said. "But I will definitely make them because more people will watch them now and it definitely won't stop me.

"My stylish green face perfectly fits the interiors of our headquarters," he said, standing in front of a colorfully painted wall. "I'm a bit worried about my teeth: they are green too! I hope they will be white again."

Navalny and his team had rented out conference space in a nearby hotel to meet with local volunteers, but the hotel's owners balked and refused to allow the gathering. They said the space could not accommodate so many people—but political pressure, fear, or both seemed more logical explanations.

Instead, Navalny met his supporters outside in the cold. With his face and hands now a faded—but more evenly spread—shade of green, he climbed onto a pile of snow to address the crowd. "This government has pumped out $3 trillion worth of oil and gas and still cannot give people $500 [monthly] salaries," he said. "Nothing good will ever come of it."

Raising Russia's minimum wage was among the planks of Navalny's presidential platform, and he spoke about the challenges Russian citizens faced to meet the rising cost of home utilities. He also urged his followers to not be afraid to gather for rallies.

"This is the main thing in politics—people who just stand together somewhere," Navalny said, his ears stained a slightly darker green than the rest of his face. "This is the biggest threat that exists for this government."

Navalny and Volkov were aggressively building their campaign operation, even though Navalny was technically barred from running because of his criminal conviction in the Kirovles case.

His original conviction had been ruled invalid by the European Court of Human Rights, in Strasbourg, France, which found that he and his friend and colleague, Pyotr Ofitserov, were tried and baselessly found guilty of doing nothing more than conducting normal business transactions. The Russian Supreme Court vacated the verdict and sent the case back to Kirov for retrial. In February 2017, the Kirov court convicted Navalny again, without any new evidence, and imposed another five-year suspended sentence. Navalny's victory in Strasbourg merely gave Russia another chance to bar him from running for office.

Navalny leveraged the *zelyonka* attack for publicity and fund-raising, turning his new look into a popular internet meme. Supporters posted photos of themselves with green faces.

Back in Moscow, six days after the incident in Barnaul, Navalny was arrested as he arrived at a protest rally that he had called to fan the fury against Prime Minister Dmitry Medvedev. It was less than a month after the release of the video *Don't Call Him Dimon*, which showed extravagant properties allegedly belonging to Medvedev. Thousands turned out in Moscow and in cities across the country. Hundreds were arrested.

After Navalny was detained, protesters tried to stop the police wagon he was in from pulling away. "Guys, I'm fine," he tweeted, urging them to continue the protest by marching along Tverskaya Street in the center of the capital. Some protesters arrived with their faces painted green. Others carried yellow rubber duckies, a nod to the "duck house" shown in the video at the center of a lake of one of Medvedev's properties.

In addition to arresting Navalny on-site, police raided the offices of the Anti-corruption Foundation and detained staffers who were livestreaming the protest.

A month after the protest, on April 27, Navalny was attacked again with brilliant green dye, this time near his office in Moscow. Video of the incident showed a man walking up just as Navalny was about to climb into a waiting car, throwing the liquid in his face and bolting off in a run. Navalny was left hunched over, wincing in pain.

Paramedics who responded to the scene wrapped bandages around Navalny's head, covering his right eye. He once again posed for a photo with staffers, but this time Navalny was not in such good humor. He was hurt. Doctors diagnosed a chemical burn. "It looks comical," he tweeted. "But the eye burns like hell."

In early May, Navalny said he had been advised to have eye surgery at a specialized clinic abroad. Pro-Kremlin news outlets reported that Navalny "had been reminded" by the Federal Penitentiary Service that he was not allowed to travel outside the country because of his suspended criminal sentences.

Curiously, though, on the same day, Navalny reported that he had received a call from prison officials telling him that he could come pick up his passport. Navalny thought it was a prank but, in fact, the passport was waiting for him.

Navalny's lawyer, Vadim Kobzev, said Navalny intended to go abroad for surgery despite the warning that doing so was a violation of the terms of his suspended sentence. Within days he and his wife, Yulia, were on a plane to Barcelona. Life News, the Kremlin-connected television station, posted photos, which it said had been submitted by a "citizen journalist," of Navalny sitting in a window seat, wearing a pink T-shirt. Yulia was next to him. Both were focused on their mobile phones.

Navalny's need for treatment coincided with Russia's May holidays, when the couple often went on vacation. On May 9, while Russia was celebrating Victory Day—the annual commemoration of the Soviet Union's triumph over Nazi Germany—Navalny posted on Instagram from Spain, announcing that he had eye surgery but that the doctors told him it would take another several months for his eyesight to recover.

He posted a photo of himself with his right eye looking bloodshot, but he seemed to be in good spirits. "When I asked them to give me x-ray or infrared vision in the hospital," he wrote, "they answered with a categorical refusal. Another manifestation of Russophobia." Navalny had still not given up on the idea of becoming a superhero.

It would be silly and naïve not to recognize the restoration of Navalny's passport as part of the Kremlin's hope that Navalny would finally just give up and stay abroad. If he returned, the unauthorized trip would provide another potential legal justification for converting his suspended sentence into a real one and throwing him in prison.

Moskovsky Komsomolets, quoting anonymous sources, reported that Navalny had appealed directly to the Kremlin for permission to travel abroad. And Volkov initially declined to comment when journalists asked about reports in government-connected news outlets that Navalny had left the country. Volkov claimed not to know Navalny's whereabouts, an assertion that defied credibility.

* * *

Such incidents—in which the Russian regime inexplicably seemed to extend Navalny a bit of kindness after likely being behind an attack on him in the first place—have fueled conspiracy theories that Navalny is actually an agent of the Kremlin, part of the never-ending Kabuki theater of Russian politics.

In his conversations with Navalny, which were turned into a book, Michnik, the Polish historian, drew a parallel to efforts in Poland to expose Lech Wałęsa, the Solidarity leader, as an operative of the Security Service. "In Russia, you'll get radicals claiming that 'Navalny is a Kremlin project!' either on account of their own stupidity or just to line their own pockets," Michnik said.

"Many people do say that," Navalny replied.

In the same part of their conversation, which took place in 2015, Navalny noted that he was working to form a political party with Mikhail Kasyanov, who had served as prime minister under Putin for nearly four years from May 2000 to February 2004. In 2015, Kasyanov had become a leader of the People's Freedom Party, PARNAS, along with Boris Nemtsov, and there was hope that the still-disparate democratic forces in Russia could unite in time for elections to the State Duma, which would be held in September 2016.

At the time of negotiations with Kasyanov, Navalny was the leader of the Progress Party, a name that he and Volkov settled on after the Russian election authorities refused to register the People's Alliance Party because, they said, another party with the same name already existed. Volkov had founded the People's Alliance in 2012, but Navalny initially refrained from joining, convinced that the authorities would kill the party if he was formally associated with it.

"People's Alliance is my party," Navalny said at a party congress in December 2012. But he also explained that he would not formally join, citing the criminal investigations proceeding against him and the lawsuits that he was entangled in related to his shareholder activism. A year later, after his bid for mayor of Moscow fell short, Navalny agreed to become the leader of the People's Alliance. In February 2014, it became the Progress Party.

In early 2014, the Kremlin was focused on one of Putin's most beloved pet projects—the Winter Olympic Games in Sochi. Its other focus was the volatile political situation in neighboring Ukraine, where prodemocracy demonstrators were occupying Maidan Nezalezhnosti—Independence Square—in the center of Kyiv, the capital. Ukraine's Orange Revolution of 2003–2004 had set off panic in Moscow, and this time it was worse.

Initially, the demonstrations on Maidan were a protest against then-president Viktor Yanukovych's decision, under Russian pressure, to not sign far-reaching political and economic agreements with the European Union. Yanukovych had promised to sign the accords, and his refusal to do so, at a European Union meeting in Vilnius in November 2013, left many Ukrainians feeling utterly betrayed. The protests, however, morphed into an unstoppable force after the Ukrainian riot police, acting on orders from the president's office, savagely beat some of the young demonstrators gathered on Maidan. That violence prompted thousands of people previously not motivated to take to the streets in fury.

Navalny, for his part, opened 2014 by releasing an investigation into cost overruns and corruption related to the Sochi Olympics, which was costing Russia more than $45 billion. He and his team created an interactive website, sochi.fbk.info, laying out the vast sums of taxpayer money that were being poured into projects that would never generate sufficient return on investment. The site also described how state-controlled corporations, including Gazprom and Russian Railways, had been forced to take on huge projects related to the Olympics that would almost certainly result in losses to taxpayers and shareholders.

Oligarchs had also been pressed into service, but many were overseeing projects using money loaned by the government-owned Vnesheconombank. "All major private investors—billionaires Vladimir Potanin, Oleg Deripaska and Viktor Vekselberg—have received substantial financial support from Vnesheconombank, reaching 90 percent of the whole project costs," Navalny's investigation concluded. "Out of 20 Vnesheconombank loans for $7.6 billion, nine loans for $5.8 billion need to be restructured. According to the business newspaper *Vedomosti*, these projects are unprofitable with loans being unrecoverable without additional support."

In putting a spotlight on corruption related to the Olympics, Navalny had to be mindful that hosting the games was a matter of national pride and that many Russian voters were excited about it.

"We are proud that Sochi hosts the Winter Olympic Games," the Anti-corruption Foundation posted on the website's home page. "This is a unique sports event for everybody. However, officials turned the Olympics into a source of their income. The Anti-corruption Foundation proves that with figures and facts. Learn who cashed in on the most expensive Olympic games ever."

On February 22, 2014, while the games were still underway, the protests in Kyiv turned deadly. Riot police shot and killed more than one hundred demonstrators. Yanukovych fled the capital, abandoning his presidency, and sought shelter in Russia—a cowardly move that would stand in stark contrast to President Volodymyr Zelensky's decision eight years later to stay in Kyiv even as the Russian military invaded his country and Western nations offered to evacuate him.

Within days of Yanukovych's gutless departure, Putin ordered the invasion and annexation of Crimea, and Russia began fomenting a separatist war in the eastern Ukrainian region of Donbas. These events, entangling Russia in military conflict for years to come, further reduced the Kremlin's already miniscule tolerance for political dissent.

In spring 2014, the Russian authorities also opened a criminal case against Vladimir Ashurkov, the former Alfa Group executive who had quit his lucrative corporate career to take on a full-time role as executive director of the Anti-corruption Foundation. Ashurkov and his partner, Alexandrina Markvo, left Russia for Britain shortly after he received a summons from the Investigative Committee in an embezzlement case, which was connected with fund-raising he had done for Navalny's mayoral campaign. The couple applied for political asylum, which was granted the following year.

By 2015, Russian opposition politicians—and their supporters—were under intense pressure.

On February 27, Boris Nemtsov was murdered on a bridge near the Kremlin. Months earlier, Nemtsov had issued his own report on corruption surrounding the Sochi Olympics. Together with another opposition politician, Leonid Martynyuk, Nemtsov alleged that $25 billion to $30 billion had been stolen in Sochi.

An assassin shot the fifty-five-year-old Nemtsov six times in the back as he walked across the bridge with his twenty-two-year-old girlfriend, Anna Durytska, a fashion model and finalist in the Miss Ukraine Universe pageant of 2018.

Navalny was confined under house arrest at the time and learned the news the next day. He was shattered.

"I'm in such shock that it's hard to even find words," he wrote on his blog. "Boris came here to visit me a couple of days ago, he was as usual energetic, cheerful, full of plans. He charmed the policemen, chatted merrily with them, explained how it was beneficial for them to support the demands of the Spring march, handed out brochures with his report. I can't even imagine not seeing him again.

"This is a terrible tragedy and loss for all of us; Borya was a very good decent person," Navalny wrote, referring to Nemtsov by an affectionate diminutive. "A big, genuine politician and a decent person—this is not so common. My most sincere condolences to his family, relatives, friends, and indeed to everyone. We really lost something that cannot be replaced."

Navalny added that he would not speculate about the killing, but he expressed a desire to pay his last respects. "I hope they will give me the opportunity to get to say goodbye to Boris."

Within hours, however, Navalny felt compelled to share another observation: The Russian security services must have known—immediately—who killed Nemtsov. "A short remark, which I think is important to say now, while the investigation is in 'hot pursuit,' " Navalny wrote.

"For all practical purposes, I rule out that Boris Nemtsov was not under surveillance last night," Navalny wrote.

He had met with Nemtsov at the end of January and they had discussed and agreed to hold a demonstration on March 1 to protest Russia's military intervention in Ukraine. The meeting was not public knowledge, but shortly afterward, a journalist from Tass had called Nemtsov demanding to know what he had agreed with Navalny.

"The key organizers of large opposition rallies / marches are *always* under surveillance the day before. That is, even for those for whom 'in ordinary life' [surveillance] is not carried out," Navalny wrote. "Boris was exactly that kind of key organizer. You can easily see both from his latest recordings and from his public appearances. And of course, we all have seen the publication of operational materials (filming, wiretapping) about Nemtsov many times, showing how tightly he was" watched, Navalny added.

"Based on experience and practice, I cannot allow that last night he could walk towards the Kremlin without prying eyes," Navalny concluded.

Five Chechen men were eventually convicted of Nemtsov's killing, which was supposedly a murder-for-hire scheme, but who ordered the killing was never determined. Nemtsov had recently warned publicly about the strongman Chechen leader, Ramzan Kadyrov, and how he had amassed a personal army. One theory was that Kadyrov ordered the killing, either to be rid of a nagging critic or as a favor to Putin. Another theory was that Kadyrov, who was locked in a rivalry with the Russian special services in Moscow, wanted to show them that he was untouchable.

The protest march that had been intended to denounce Russia's military intervention in Ukraine instead became a procession of mourning. Supporters left piles of flowers on the bridge at the location where Nemtsov was killed.

Nemtsov's murder marked the crossing of a red line in Russian politics that Navalny must have recognized as a threshold moment. Russian politicians who had fallen out of favor, or joined the opposition, were frequently jailed and harassed, but had never been assassinated.

In July 2015, the Russian government took aim at Boris Zimin, Navalny's longtime patron, and his father, Dmitry Zimin.

Their family's charitable foundation, called Dynasty, which had financed numerous scientific and educational projects, was branded a "foreign agent" under the 2012 law intended to stigmatize organizations that received funding from abroad.

In the Zimins' case, Dynasty provided financing for numerous worthy Russian projects, and the money had come from Dmitry Zimin's own work in the Russian telecommunications industry. The authorities said that the law applied because the accounts holding Dynasty's money were located abroad. Boris Zimin was already living outside Russia, and Dmitry Zimin had left the country a month earlier. Instead of accepting the insulting label, they simply closed the foundation.

Navalny's effort to form a democratic coalition with Kasyanov, the former prime minister, fell apart in early 2016. There were numerous and predictable disagreements over candidates and places on party lists. But another major factor was an investigative documentary broadcast by NTV, the Kremlin-connected channel, which obtained secretly recorded video of Kasyanov with Natalya Pelevina, a member of the PARNAS general council who was also Kasyanov's lover.

The documentary showed intimate scenes of Kasyanov, who was married, and Pelevina in bed. But the bigger political damage came from their surreptitiously recorded conversations, in which they trashed other opposition leaders, including Navalny. In the footage, Pelevina described Navalny as "shit" both as a person and as a politician, but she and Kasyanov acknowledged a need to work with him because of his media appeal.

Pelevina also derided Ilya Yashin as "a beast," "complete scum," and "without principles." *Komsomolskaya Pravda*, reporting on the NTV exposé, noted that "the ostentatious solidarity and public unity shown at forums and events" with Navalny "turned out to be pure lies."

The NTV revelations were predictably devastating. Yashin, then a deputy chairman of PARNAS, called for removing Kasyanov from the top slot on the coalition's candidate list for the September 2016 Duma elections. Volkov and others agreed, and demanded that Kasyanov compete in a primary election with other contenders.

In the end, however, it was too big of a breach. In late April 2016, Navalny and Vladimir Milov, still the chairman of Democratic Choice, decided to break with Kasyanov. Around the same time, conspiracy theories were spreading about Navalny as an operative of foreign intelligence services, including MI6 and the CIA.

One report broadcast on Russian state television alleged that Navalny was working in cahoots with Bill Browder, the former head of Hermitage Capital and champion of the Magnitsky Act. Among the preposterous assertions in the report were that Browder, given the code name "Agent Solomon," paid for Navalny to carry out corporate blackmail. It also claimed that Browder and Navalny were part of a CIA operation initiated in 1986—when Navalny was just ten years old—aimed at changing the constitutional systems of countries in Eastern Europe and the Soviet Union.

Harassment by the law enforcement authorities, and violence, also continued.

In mid-May 2016, Navalny and Volkov led staffers of the Anti-corruption Foundation and their families on an outing in Russia's Krasnodar Region. Their group, of parents and children, including Navalny's daughter and son, was accosted upon its arrival at Krasnodar airport. Then, the families were followed on their trip by guys in a jeep, including on segments of their hike through a forest.

Two colonels from the Ministry of Emergency Situations even demanded that Navalny give signed, written assurance that the group would not hold rallies and fireworks in the mountains, according to a summary of the trip that he posted on his blog.

At one point, the bus carrying the group was stopped by the police. The families were detained for about an hour and a half, supposedly as part of a national antiterrorism campaign called Operation Anaconda, aimed at rooting out individuals with ties to the Islamic State.

Finally, while they were trying to fly home from an airport in Anapa, Russia, they were accosted by a group of Cossacks who threw the men, including Navalny, to the ground while kicking, punching, and beating some of them. One of Navalny's associates, Artem Torchinskiy, was hospitalized after being kicked repeatedly in the head and went home with his right eye swollen shut.

"The action was clearly coordinated by the police," Navalny said, adding, "The police no longer just protect the attackers, but work with them."

Navalny likened the situation to Latin America in the 1970s and '80s. "A standard intimidation tactic for authoritarian regimes is to recruit informal but controlled groups to carry out violent actions," he wrote. "No elections and no public outcry will be able to influence this...

"Just take to the streets. We need real solidarity in the face of a semi-fascist state."

* * *

Under the headline "Surely I Should Apologize," Navalny, on his blog on May 5, 2016, offered a remorseful mea culpa about the collapse of the attempted democratic coalition with Kasyanov.

"I apologize to everyone who, from the creation of the democratic coalition a year and a half ago, I promised that everything would be different for us." He had promised candidates would be chosen through competitive primaries, that disputes would be settled by voting, that the strongest nominees, not those favored by party leaders, would be put forward to run.

"Alas, nothing happened," Navalny wrote, adding, "It's a pity... This is my personal defeat as a big supporter of internal elections. A year and a half wasted.

"OK, let's draw conclusions and move on," he wrote. "In general, my position has not changed since 2011: the government will not change as a result of elections."

Navalny linked back to an interview he had given to Yevgenia Albats and *New Times* in 2011, in which he delivered a long discourse that amounted to his same comment after the attack by Cossacks in Anapa: Just take to the streets.

"Power in Russia will not change as a result of elections," Navalny had declared in 2011, predicting that Russia would have its own version of the Arab Spring. "We call it the Tunisian scenario because there is no other name. It is clear that in Russia the scenario will be some other, and no one understands which one. There will be some kind of confrontation between the corrupt elite and the broad masses of the people."

Albats asked if he was just waiting then for the wave to materialize.

"My idea is that we do not know when this moment will happen, but we can bring it closer with all our might," Navalny replied. "They are crooks and thieves. We need to fight them, create problems and stress for them, involve more and more people in creating problems. The more actively we work in this direction, the closer is the moment when everything will change."

Navalny, in 2011, had expressed confidence that change would come, and he allowed that softer change might be possible, as in the 1989 Velvet Revolution in Czechoslovakia.

"One way or another, the regime changed as a result of pressure from broad sections of society on the authorities," he said. "This pressure can be of different intensity: from negotiations to standing on the street and crowds of people who throw officials out of their offices and hang them. And the sooner the government itself, its most far-sighted representatives enter into negotiations, the less likely the scenario becomes in which they will simply be dragged out by the collar. I don't think it's possible with the help of cunning political technology or Twitter to make people take to the streets, chase away thieves and swindlers, and normal people come in their place. The moment will come."

Navalny's belief that Russia's government would only change through upheaval was not the only long-standing view he was clinging to with fervent conviction. He also still insisted that Russia must clamp down on immigration and impose a visa regime on the former Soviet republics in Central Asia.

A few days before Victory Day that year, Russia's security services claimed to have disrupted a plot by "immigrants from Central Asia" to carry out terror attacks during the May holidays. Navalny, however, insisted that the Russian government itself was at fault.

"I just want to make an important correction right away: there is no need for any immigrants from Central Asia to 'penetrate' into the territory of Russia. You just need to buy a ticket on your national passport and board a plane—and you can bring instructions here from ISIS, even from the Nicaraguan Contras," Navalny wrote. "No control, no background checks and connections, no serious questioning, no chance of rejection. Why does it happen that it is so easy to come here from countries neighboring Afghanistan and others with high terrorist risks?"

He answered his own question: "Because a certain V.V. Putin and United Russia in his pocket have long and consistently rejected all proposals to introduce a visa regime with the countries of Central Asia."

Navalny expressed dismay that travelers to Russia from Norway and Finland must obtain a visa but not those from Tajikistan or Uzbekistan. "I don't know what benefits I have from the fact that people from Norway can enter here only with a visa, and from Tajikistan even without a passport," he wrote. "I estimate the probability of penetration of terrorists from Norway as lower. I estimate the probability of importing heroin from Iceland as lower. I assess the probability of a flow of refugees from Luxembourg as lower than in Uzbekistan. Only with Norway, Iceland and Luxembourg do we have barriers and borders, but not with Uzbekistan."

Navalny could certainly boast of consistency in his views. What he did not anticipate, however, was that the visa-free regime with Central Asia would end up allowing hundreds of thousands of Russian men to flee and escape military conscription in the fall of 2022.

Navalny had long said that Putin's true power lay in his genuine political popularity, and that his main weapon was "his ability to bribe the population."

But for all of Navalny's fatalism about the inability to change Russia through elections, he insisted on participating in them and trying to find ways to break the grip of Putin and United Russia at every level, from local municipal councils to the presidency.

In an interview with Nataliya Vasilyeva of the Associated Press, while under house arrest in December 2015, Navalny reiterated his view about the pointlessness of elections in Russia. "The regime in Russia will not change as a result of an election," he said. "In a situation where we are barred even from running, I don't see how it can."

He also said that Putin's claimed approval rating of 84 percent was a lie. "Eighty-four percent means nothing in an authoritarian state. Why can't they allow us to run?" He added, "Many people in Russia simply don't believe that Russia has a future."

In October 2017, the European Court of Human Rights sided with Navalny again, ruling that his rights and those of his brother, Oleg, had been violated in the Yves Rocher embezzlement case. But Russia's Central Election Commission nonetheless ruled that Navalny could not run for office until 2028, a decision affirmed by the Russian Supreme Court. Navalny, furious over the court's decision, tweeted: "We don't recognize elections without competition."

Barred from the ballot, Navalny called for a boycott. The refusal to let him run prompted criticism from the United States. Asked about that criticism, Putin derided Washington for only complaining about one of several would-be candidates who did not meet the qualifications to run.

"The character you mentioned is not the only one who was banned," Putin said at his news conference in December 2017, once again refusing to utter Navalny's name. "For some reason others were not mentioned. This seems to reveal the U.S. administration and other nations' preferences regarding who they would like to promote in Russia's politics and who they would like to see among the country's leadership, if not the leader. And apparently, these are the people they count on, they rely on. And in this case, they gave themselves away, they would have done better if they had kept silent."

Putin went on to win the March 2018 presidential election with 77.5 percent of the vote, defeating a field of mostly tired, systemic opposition candidates, including Grigory Yavlinsky of Yabloko, who Navalny had urged to step aside to make way for young leadership back in 2007.

* * *

In May 2018, Navalny changed the name of his party to Russia of the Future. He and Volkov also advanced their "Smart voting" strategy by launching a website and cell phone app to help voters select the candidates most likely to defeat those running for United Russia.

That system, as well as the network of more than eighty campaign offices that Navalny had opened while campaigning for president, positioned Russia of the Future to make gains in local elections, especially in Moscow in 2019, and in regional elections, as in Novosibirsk and Tomsk after Navalny was poisoned in 2020.

But darker designs were underway in the Kremlin, including planned changes to the Russian Constitution to let Putin be leader for life, and even grimmer plans for the war against Ukraine. There was little patience left for Navalny and his band of aspiring democracy superheroes flying their drones over important officials' country estates and harping about corruption.

In 2019, Putin's regime shifted into a systematic effort to put Navalny and the Anti-corruption Foundation out of business.

A fraud case was opened against Volkov, and he left Russia that summer. In April, a catering company called Moscow Schoolchild reportedly connected to Yevgeny Prigozhin, the founder of the Wagner mercenary group, sued Navalny and his colleague, Lyubov Sobol, for defamation, claiming economic harm. A Navalny investigation had accused the company of serving tainted lunches that set off an outbreak of dysentery among Moscow schoolchildren. Prigozhin, nicknamed "Putin's chef" after earning a fortune off of government catering contracts, denied any connection to the company.

As persecution of Navalny by the Russian courts continued, so did the rebukes of Russia by the European Court of Human Rights. In April, the

Strasbourg court ruled that Navalny's rights were violated when he was put under house arrest. He was awarded €20,000 in damages.

Navalny and his wife strive not to show signs of the stress that his political work puts on their family. And Yulia Navalnaya, in particular, has said she makes it her duty to keep life as normal as possible for their children.

The pressure, however, is omnipresent, and that June it almost boiled over. "I remember... a simple everyday story about our family," Navalnaya later recounted. Their daughter, Darya, was graduating from high school, but on the day of the ceremony, Russian authorities arrested a journalist, Ivan Golunov, after apparently framing him on drug charges. A spontaneous rally was called, and Navalny felt compelled to go.

"Alexey called me, realizing that he was not getting to Dasha's graduation, and said: 'Well, you understand that I can't not go to this rally?'" Navalnaya recalled. "I answered briefly: 'Of course, I understand.'

"It was the only time, in all the years, when I burst into tears after the call," she said. "I felt sorry for both Dasha and my husband, it was very important for our whole family and for the two of them too, because Dasha is 'daddy's daughter.' But he could not do otherwise, and I had no right to dissuade him. Three people were arrested at the rally; one of them is Alexey."

In the end, Navalny was released from the police station in time to get to Dasha's graduation. Photographs showed her in a sparkly silver dress, clutching her diploma, her father in a dark suit and thin red necktie.

That summer of 2019, the Moscow election authorities refused to register a slew of independent candidates for the September City Council elections, citing irregularities with the required signatures they had collected to get on the ballot. Among the rejected candidates were several Navalny associates and allies, including Lyubov Sobol, Ivan Zhdanov, and Ilya Yashin. On July 14, dozens were detained during a protest outside the Election Commission offices in Moscow. Smaller daily protests continued at Moscow's Trubnaya Square until July 20 when a larger rally, estimated at more than twenty thousand people, was held on Sakharov Avenue.

Navalny issued an ultimatum warning of another rally on July 27 if the authorities did not accept the registration of the independent candidates. On July 24, Navalny was detained outside his apartment building and put under arrest for thirty days for calling the unauthorized rally. In between, Navalny and his team had published an investigation showing that Vladimir Solovyov, one of the Kremlin's loudest propagandists on state television, had obtained a permanent residence permit in Italy. On July 27, the day of the protest, more than one thousand people were arrested, including many of the rejected candidates. Their homes and offices were also searched.

In September, despite the effort to stack the ballot, United Russia suffered a stinging defeat, losing fifteen of the forty seats that it had held on the forty-five-member City Council. Three recognized opposition parties—the Communists, A Just Russia, and Yabloko—picked up the seats. United Russia retained a slim majority of twenty-five seats, but it was still a stunning blow. The unexpected losses demonstrated the potential power of Navalny's "Smart voting" strategy even if his own party's candidates were barred from running. In response, the authorities carried out a series of raids against the Anti-corruption Foundation and Navalny's offices across Russia.

In October, a Moscow court ruled in favor of Moscow Schoolchild in the tainted lunches case and ordered Navalny and Sobol to pay $1.15 million for damages.

"So, they poisoned children in schools and kindergartens. Cases of dysentery were proven with documents. But we should pay," Navalny wrote on Instagram. Prigozhin, the mercenary boss, paid the debt to Moscow Schoolchild so that Navalny's penalties would be owed personally to him. Prigozhin later threatened to bankrupt Navalny's operation. "I intend to strip this group of unscrupulous people of their clothes and shoes," he said in a statement. After his statement, the court froze Navalny's bank accounts and put a lien on his apartment.

That same month, in October 2019, the Anti-corruption Foundation was branded as a foreign agent. In July 2020, Navalny announced that he was dissolving the foundation because it could not afford to pay the judgment to Prigozhin, or court-ordered damages in other lawsuits.

"S.O.S. Liquidation of the F.B.K.," the headline on Navalny's blog declared, using the foundation's Russian acronym.

"You know what stores often do, they write in big letters: LIQUIDATION. THE STORE IS CLOSING. LAST SALE," Navalny wrote. "People buy into this publicity stunt, sweep away supposedly discounted goods, but in fact, no one closes. In our case, we really have to say that the non-profit Anti-corruption Foundation, which I founded nine years ago, has come to an end, because it was simply taken away from us."

In his post, Navalny described constant raids, hundreds of searches of his offices nationwide, and the repeated confiscation of equipment, "from phones and laptops to lamps and kettles.

"We were illegally recognized as foreign agents, even though we never received a penny of foreign money," Navalny said. "They fabricated criminal cases against us. Bank accounts of FBK and all other legal entities were frozen. The accounts of hundreds of employees and members of their families were frozen. My accounts were frozen and my father's, mother's, wife's and even those of my children."

The major problem was the giant judgment owed to Prigozhin. Navalny noted with dismay that the verdict was allowed to stand even though Sobol's investigations had proven Prigozhin's company was liable for the dysentery outbreak among schoolchildren, and another court had ordered damages paid to the victims' families.

"Something happened that can only happen in Putin's court," Navalny wrote. "Despite the fact that we have proven poisoning. Despite the fact that Prigozhin paid compensation in court. He sues me, Sobol and FBK, declares that he did not poison anyone, and demands an unthinkable amount from us.

"A separate irony is that having poisoned hundreds of children, he paid them," Navalny wrote, "and we who forced him to pay, must pay him 293 times more."

Navalny said it was clear that he and Sobol would never be able to pay the debt, and would have to live indefinitely with their accounts and assets frozen. "Now the question," he said, "is what to do with the FBK? We already have nothing. Everything was taken from previous searches. And now they will take away both the organization itself and the current account. Our name is dear to us, but, as I have said many times: FBK is not an office or a piece of paper from the Ministry of Justice. FBK is people. It is those who come here to fight corruption and you who support it.

"We will switch to another legal entity, and let Putin and Prigozhin choke on it," he wrote. In 2019, he said, 21,467 people donated to the foundation, and most crucial were the 7,607 who had registered to make monthly donations. He urged them to sign up to donate to the new legal entity.

* * *

Three weeks before Navalny's SOS announcement, the FSB assassins trailed him on vacation to Kaliningrad, where they may have mistakenly poisoned Yulia Navalnaya. A month later, the alleged kill team followed Navalny to Tomsk, according to the *Bellingcat*-led investigation, snuck into his hotel room while he was out for a swim in a local river, and laced his underpants with a chemical weapon.

On the anniversary of Navalny's poisoning, German chancellor Angela Merkel traveled to meet Putin at the Kremlin on her last visit to Russia before retiring in December 2021.

"Of course, we discussed the very depressing situation with Alexey Navalny," Merkel said at a news conference after their meeting. "From our perspective, his sentence and imprisonment in a correctional facility were based on a court ruling that the [European Court of Human Rights] found unobvious and disproportionate. This is unacceptable to us. I once again demanded that the president of Russia release Alexey Navalny and stressed that we would continue to monitor this case."

Putin pushed back hard. "With regard to the subject you just mentioned, he was not convicted for his political activities, but a criminal offense against foreign partners," Putin said in response to a reporter's question. "As far as political activity goes, no one should be using political activity as a front to carry out business projects, which, on top of that, violate the law."

But Putin quickly turned to his classic whataboutism, accusing the United States of squashing protesters from the Occupy Wall Street movement, and France of doing the same with the Yellow Vest demonstrators, who demanded lower taxes and higher minimum wages. Putin also referred to the prosecutions in the United States of people who had breached the U.S. Capitol building seeking to overturn Donald Trump's defeat.

"As for us, our political system is evolving, and all citizens of the Russian Federation have the right to express their opinions on political issues, form political organizations, and participate in elections of all levels," Putin said in comments that defied reality. "However, this must be done within the limits of applicable law and the Constitution. We will do our best to keep the situation in Russia stable and predictable.

"Russia exhausted its limit on revolutions back in the twentieth century," he continued. "We do not want revolutions. What we want is evolutionary development of our society and state. I hope that this will be so. As for the decision of the judicial authorities of the Russian Federation, please treat these decisions with respect. Fighting corruption is critically important, but it should not be used as a tool in a political struggle. We, as well as you, are well aware that this toolkit is used to achieve political goals."

Merkel did not let Putin go unanswered. "I would like to emphasize that we have talked at length about the way we understand political systems and freedoms. I believe that the questions of good governance and fighting corruption are actually entwined."

She added, "Within the European Union we believe in the need to discuss these matters, since there is a genuine link between corruption and political activity, no matter where it takes place. This includes Germany, I believe. Fighting corruption requires independent courts, a free press, as well as non-profit organizations that refuse to play along."

* * *

Navalny himself could not have made the point any plainer. But Putin had long stopped caring about the views of Merkel or any other Western leader. He had outlasted them all.

Russia's brutal invasion of Ukraine in February 2022 showed that even Navalny's darkest warnings about Putin had not anticipated the Russian leader's willingness to wreak death and destruction, and the war quickly distracted from Navalny's fate.

But in April 2022, after the liberation of the Kyiv suburb of Bucha, where Russian forces committed atrocities against the civilian population, Navalny noted that even in Ukraine, the birthplace of his father and paternal grandparents, there were signs of the Kremlin's animosity toward him.

"A passport with the surname Navalny lies next to the dead body on the ground," he wrote in a statement posted by his team on social media. "This is one of the people killed in the Ukrainian village of Bucha. Ilya Ivanovich Navalny. Everything indicates that they killed him because of his last name. That's why his passport was defiantly thrown nearby. A completely innocent person was killed by Putin's executioners (what else can I call them? definitely not 'Russian soldiers') because he is my namesake. Apparently, they hoped he was a relative of mine. I don't know if he is related to me. He is from the same village as my father.

"Maybe he is my relative, but there are generally lots of Navalnys in that village," Navalny continued. "I remember that, as a child, I was amazed when I looked at the monument to those who died in the Great Patriotic War. I'm used to the fact that my last name is rare, but there were several Navalnys in a row there. Well, now there will be another monument in Ukraine to those who died in the war, and the name of Ilya Ivanovich Navalny, born in 1961, will be there among others."

Navalny urged Russians to protest, but most of the political opposition had either been arrested or had fled. Within months, hundreds of thousands more Russians would escape to neighboring countries, seeking to avoid conscription.

"This war was also unleashed by a raving maniac obsessed with some nonsense about geopolitics, history and the structure of the world," Navalny wrote, comparing Putin to Hitler. "This maniac will not stop himself. He, like a drug addict, got hooked on death, war and lies—he needs them to maintain his power. It is now everyone's duty to make at least some, even the smallest contribution to stop this war and remove Putin from power. Protest wherever and however you can. Agitate however you can and whomever you can. Inaction is the worst possible thing. And now its consequence is death."

Just before the first anniversary of Putin's full-scale invasion of Ukraine, Navalny posted a blunt restatement of his opposition to the war in which he called—unequivocally this time—for the respect of Ukraine's internationally recognized border as defined in 1991, which included Crimea. He did not mention the illegally annexed peninsula by name, but he also did not repeat his "bologna sandwich" remark asserting that Crimea would not be returned.

"What are Ukraine's borders? They are the same as Russia's—internationally recognized and defined in 1991," Navalny wrote. "Russia also recognized these borders back then, and it must recognize them today as well. There is nothing to discuss here."

"Almost all borders in the world are more or less accidental and cause someone's discontent," he added. "But in the twenty-first century, we cannot start wars just to redraw them. Otherwise, the world will sink into chaos."

In his post, which he called "15 points from a Russian citizen who wishes the best for his country," Navalny declared that Russia's military defeat was inescapable, and he called for immediately ending the war and withdrawing Russia's troops, for the investigation of war crimes, and for Ukraine to be compensated for damages using Russia's oil and gas revenues.

He blamed the war on Putin and reiterated his call for the reformation of Russia's government as a parliamentary republic, with free elections and an independent judiciary.

Navalny also pushed back on the view, increasingly prevalent in Ukraine, that all Russians harbor imperialist aspirations to subjugate Ukraine and other neighboring countries.

"Are all Russians inherently imperialistic?" Navalny asked. "This is bullshit. For example, Belarus is also involved in the war against Ukraine. Does this mean that the Belarusians also have an imperial mindset? No, they merely also have a dictator in power.

"There will always be people with imperial views in Russia, just like in any other country with historical preconditions for this, but they are far from the majority," he continued. "There is no reason to weep and wail about it. Such people should be defeated in elections, just as both right-wing and left-wing radicals get defeated in developed countries."

Navalny, while blaming Putin, argued that most Russian people do not support the war—a point that is contradicted by public opinion polls, although amid a brutal crackdown on dissent it is hard to know if Russians are sharing honest views. "The real reasons for this war are the political and economic problems within Russia, Putin's desire to hold on to power at any cost, and his obsession with his own historical legacy," Navalny wrote. "He wants to go down in history as 'the conqueror tsar' and 'the collector of lands.'"

Navalny urged that Russia cut its losses as quickly as possible and begin addressing the damage. He reiterated the need to compensate Ukraine. "We have hit rock bottom, and in order to resurface, we need to bounce back from it," he wrote. "This would be ethically correct, rational, and profitable. We need to dismantle the Putin regime and its dictatorship, ideally through conducting general free elections and convening a constitutional assembly. We need to establish a parliamentary republic based on the alternation of power through fair elections, independent courts, federalism, local self-governance, complete economic freedom, and social justice."

He concluded: "Recognizing our history and traditions, we must be part of Europe and follow the European path of development. We have no other choice, nor do we need any." Since February 20, 2023, the post has been pinned to the top of Navalny's Twitter feed, which as of this writing has 2.9 million followers.

* * *

In March 2023, the movie that Navalny and his team helped make about his poisoning, filmed during his recovery in Germany, won the Oscar for best documentary.

Yulia Navalnaya and her children, Dasha and Zakhar, joined the filmmakers onstage to accept the golden statue, along with the *Bellingcat* journalist, Christo Grozev, and the head of the Anti-corruption Foundation's investigative unit, Maria Pevchikh.

"To the Navalny family, Yulia, Dasha and Zakhar, thank you for your courage. The world is with you," the film's director, Daniel Roher, said. "And there is one person who couldn't be with us here tonight. Alexey Navalny, the leader of the Russian opposition, remains in solitary confinement... I would like to dedicate this award to Navalny, to all political prisoners around the world. Alexey, the world has not forgotten your vital message to us all. We cannot, we must not be afraid, to oppose dictators and authoritarianism wherever it rears its head."

Roher asked Yulia Navalnaya to come to the podium. "Thank you, Daniel, and thank you to every- everybody here," she said in halting but perfect English. "My husband is in prison just for telling the truth. My husband is in prison just for defending democracy. Alexey, I am dreaming of the day when you will be free, and our country will be free. Stay strong, my love. Thank you." In June 2023, Navalny was put on trial on new charges, of extremism and running an extremist organization, the Anti-corruption Foundation.

But when Navalny appeared for a hearing, emerging from the prison colony in which he was cut off from the outside world and denied access to any news, he was shocked to discover that the Wagner mercenary boss, Yevgeny Prigozhin, had led a rebellion, in which he briefly sent a column of fighters rolling toward Moscow.

In a Twitter thread, posted by his team on June 27, Navalny described being thunderstruck at the news that Russia had briefly faced the prospect of a civil war. But he was even more astounded that Putin had cut a deal to drop insurgency charges against Prigozhin and allow him to leave Russia for Belarus.

Navalny, whose only crime had been working to expose corruption and pleading for a chance to run in a free and fair election, was on trial for extremism charges. And the murderous warlord Prigozhin, "Putin's Chef" because he became a billionaire off of government contracts, would face no criminal charges despite having led a mutiny in which more than a dozen Russian soldiers were killed.

"The prosecutor came in and we continued the trial in which I stand accused of forming an organization to overthrow President Putin by violent means," Navalny wrote.

"While listening to these accusations, I looked at the photo of a roadblock with a grenade launcher in Moscow's Yasenevo district," Navalny tweeted, adding: "I read about how one group of Russian troops 'took positions on the Oka River' to defend themselves against another group of Russian troops.

"There is no greater threat to Russia than the Putin regime," Navalny wrote. "It wasn't the West or the opposition that shot down Russian helicopters over Russia. It wasn't the [Anti-corruption Foundation] that brought Russia to the brink of civil war." He added: "It was Putin who personally did this."

Prigozhin, of course, had been behind the lawsuits that bankrupted the Anti-corruption Foundation, and as an ally of Putin he was the beneficiary of years of favoritism.

Now, however, he had turned against the Kremlin. Decades of corruption and malfeasance, and the strains of a brutal war in Ukraine, had combined to confront Putin with the greatest threat of his twenty-three years in power. But after the failed mutiny, Putin was still in charge, and Navalny was still on trial.

In his defendant's "last word" for the extremism trial, on July 20 2023,

Navalny noted that no justice could be achieved in a Russian court, and he said that the authorities were even trying to deny the right for his statement to be heard by ordering a closed trial.

"Nevertheless," he said, "I must take every opportunity to speak out, and speaking now before an audience of eighteen people, seven of which are wearing black masks on their heads that cover their faces, I wish not only to explain why I continue to fight the unscrupulous evil that calls itself 'the state authorities of the Russian Federation,' but also to urge you to do so along with me."

"The question of how to act is the central question of humanity," Navalny said, adding: "People have searched high and low for the formula of doing the right thing, for something to base the right decisions on. I really like the wording of our compatriot, the doctor of philological sciences Professor Yuri Lotman. Speaking to students, he once said: 'A man always finds himself in an unforeseeable situation. And then he has two legs to rest on: conscience and intellect.' "

"I love Russia," Navalny said. "My intellect tells me that living in a free and prosperous country is better than living in a corrupt and destitute one. And as I stand here looking at this court, my conscience tells me that there will be no justice in such a court for me or anyone else. A country without fair courts will never be prosperous. So my intellect raises its voice again and says it would be wise and right for me to fight for an independent court, for fair elections, and against corruption, because then I would reach my goal and be able to live in my free, prosperous Russia."

"It may seem to you now that I am crazy, but you are all normal—after all, one cannot swim against the current," he added. "But in my opinion, it's you who are crazy. You have one God-given life, and this is what you choose to spend it on? Putting robes on your shoulders and black masks on your heads to protect those who rob you? To help someone who already has ten palaces to build an eleventh?"

Navalny said that not everyone has to go to prison, but he urged all Russians "to make some kind of sacrifice, some kind of effort."

Navalny's speech was unlike others he had given—not the closing argument of a defendant but the potential last word of a dissident, demanding freedom and other ideals for his nation. His imprisonment was "a lottery," he said, "and that ticket has been drawn for me."

He concluded: "I am accused of inciting hatred against representatives of the government and security services, judges, and members of the United Russia Party. But no, I am not inciting hatred. I merely remember that every person has two legs: conscience and intellect."

Navalny was convicted of the extremism charges and on August 4, 2023, was sentenced to an additional nineteen years—this time in a "special regime" prison colony, which would bar him from family visits and even letters for a decade. That sentence, if he survives it, could keep Navalny locked up until he is seventy-four years old; Putin would be ninety-eight.

"Navalny got horror," Sergei Markov, a former close adviser to Putin and still a strong supporter of the Russian president, posted on Telegram after the sentence was announced. "Isn't that too much? Why these cruelties? Why can't Navalny see his wife? He's not a killer."

Navalny's torture, however, was underway well before his latest sentencing.

In July 2023, Navalny's family announced a lawsuit against the penal colony where he was being held, saying his rights as a prisoner were being violated. In the previous year, they said, Navalny had not been allowed any family visits, and only two phone calls, eleven months earlier.

In a social media post after the August 4 sentencing, Navalny wrote: "I perfectly understand that, like many political prisoners, I am sitting on a life sentence, where life is measured by the term of my life or the term of life of this regime."

Navalny urged Russians to resist the regime, which he called a "gang of traitors, thieves, and scoundrels." He added: "Putin must not achieve his goal."

And in a blog post published a week after the sentencing, Navalny finally seemed to accept his status as a dissident. Navalny said that in his isolation cell, or SHIZO, he had been reading Natan Sharansky's book

Fear no Evil, which describes how Sharansky, too, was held in solitary confinement while imprisoned from 1977 to 1986.

"While reading his book, I sometimes shake my head to get rid of the feeling that I am reading my personal file," Navalny wrote in his post, and he called again for Russians to fight corruption and demand democracy: "So that no one in 2055 will be reading Sharansky's book in the SHIZO, thinking: *Wow, it's just like me.*"

* * *

In 2011, before the street protests that made him famous, before the campaigns for mayor and for president, before the endless arrests, the poisoning attempts and the green dye thrown in his face, Navalny had told his political mentor, Yevgenia Albats, that he was prepared for a long struggle. He said that he did not expect Russia would ever change as a result of elections. He was honest about his ambitions but measured in his expectations. Change would come, he said, but it was unclear when.

"It would be foolish to say that I want to investigate a little here, to catch a few corrupt officials by the hand, but politics does not interest me," Navalny said. "It would be obvious to everyone that I am: a) flirting, b) lying, or I'm just a fool. Because if you are seriously fighting corruption in Russia, you cannot fail to understand that it is impossible to defeat it without serious political changes. It cannot be defeated without the possession of levers of power. This is obvious to all reasonable people, and I'm not going to fool anyone."

Albats, addressing him affectionately, asked: "Alyosh, do you believe there will be light at the end of the tunnel?"

"Maybe it sounds ridiculous and naïve, but I believe in the victory of good over evil," Navalny said. "That is, I believe that the obvious injustice that is happening, the obvious stupidity, nonsense—they will end. Because people understand what is good and what is bad."

NOTES and WORKS CONSULTED

As a news-driven, unauthorized biography, this book owes much to contemporaneous news accounts by Russian and international journalists who have covered Alexey Navalny and his rise as Russia's leading political opposition figure, and to the author's own reporting, including as a Moscow-based correspondent for the *New York Times* from 2011 to 2015.

The book also relied to the greatest extent possible on primary source audio and video, including Navalny's many public appearances, court proceedings, radio and television interviews, and Navalny's own words in his LiveJournal blog, as well as on social media and in the video investigations produced by his Anti-corruption Foundation.

Two nonjournalistic works provided essential insights into Navalny's thinking. These were an early biography, *Threat to Crooks and Thieves*, written by Konstantin Voronkov, a friend and colleague of Navalny's, published in Russia in 2012, and *Opposing Forces: Plotting the New Russia*, a compilation of conversations between Navalny and Polish historian Adam Michnik, published in 2015.

Introduction

"The Trial of Navalny. Online," *Insider*, February 2, 2021. https://theins.ru/politika/239043.

Chapter 1. Poisoning

Dasha Veledeeva, "Yulia Navalnaya: 'If Everything Is Great Today, Then I Am Already Happy. Because Tomorrow Everything Can Definitely Change, and I Will Be Very Disappointed,'" *Symbol*, February 17, 2021. https://www.thesymbol.ru/heroes/the

-symbol/yuliya-navalnaya-svoyu-glavnuyu-zadachu-ya-vizhu-v-tom-chtoby-u-nas-v-seme-nichego-ne-izmenilos-deti-byli-detmi-a-dom-domom/.

"Navalny Was Urgently Hospitalized with Poisoning in Omsk," *Taiga.info*, August 20, 2020. https://tayga.info/158458.

Svetlana Reiter, "Navalny's Team Reveals Hotel Room Search That Uncovered Water Bottle with Traces of Novichok-Type Poison": *Meduza*, September 17, 2020. https://meduza.io/en/feature/2020/09/17/navalny-s-team-reveals-hotel-room-search-that-uncovered-water-bottle-with-traces-of-novichok-type-poison.

Marcel Rosenbach, "Suddenly the Ones in the Gray Suits Gave the Diagnosis," *Der Spiegel*, August 21, 2020. https://www.spiegel.de/ausland/alexej-nawalny-vertrauter-wolkow-auf-einmal-gaben-diejenigen-in-den-grauen-anzuegen-die-diagnose-vor-a-71cb3878-b073-4c9f-8f70-3a9242e0a42b.

Farida Rustamova, "Navalny Ended Up in Intensive Care in a Serious Condition When He Was Returning from Siberia. What Was He Doing There?" *Meduza*, August 20, 2020. https://meduza.io/feature/2020/08/20/vo-vremya-poezdki-v-sibir-navalnyy-popal-v-reanimatsiyu-v-tyazhelom-sostoyanii-a-chto-on-tam-delal.

Irina Kravtsova, "'He Needs to Be Evacuated to Europe': Interview with Yaroslav Ashikhmin, Alexey Navalny's Doctor, About His Poisoning in Siberia, Possible Causes and Necessary Treatment," *Meduza*, August 20, 2020. https://meduza.io/feature/2020/08/20/ego-nuzhno-evakuirovat-v-evropu.

"A Day and a Half in a Coma: Online Broadcast About Alexey Navalny in BSMP-1," *NGS55online.ru*, August 20, 2020. https://ngs55.ru/text/incidents/2020/08/20/69430861.

Sabine Siebold, Anton Zverev, Catherine Belton, and Andrew Osborn, "Special Report: In Germany's Black Forest, Putin Critic Navalny Gathered Strength and Resolve," Reuters, February 25, 2021. https://www.reuters.com/article/russia-politics-navalny-germany-specialr-idUSKBN2AP1BH.

"The Chief Omsk Toxicologist Linked Navalny's Hospitalization to His Diet," *Kommersant*, September 4, 2020. https://www.kommersant.ru/doc/4477083.

"Novichok Trolling," *Kommersant*, September 3, 2020. https://www.kommersant.ru/doc/4476810.

Christo Grozev, Pieter van Huis, Aric Toler, and Yordan Tsalov, "FSB Team of Chemical Weapon Experts Implicated in Alexey Navalny Novichok Poisoning," *Bellingcat*, December 14, 2020. https://www.bellingcat.com/news/uk-and-europe/2020/12/14/fsb-team-of-chemical-weapon-experts-implicated-in-alexey-navalny-novichok-poisoning/.

Anna Pushkarskaya, Elena Berdnikova, Timur Sazonov, Andrey Soshnikov, and Ksenia Churmanova, "Who Saved Navalny's Life, and How, in the First Two Hours," BBC News Russian Service, September 2, 2020. https://www.bbc.com/russian/features-54002575.

Victoria Chumakova, "Navalny's Entire Route Tracked Before the Poisoning: He Swam," *Moskovsky Komsomolets*, August 21, 2020. https://www.mk.ru/incident/2020/08/21/otslezhen-ves-marshrut-navalnogo-pered-otravleniem-on-kupalsya.html.

Robyn Dixon, "Inside Room 239: How Alexei Navalny's Aides Got Crucial Poisoning Evidence out of Russia," *Washington Post*, October 4, 2020. https://www.washington

post.com/world/europe/russia-navalny-hotel-poisoning/2020/10/03/b70392b4-034a-11eb-b92e-029676f9ebec_story.html.

Eric Campbell and Matt Henry, "Maria Pevchikh: The Young Investigator Uncovering 'the Hidden World of Vladimir Putin,'" ABC News Australia, February 15, 2021. https://www.abc.net.au/news/2021-02-16/maria-pevchikh-vladimir-putin-alexei-navalny/13150492.

"'If It Hadn't Been for the Prompt Work of the Medics': FSB Officer Inadvertently Confesses Murder Plot to Navalny," *Bellingcat*, December 21, 2020. https://www.bellingcat.com/news/uk-and-europe/2020/12/21/if-it-hadnt-been-for-the-prompt-work-of-the-medics-fsb-officer-inadvertently-confesses-murder-plot-to-navalny/.

Chapter 2. Navalny vs. Putin

Leonid Parfenov, "Yulia Navalnaya: 'The Children Know Where Dad Is When They Imprison Him,'" TV Rain, April 14, 2013. https://tvrain.tv/teleshow/parfenov/julija_navalnaja_deti_znajut_gde_papa_kogda_ego_sa-341087/.

"Alexey Navalny, About Crooks and Thieves, Mushrooms and Shwarma, Black Grouse and Nationalism," *Esquire* (Russia), December 2011. https://www.buro247.ru/beauty/3883.html.

David M. Herszenhorn, "Putin Says Russia Could Have 'Finished' Navalny," *Politico* Europe, December 17, 2020. https://www.politico.eu/article/vladimir-putin-says-russia-could-have-finished-alexei-navalny/.

Aleksey Navalny and Adam Michnik, *Opposing Forces: Plotting the New Russia* (Moscow: Novoe Izdateltsvo), 2015.

Chapter 3. Revenge

"Medvedev Against Corruption," *Vzglyad*, May 19, 2008. https://vz.ru/politics/2008/5/19/169261.html.

Roman Anin, "Presidencies: For Whom Is the 'Gift' on the Bolshoi Utrish? Following the 'Putin's Palace,' We Decided to Study the Objects That Are Associated with President Medvedev," *Novaya Gazeta*, February 15, 2011. https://web.archive.org/web/20120414191448/http://www.novayagazeta.ru/inquests/7094.html.

Scott Shane, "From Success at Putin's Side to Exposing Corruption," *New York Times*, February 3, 2012. https://www.nytimes.com/2012/02/04/world/europe/sergei-kolesnikov-aims-to-expose-corruption-of-putin-era.html.

Matt Bivens, "Rybkin Affair Is No Laughing Matter," *Moscow Times*, February 16, 2004. https://www.themoscowtimes.com/archive/rybkin-affair-is-no-laughing-matter.

Yevgenia Albats, "Clean, Concrete Candidate (Audio Files Added)," *New Times*, February 27, 2012. https://newtimes.ru/articles/detail/50206.

Viktor Feshchenko, "Riding a Hype: What's Under the Hood of Alexei Navalny's Media Machine," *Firm's Secret*, September 22, 2017. https://secretmag.ru/navalnyi/.

"The Head of the National Guard, Zolotov, Challenged Navalny to a Duel. And Did It Against All Dueling Rules," *Meduza*, September 11, 2018. https://meduza.io

/feature/2018/09/11/glava-rosgvardii-zolotov-vyzval-navalnogo-na-duel-i-sdelal-eto-protiv-vseh-duelnyh-pravil.

Andrew Roth, "Russian Officials Appropriating Jets for Family and Lovers, Says Activist," *Guardian*, December 4, 2019. https://www.theguardian.com/world/2019/dec/04/russian-officials-appropriating-jets-for-family-and-lovers-says-activist.

Pyotr Mironenko and Irina Pankratova, "Patriarch Kirill Used the Company's Business Jet from Navalny's Investigation," *Bell*, December 26, 2019. https://thebell.io/patriarh-kirill-polzovalsya-biznes-dzhetom-kompanii-iz-rassledovaniya-navalnogo.

Chapter 4. Early Years

Vitaly Chervonenko and Tatiana Yanutsevich, "Navalnys' Village. What Ukrainian Compatriots and Relatives Say About Putin's Main Enemy," BBC News Ukraine, February 4, 2021. https://www.bbc.com/ukrainian/features-russian-55922932.

Irina Guk, "Chernobyl Childhood of Alexei Navalny," *Vesti*, October 17, 2013. https://vesti.ua/strana/21302-ukrainskie-rodstvenniki-navalnogo-rasskazali-o-ego-mestnyh-kornja.

Dmitry Sokolov and Zyubov Pavel, "Butyn as a Mirror of Russia: Navalny's Native Village Is Mired in Poverty and Corruption," *Sobsednik*, June 4, 2020. https://sobesednik.ru/politika/20200603-butyn-kak-zerkalo-rossii-rodno.

Yevgenia Albats, "Enemy No. 1: Interview with the Mother of Alexey Navalny," *New Times*, April 22, 2013. https://newtimes.ru/articles/detail/65807/.

Lesley Stahl, "The Man Trying to Beat Putin," CBS News, July 29, 2019. https://www.cbsnews.com/news/alexey-navalny-the-man-trying-to-beat-putin-60-minutes-2019-07-29/.

Konstantin Voronkov, *Threat to Crooks and Thieves* (Moscow: Eksmo, 2012).

Oleg Bocharov, "The Story of One Photo: Schwarzenegger Meets His Idol Yuri Vlasov, 1988," *Maxim*, April 24, 2022. https://www.maximonline.ru/longreads/istoriya-odnoi-fotografii-shvarcenegger-vstrechaet-svoego-kumira-yuriya-vlasova-1988-id727832/.

Simon Shuster, "Can Crusading Blogger Alexei Navalny Save Russia?" *Time*, January 23, 2012. https://content.time.com/time/subscriber/article/0,33009,2104221,00.html.

Simon Shuster, "The Anti-Putin Movement: An Interview with the Blogger in Chief," *Time*, January 18, 2012. https://content.time.com/time/world/article/0,8599,2104445,00.html.

Julia Ioffe, "'These Bastards Will Never See Our Tears': How Yulia Navalnaya Became Russia's Real First Lady," *Vanity Fair*, July 8, 2021. https://www.vanityfair.com/news/2021/07/how-yulia-navalnaya-became-russias-real-first-lady.

Irina Mokrousova and Irina Reznik, "How Alexei Navalny Earns a Living," *Vedomosti*, February 13, 2012. https://www.vedomosti.ru/library/articles/2012/02/13/pesnya_o_blogere#ixzz1mLIgNsyq.

Chapter 5. Making of a Politician

"The Committee for the Protection of Muscovites agreed with Don-Stroy," *Rosbalt*, November 4, 2004. https://www.rosbalt.ru/main/2004/11/04/184071.html.

"New Politics: Who Is Navalny?" *Afisha*, February 27, 2012. https://daily.afisha.ru/archive/gorod/archive/new-politics-navalny/.

Julia Gutova, "Navalny, Who Are You?!" *Russian Reporter*, March 10, 2011. https://expert.ru/russian_reporter/2011/09/navalnyij--tyi-kto_i/.

Olga Khvostunova, "Who Is Mr. Navalny?," Institute of Modern Russia, January 18, 2012. https://imrussia.org/en/politics/183-who-is-mr-navalny.

Julia Ioffe, "Net Impact: One Man's Cyber Crusade Against Russian Corruption," *New Yorker*, March 28, 2011. https://www.newyorker.com/magazine/2011/04/04/net-impact.

Yulia Ignatyeva, "College Students Kicked Out of the Center," *Izvestia*, September 28, 2006. https://web.archive.org/web/20071011202544/http:/www.izvestia.ru/moscow/article3097073/.

Rimma Polyak, "LJ Conquers Space," Russian Nights, Russian Journal, November 4, 2006. https://web.archive.org/web/20061104083143/http:/nights.russ.ru/events/111722334.

Rimma Polyak, "Debates—Yes?" Russian Nights, Russian Journal, November 30, 2007. https://web.archive.org/web/20071130033925/http:/nights.russ.ru/events/115959746.

Roman Ukolov, "Dispute with Scuffle and Shooting," *Nezavisimaya Gazeta*, November 1, 2007. https://www.ng.ru/events/2007-11-01/7_disput.html.

" 'I Shot the Whole Clip': How Navalny Managed to Avoid Responsibility for a Fight with a Weapon in 2007," RT in Russian, August 11, 2020. https://russian.rt.com/russia/article/771393-navalnyi-klub-draka-strelba-delo.

Masha Gessen, "The Evolution of Alexey Navalny's Nationalism," *New Yorker*, February 15, 2021. https://www.newyorker.com/news/our-columnists/the-evolution-of-alexey-navalnys-nationalism.

" 'Political Nationalists' Signed a Cooperation Pact," *Grani.ru*, June 8, 2008. https://graniru.org/Politics/Russia/Parties/m.137589.html.

Chapter 6. Anti-corruption Crusader

Peter Carlson, "The Stock Character," *Washington Post*, April 20, 2003. https://www.washingtonpost.com/archive/lifestyle/2003/04/20/the-stock-character/f03271e1-74ee-4cad-918e-c18ef7d0f2d9/.

"Wanted: Minority Shareholders of Surgutneftegaz Want to Know Its Real Owners," *Izbrannoe*, May 4, 2008. https://web.archive.org/web/20101129073921/http://www.izbrannoe.ru/34843.html.

Elena Mazneva and Irina Malkova, "Bogdanov Does Not Know the Owners of Surgut," *Vedomosti*, April 30, 2008. https://www.vedomosti.ru/library/articles/2008/04/30/bogdanov-ne-znaet-hozyaev-surguta.

"Rebellion of Surgutneftegaz Minority Shareholders: At the Annual Meeting of Shareholders They Asked Bogdanov Several Uncomfortable Questions," *Ura.ru*, May 05, 2008. https://ura.news/news/38110.

Svetlana Ivanova, Vera Surzhenko, and Ekaterina Derbilova, "Billions Out of Control," *Vedomosti*, March 24, 2008. https://www.vedomosti.ru/newspaper/articles/2008/03/24/beskontrolnye-milliardy.

Elena Mazneya and Alexey Nikolsky, "Gas Arithmetic," *Vedomosti*, December 24, 2008. https://www.vedomosti.ru/newspaper/articles/2008/12/24/gazovaya-arifmetika.

Richard L. Cassin, "Moscow Activist Questions International Auditors," *FCPA Blog*, December 28, 2010. https://fcpablog.com/2010/12/28/moscow-activist-questions-international-auditors/.

Miriam Elder, "Russia's Chief Whistleblower Wants to Jail the Corrupt," *Guardian*, February 23, 2011. https://www.theguardian.com/world/2011/feb/23/russia-whistleblower-corruption.

"Navalny Published Part of the Classified Report on the 'Sawing' in Transneft," *Lenta.ru*, November 16, 2010. https://lenta.ru/news/2010/11/16/transneft/.

Alexei Navalny and Maxim Trudolyubov, "Russian Journalists Need Help in Exposing Corruption," *Nieman Reports*, April 20, 2011. https://niemanreports.org/articles/russian-journalists-need-help-in-exposing-corruption-2/.

Andrew Roth, "Russian Court Outlaws Alexei Navalny's Organisation," *Guardian*, June 9, 2021. https://www.theguardian.com/world/2021/jun/09/russian-court-expected-to-outlaw-alexei-navalnys-organisation.

Yulia Kalinina, "Blog Will Punish: Well-Known Anti-corruption Fighter Alexei Navalny: 'The Fight Against Crooks and Thieves Is My Political Campaign, My Struggle for Power,'" *Moskovsky Komsomolets*, June 9, 2011. https://www.mk.ru/politics/2011/06/09/596335-blog-nakazhet.html.

Chapter 7. Blogger, Street Fighter, Politician

Ksenia Veretennikova, "Internet and Samizdat: The Opposition Discussed Its Future in Federal Election Campaigns," *Vremya*, June 17, 2010. http://www.vremya.ru/2010/103/4/256034.html.

Maksim Ivanov, "Democrats Consulted But Did Not Agree," *Kommersant*, June 16, 2010. https://www.kommersant.ru/doc/1387124.

Pavel Sheremet and Olga Filina, "On a Closed Circle of Questions," *Spark Magazine*, *Kommersant*, June 21, 2010. https://www.kommersant.ru/doc/1386111.

Konstantin Sonin, "The Kuzimov vs. Navalny Debate," *Moscow Times*, March 23, 2011. https://www.themoscowtimes.com/2011/03/23/the-kuzminov-vs-navalny-debate-a5830.

Dmytry Lanin, "Blogger Navalny and Rector Kuzminov Did Not Hear Each Other," *BFM.ru*, March 19, 2011. https://www.bfm.ru/news/132567.

Natalia Raibman, "Navalny Wants to Become President," *Vedomosti*, April 15, 2013. https://www.vedomosti.ru/politics/articles/2013/04/05/navalnyj_hochet_stat_prezidentom.

Anastasia Kornya, Olga Churakova, and Roman Shleynov, "Navalny's Investigation into the Business of the Sons of the Prosecutor General Is Not Yet of Interest to the Authorities," *Vedomosti*, December 2, 2015. https://www.vedomosti.ru/politics/articles/2015/12/03/619391-genprokurora-vlast-ne-interesuet.

"Chaika Called the Revelations of the Anti-corruption Foundation Made-to-Order and False," Interfax, December 3, 2015. https://www.interfax.ru/russia/482923.

"Elections of the Mayor of Moscow," *Gazeta.ru*, October 8, 2010. https://www.gazeta.ru/politics/2010/10/07_a_3426748.shtml.

Elena Ovchinnikova, "FSB Loves from Behind," *Vyatsky Observer*, January 14, 2010. https://web.archive.org/web/20100117185759/http://www.nabludatel.ru/numers/2010/3/36.htm.

Olga Kuzmenkova, "'Then It Screamed from the Heart': How Alexei Navalny Did Not Want to Go to Chistye Prudy, and Ksenia Sobchak Decided to Perform on Sakharov Avenue," *Gazeta.ru*, December 5, 2012. https://www.gazeta.ru/politics/2012/12/04_a_4878797.shtml.

Zoya Svetova, "We Are All Deprived of Liberty Completely Illegally," *New Times*, December 12, 2011. https://newtimes.ru/articles/detail/47446.

Vladimir Antipin, "Weirdo with the Letter W," *Russian Reporter*, February 4, 2010. https://expert.ru/russian_reporter/2010/04/volkov/.

Pavel Sergeev, "Leonid Volkov: Biography, Politics and Personal Life of Navalny's Ally," *Anews*, February 5, 2021. https://web.archive.org/web/20210205132646/https://anews.com/136480937-leonid-volkov-biografija-politika-i-lichnaja-zhizny-soratnika-navalynogo.html.

Chapter 8. Prosecution, Persecution, Prison

"Votinov was Taken into Custody Right in the Courtroom," *Newsler.ru*, May 17, 2012. https://www.newsler.ru/incidents/2012/05/17/votinov17.

"Another Adviser to Nikita Belykh Is Suspected of Fraud," *Newsler.ru*, June 3, 2010. https://www.newsler.ru/incidents/2010/06/03/navalny.

Oleg Suchkov, "Unsanitary Forest," *Vek*, June 3, 2010. https://wek.ru/antisanitar-lesa.

Igor Degtyarev, "Adviser to the Governor of the Kirov Region May Be Involved in a Criminal Case on the Fact of Fraud," *Rossiyskaya Gazeta*, June 11, 2010. https://rg.ru/2010/06/11/sovetn-gubern.html.

Mikhail Agafonov, "Alexey Navalny's Fraud Case Reached the UPC," *Marker*, December 9, 2010. https://web.archive.org/web/20140904085727/http:/marker.ru/news/2902.

"Nikita Belykh Called Accusations Against Navalny 'Ridiculous,'" *Newsler.ru*, December 10, 2010. https://www.newsler.ru/politics/2010/12/10/navalny041.

David M. Herszenhorn, "Putin Critic Gets 5-Year Jail Term, Setting Off Protests," *New York Times*, July 18, 2013. https://www.nytimes.com/2013/07/19/world/europe/russian-court-convicts-opposition-leader-aleksei-navalny.html.

David M. Herszenhorn, "Aleksei Navalny, Putin Critic, Is Spared Prison in a Fraud Case, but His Brother Is Jailed," *New York Times*, December 30, 2014. https://www.nytimes.com/2014/12/31/world/europe/aleksei-navalny-convicted.html.

Yulia Chernukhina, "The Man Who Announced the Verdict on Navalny," *New Times*, April 15, 2013. https://newtimes.ru/articles/detail/65311/.

Mikhail Rubin, Olga Churakova, and Roman Badanin, "Enemy Number One: The Story of How the Authorities Are Fighting with Alexei Navalny," *Proekt*, August 24, 2020. https://www.proekt.media/narrative/kreml-protiv-navalnogo/.

Evgeny Feldman and Ivan Zhilin, "The Court Changed Navalny and Ofitserov's Punishment from Real to Suspended (Chronicle)," *Novaya Gazeta*, October 16, 2013. https://web.archive.org/web/20131018235427/http:/www.novayagazeta.ru/news/132691.html.

Chapter 9. Mayoral Candidate, Statesman

"Navalny Prepared a Truckload of Complaints About Election Violations," *Lenta.ru*, September 11, 2013. https://lenta.ru/news/2013/09/11/claim/.

Ekaterina Vinokurova, "Navalny Will Add Legitimacy to the Elections," *Gazeta.ru*, July 10, 2013. https://www.gazeta.ru/politics/2013/07/09_a_5419993.shtml?updated.

Ekaterina Vinokurova, "Navalny Collected Signatures Without Asking," *Gazeta.ru*, July 8, 2013. https://www.gazeta.ru/politics/2013/07/08_a_5417225.shtml?updated.

"Sobyanin Resigns to Participate in New Elections," BBC News Russian Service, June 4, 2013. https://www.bbc.com/russian/international/2013/06/130604_moscow_sobyanin_resigns.

Eduard Limonov, "Your Lyosha," *Svobodnaya Pressa*, October 4, 2012. https://svpressa.ru/society/article/59369/.

"Navalny Launches Campaign Platform, Promises 'Wonderful Future' for Russia," *Moscow Times*, December 14, 2017. https://www.themoscowtimes.com/2017/12/14/navalny-campaign-promises-wonderful-future-russia-a59935.

Chapter 10. Prisoner

Arkady Ostrovsky, "'I've Mortally Offended Putin by Surviving': Why Alexei Navalny Keeps Fighting," *1843 Magazine*, *Economist*, May 2, 2012. https://www.economist.com/1843/2021/05/02/ive-mortally-offended-putin-by-surviving-why-alexei-navalny-keeps-fighting.

Masha Gessen, "Why Alexey Navalny Returned to Russia," *New Yorker*, April 13, 2021. https://www.newyorker.com/news/our-columnists/why-alexey-navalny-returned-to-russia.

Daria Garmonenko, "The Kremlin Will Have Time to Prepare for the Return of Navalny," *Nezavisimaya Gazeta*, January 13, 2021. https://www.ng.ru/politics/2021-01-13/1_8055_politics1.html.

Max Seddon, "Alexei Navalny Protests Breathe New Life into Anti-Putin Feeling," *Financial Times*, January 29, 2021. https://www.ft.com/content/c2a8c193-6243-41d8-b53b-b7854d5af8f2.

"Plane with Navalny Redirected from Vnukovo to Sheremetyevo," *Kommersant*, January 17, 2021. https://www.kommersant.ru/doc/4652414.

Masha Gessen, "Alexey Navalny Has the Proof of His Poisoning," *New Yorker*, October 18, 2020. https://www.newyorker.com/culture/the-new-yorker-interview/alexey-navalny-has-the-proof-of-his-poisoning.

Andrew Roth, "Kremlin Could Try to Keep Navalny Locked Away for Years," *Guardian*, January 17, 2021. https://www.theguardian.com/world/2021/jan/17/kremlin-try-keep-alexei-navalny-locked-away-years-vladimir-putin.

Andrew E. Kramer, "In First Interview from Jail, an Upbeat Navalny Discusses Prison Life," *New York Times*, August 25, 2021. https://www.nytimes.com/2021/08/25/world/europe/navalny-jail-prison.html.

"What Is Known About the Colony Where Alexei Navalny Was Taken," *Kommersant*, June 14, 2022. https://www.kommersant.ru/doc/5410316.

Maria Starikova, "The Food Is Better Than in IK-2," *Kommersant*, January 18, 2023. https://www.kommersant.ru/doc/5774185.

Denis Telmanov, " 'I Am a Threat to US National Security': Butina About Foreign Agents, Navalny and Barbie Dolls," *Gazeta.ru*, December 20, 2021. https://www.gazeta.ru/politics/2021/12/19_a_14332765.shtml.

Alexey Navalny, "Alexei Navalny: This Is What a Post-Putin Russia Should Look Like," *Washington Post*, September 30, 2022. https://www.washingtonpost.com/opinions/2022/09/30/alexei-navalny-parliamentary-republic-russia-ukraine/.

Chapter 11. Last Word

"The Speed of Obtaining Navalny's Passport Turned Out to Be Amazing," *Moskovsky Komsomolets*, May 8, 2017. https://www.mk.ru/politics/2017/05/08/skorost-polucheniya-navalnym-zagranpasporta-okazalas-izumitelnoy.html.

Sergey Polosatov, "Kasyanov and His Mistress Shook The Dirty Linen of the Opposition," *Komsomolskaya Pravda*, April 1, 2016. https://www.kp.ru/daily/26512.7/3380893/.

David M. Herszenhorn, "Navalny Accuses Russian Forces of Killing a Namesake in Ukraine," *Politico* Europe, April 19, 2022. https://www.politico.eu/article/navalny-accuses-russian-forces-of-killing-a-namesake-in-ukraine/.

"Alexei Navalny Was Doused with Green Paint in Barnaul," *Vesti*, March 20, 2017. https://www.vesti.ru/article/1567276.

Yevgenia Albats, "Interview: 'I Think Power in Russia Will Not Change Because of Elections," *New Times*, July 19, 2011. https://newtimes.ru/articles/detail/38107/.

Robyn Dixon, "Navalny is sentenced to 19 years for 'extremism' as Kremlin crushes dissent," *Washington Post*, Aug. 4, 2023. https://www.washingtonpost.com/world/2023/08/04/alexei-navalny-sentenced-russia-opposition/.

ACKNOWLEDGMENTS

Thanks goes first and foremost to Sean Desmond, my editor and above all a great friend, for being the godfather and champion of this project and for his patient persistence as Russia's war in Ukraine upended our plans and rewrote the calendar, and to my dear friend Susan Cordaro, for her impeccable taste and encouraging Sean and I to work together.

This book would also never have been possible without many great colleagues and friends at the *New York Times*, *Politico Europe*, and the *Washington Post*. Special thanks are due to Bill Keller and Susan Chira, who offered me a dream assignment as a *New York Times* correspondent based in Moscow, and to my editors during that assignment, Joe Kahn and Michael Slackman. Thanks also to Clifford J. Levy, who preceded me for the *Times* in Moscow and who, along with his wonderful family, introduced my family to the Novaya Gumanitarnaya Shkola—the New Humanitarian School—and to my fellow correspondents, especially Ellen Barry, Andrew E. Kramer, Steven Lee Myers, and Andrew Roth.

I owe a tremendous debt to the *New York Times* Moscow Bureau's longtime magician-translators, Nikolay Khalip and Viktor Klimenko, who taught me how to work effectively as a foreign journalist in Russia. As Nik often said, "We don't want an interview, we just want to chat." I also owe huge thanks to my Russian teacher, the late Boris Shekhtman, whose wonderous techniques and great sense of humor helped train generations of Russian correspondents for the *New York Times* and other news organizations. Thanks also to my dearest mentors at the *Times*—Sara Rimer, John Kifner, Robert D. McFadden, Dan Barry, Suzanne Daley, Alison Mitchell, Carl Hulse, and the late Robert Pear.

Carrie Budoff Brown and Matthew Kaminsky brought me to Brussels to be part of the exciting *Politico Europe* project. They, along with Stephen Brown, who is dearly missed, allowed me to keep reporting on Russia and Ukraine as an extension of the European Union and transatlantic relations. To my great friends at *Politico Europe*, especially Jacopo Barigazzi, Florian Eder, and Rym Momtaz, who proved every day that it is possible to get the scoop and get the joke—often at the same time. And thanks to my colleagues at the *Washington Post*, especially Douglas Jehl and Sally Buzbee, who brought me back to the Russia beat full-time, and also to the fabulous and brave *Washington Post* Russia and Ukraine correspondents with whom I work every day.

Thank you to all of the Russian and international journalists, an incredible cadre of professionals, whose extensive and exhaustive coverage of Navalny—in real time—provided the factual foundations of this book.

I can't say enough about the terrific staff at Twelve, especially Bob Castillo and Zohal Karimy, who made the production process seem effortless.

Deep thanks to ace photographer Evgeny Feldman for the photos from his many years of unparalleled coverage of Navalny, including from his remarkable *This Is Navalny* project. And *ogromnoe spasibo* to Anna Berezniatskaia for some clutch translation help with tricky Russian phraseology.

Of course, any mistakes in this book are my responsibility and mine alone.

A special thanks to my uncle, Moises "Mo" Herszenhorn, for teaching me to be brave, to bet on adventure, and "to keep our name high." Of course, this book would not have been remotely possible without the patient, steadfast love and support of my wife, Christina Pan Marshall, and our sons, Miles, Isaac, and Ellis Herszenhorn, who made enormous sacrifices to allow me to follow the news wherever it led.

INDEX

ABOUT THE AUTHOR

David M. Herszenhorn recently joined the *Washington Post* as Russia, Ukraine, and East Europe editor. He is the former chief Brussels correspondent of *Politico*. Before joining *Politico*, David worked for more than twenty years at the *New York Times*, as a reporter, Washington correspondent, and foreign correspondent based in Moscow.